DIDACTIC CLASSROOM STUDIES

KRITERIUM

Didactic classroom studies

A potential research direction

Edited by
Christina Osbeck, Åke Ingerman
& Silwa Claesson

NORDIC ACADEMIC PRESS

CHECKPOINT

Nordic Academic Press
P.O. Box 148
SE-221 00 Lund
Sweden
www.nordicacademicpress.com

For enquiries concerning printing/copying this work
for commercial or extended use please contact the publisher.

Typesetting: Stilbildarna i Mölle, Frederic Täckström
Cover design: Fugazi form
ISBN 978-91-88661-45-6 (print)
ISBN 978-91-88661-50-0 (epdf)
ISSN 2002-2131 Kriterium (Online)
DOI 10.21525/Kriterium.14

Contents

CHAPTER 1

An introduction to didactic classroom studies

Christina Osbeck, Åke Ingerman & Silwa Claesson

Didaktik – an ambiguous concept

Didaktik is the term used in the Scandinavian countries and Germany for a special area of educational science, but it tends not to translate well into English, where didactic has partly negative connotations related to conveying and sententious processes (Gundem 2011). One solution has been simply not to translate the term—Hudson (2007), for example, uses its German form, *Didaktik*—but given that the Continental European and Scandinavian meaning of didactics is now standard in the anglophone educational sciences (Riquarts & Hopmann 1995; Klette 2007) and its relation to 'curriculum studies' has been discussed (Gundem & Hopmann 1998), we have chosen to translate *didaktik* as didactics, being the best of the necessary elisions when writing in English.

Didactics is a field of research that encompasses the collective knowledge of all teachers at the point where academic knowledge and practice intersects (Fensham 2004; Gundem 2011). It is understood as both the science of the teaching profession and the professional knowledge that teachers possess (Ingerman & Wickman 2015; Kindenberg & Wickman 2018; Seel 1999), with the latter frequently referred to as the art of teaching (for example, Bronäs & Runebou 2010). This double meaning can be confusing for the uninitiated, but it reveals just how closely related theory and practice in didactics are, or, as Klafki has it, how little separated these two realities are when it comes to educational processes (Gundem 2011). Our aim here is thus first and foremost to contribute to didactics as an empirical science—articulating classroom studies as a potential research direction for didactic studies, and suggesting directions that will put such studies at the cutting edge. However, since the findings of didactic classroom studies are important for the development of practice this means that ours is also a contribution to classroom practice—our empirical studies and their findings have 'didactical consequences' for teachers, as we have chosen to phrase it here.

Although didactics is today a distinct field of educational science in Sweden, and is one with deep roots in all the Scandinavian countries and Germany, didactics as a concept was noticeable by its absence in the period between the Second World War and the 1980s (Werler et al. 2016). Its return to favour as a concept was linked to the educational reforms in teaching in the late eighties, when it became important to invoke the long tradition of didactics (for example, Kroksmark 1989). This tradition differs considerably in the retelling, but most accounts still begin with the Greek root of the term, and then trace it via Comenius and Herbart to Germany, where *Bildung* theory and critical theory took effect (Gundem 2011).

Not only does didactics draw on a variety of traditions and theories, but the general level of interest in it has varied. The classic distinction between general didactics and subject-matter didactics is usually the first to be noticed. Even though 'subject-matter didactics' is a well-established concept (Swedish ämnesdidaktik, Danish *fagdidaktik*, Norwegian *fagdidaktikk*), it can be thought tautological since content-centredness is implied by the word didactics. A less common but still crucial differentiation in didactics centres on the institutional setting in question. This usually corresponds to the age of the learners. Hence preschool didactics is held to be distinct from primary school didactics, lower secondary school didactics from upper secondary and university didactics, and so on. This is sometimes called 'special didactics' (Gundem 2011). In the didactic classroom studies presented in this volume, we consider a range of subject matter. The content, while shifting, is evident in all eight studies, although in a couple of studies—Hipkiss's and Lilja and Claesson's—the primary interest is the generic processes more than the specific content. This section of the book thus goes under the heading of 'The framing of teaching in the classroom', but the processes could equally be understood as disciplining processes, that have been understood, in addition to teaching and guiding processes, as a central focus in general didactics having both a relational and an organisational dimension (Oettingen 2016), as the two essays exemplify. The various didactical subareas make it possible to specialise, which while productive has also hampered the synergies that could have been beneficial for knowledge development in the field (Künzli 2000), as for example in the research approaches that are our focus here. Our empirical studies also show that the *appearance* of a distinction between studies in general didactics and subject-matter didactics varies according to the age of the pupils or students and the subject taught. The character of a didactical tradition is relevant to the research being produced, as is discussed here in Osbeck and Ingerman's essay on a potential research direction for didactic classroom studies, which looks at science and religious education.

Common characteristics of didactics

Despite the fact that different sources are cited and different points are emphasised, there are some common characteristics to be found in didactics, which we would argue are fundamental and help didactics avoid the worst of its fragmentary tendencies (Hudson & Meyer 2011). Some of these features have already been noted. Didactics is said to draw closely on practice, which is sometimes said to have become clearer as subject-matter didactics evolved. According to Gundem 'subject didactics in a way saved didactics. It brought didactics back to the content and classroom' (2011, 99). To stress practice is to stress complexity. The practice-focused character of didactics can be interpreted as visualising and embodying the full complexity of the teaching–studying–learning process (Hudson 2007). Didactic studies like the ones in this volume have an interest in understanding the complexities of classroom teaching and learning without *reductio ad absurdum* arguments, and instead stress the context in these processes.

Another common trait in didactics is its attention to the intentionality of the teaching and learning process, and in that sense its normativity.

In a school setting, teaching is a specific 'restrained teaching' (Hopmann 2007). An interest in intentionality can take many forms. It can be a critique of its ideological character, as in critical didactics (Gundem 2011)—looking at the tensions between policy, the teachers' express ambitions, observed processes, and pupil experiences. It may identify differences between explicit and implicit processes, and in that sense reveal a 'hidden curriculum' (Jackson 1968). Teaching and learning processes in the classroom always include values, and, inevitably, negotiations about which values should count (Fenstermacher et. al. 2009). Intentionality in a school context also turns on the fact that successful schooling is not just the result of socialisation in general, but rather is brought about by planned processes that centre on 'powerful knowledge' (Fredricks et al. 2004; Young 2013). In the didactical *Bildung* tradition, the intentional aspect of teaching turns on pupil or student development in an overarching, long-term perspective. There are questions about how school—and especially its selected content—contributes to character development and individual responsibility (for example, Gundem 2011; Künzli 2000). *Bildung* didactics thus pays attention not only to the tensions between individual and societal ambitions for development in schools, but also to the risk that the intention with teaching and learning might be understood in a narrow, instrumental way (Klafki 1995; Hudson 2007). In the present volume, intentionality is one of several analytical perspectives, with which teaching and learning processes are interpreted and evaluated. In-depth studies of the extent to which current teaching processes can contribute to the development of wise, responsible, and independent individuals (Oettingen 2016)—teaching processes that could be related to Biesta's function of education as being subjectification, alongside qualification and socialisation (2009)—are something for another volume.

The most commonly noted characteristic is perhaps the didactical questions used for reflective planning processes and analyses of ongoing teaching: what is being taught and learnt, how is this effected, and why—with what purpose—is this carried out (for example, Ongstad 2006; Jank & Meyer 1997). The importance of keeping the content and the working processes together is clear in such didactical questions. The perspective is often referred to as constitutive in a tradition that runs from Comenius to Pestalozzi, where it was originally expressed as an interest in finding a natural way of teaching and learning in accordance with the nature of the content (Riquarts & Hopmann 1995). Didactics scholars are often sceptical about the benefit of general theories of teaching and learning (Kindenberg & Wickman 2018), and instead favour the production of local theories; for example, articulated didactic models where the specific content is central (Wickman et al. 2018). Such didactic models have been developed to support teachers' analyses and educational choices (Duit et al. 2012; Ruthven et al. 2009), and provide a conceptual toolbox with which to tackle didactic questions. Mangling didactic models in practice (in analogy with Pickering 1993) allows for the development of the models and for knowledge interaction at the point where practice and research intersect, and as such is an important means of developing didactics. The didactic models can be understood as local theories in several ways. They can be embedded in a specific practice, or they can be local in the what and how of teaching and learning; they can also be localised in a particular subject didactics, as for example Robert's (2007) model of scientific literacy as comprising two visions (an insider and an outsider perspective).

Closely related to the didactical questions is the didactical triangle—the expression of didactical interest in the form of a triangle (for example, Hopmann 2007). The integrative ambition of didactics—the simultaneous interest in content, pupils, and teachers, and how these three components interrelate in the teaching and learning process—is plain here. The components are integrated so that one component cannot be highlighted at the expense of another without the loss of valuable information (Straesser 2007; Werler et al. 2012).

Pursuing didactical research interests with classroom studies

Our didactical research interest in this volume is classroom practice, while retaining its complexity and making its goals and intentionality visible. We have adopted a holistic, integrative perspective, which has been described elsewhere as the common and distinctive feature of the didactical tradition: 'What all these efforts have in common is the strong belief that we need an integrative approach, as intended by Herbart and Comenius, which can do justice to each corner of the *didaktik* triangle: the teacher, the content and, not least, the learner who has to come to terms with this ever more complicated world' (Riquarts & Hopmann 1995, 8–9). The three corners of the didactical triangle—teacher, pupil, content—must be understood in an integrative perspective. However, the limitations of data, method, or focus often lead to an analytical separation of these components in didactic studies, with one component commonly featuring large while the other two are explicitly or implicitly relegated to the background. This limits complexity and can hamper how classroom practice is reflected in the studies. A didactical research interest that stresses the integrative focus is one that takes steps to keep intact the contextual wholeness in relation to the practice. Uljens thus defines didactics as 'the science of the teaching–studying–learning process' (2012, 43).

In this volume, we argue for the value of classroom studies as a way of gauging the ongoing process of teaching and learning in all their complexity. We would argue that didactic classroom studies are a self-contained and fruitful research direction, and thus exemplify the characteristics of such studies with eight empirical studies, and offer suggestions as to the international research context and how it might develop and thrive.

The empirical studies

The didactic classroom studies in this volume, in accordance with the opportunities offered by such studies, offer a range of contextual perspectives and findings in which teaching, learning, and content are kept together. Nevertheless, the particular emphasis varies from essay to essay.

The teacher in the classroom

The essays that particularly focus on teachers and their work in the classroom show how different kinds of teaching strategy make different kinds of learning possible, as the objects of learning become visible to varying degrees in the classroom through the teacher's actions. Teachers' actions affect the pupils' activities, which in turn affect what teachers do. While the emphasis is on the teacher, the essays show that relationships are important in the teaching and learning processes and in the communication that is established between teachers and pupils. This is the theme of Osbeck's essay, which examines how communicative patterns in the classroom provide varying conditions for learning, and how communicative patterns are negotiated by teachers and pupils. Osbeck's concern is whether a teacher's actions enable certain speech genres to become hegemonic in the classroom—speech genres that to varying degrees can impact on the development of a subject-matter language. Kullberg and Skodras's essay shows how examples used by teachers, and the variation in their use of examples, elicit pupil understandings of various kinds. Different opportunities to identify patterns and achieve insights are offered.

The student in the classroom

Two of the essays concentrate on pupils' or students' work in small groups, and articulate the development and nature of their understandings. By focusing on the students' perspectives in classroom studies, in contrast to the opportunities provided by, say, interviews or questionnaires, one can be certain that the contextual processes, relationships, and communication are taken into account. In Ingerman and Booth's essay, work in small groups is analysed in relation to the role of the tutor, while Sofkova Hashemi's essay concentrates on pupils and their choices, how they handle tasks given to them by both teachers and fellow pupils, and how they construct tasks, taken to be a measure of the skills that the pupils have to mobilise.

The study also shows how this relates to the tasks given to them and their communication with their peers. The findings touch on what it means when pupils show or do not show certain skills under these circumstances.

The framing of teaching in the classroom

Lilja and Claesson's essay pays particular attention to the relational conditions of classroom work, while Hipkiss's focuses on the physical circumstances. Both essays can be said to concentrate on the framing and conditions of classroom work, and are more general in character, as described above (Oettingen 2016). Hipkiss's contribution gives an insight into how relationships are conditioned by the possibilities of the physical milieu of the classroom. The ways a classroom is furnished has an impact on pupils' opportunities to practise subject-specific language, demonstrating that the line between general didactics and subject-matter didactics is not always easy to draw. Even though the relational and physical aspects matter, and in one way or another are visible in all classroom studies, these two essays show the importance of taking these conditions for teaching and learning as a subject of study in their own right. A closer look at current work in the classroom reveals how different types of teaching strategy can facilitate a variety of relational patterns, and thus give pupils the opportunity to expand their horizons of understanding. These two essays together point to how relational, physical context affects teaching and learning, and that makes change possible.

Researching the classroom

The remaining two empirical essays are both based on video-recorded data from classrooms, and concentrate on methodological issues—what kinds of knowledge are made possible by these studies and how different approaches reveal different things—while stressing the importance of combining overarching and in-depth analyses. In the contribution by Kilhamn et al., specific international comparisons are demonstrated to be a useful methodological tool with which to identify possible international differences and the contextualisation of teaching. The authors also discuss how video observations are a valuable method for developing work with teachers and how together their interpretations can enrich the teaching and learning process. Rocksén's essay shows that the patterns evident in many hours of recorded data can provide a solid base for the selection of specific episodes for in-depth study. The patterns in how a teacher performs a specific action are identifiable only by studying a certain number of lessons, as it is only then one can distinguish between the rule and the exception. Sequential observations are fundamental when studying progression in communication patterns and language, especially if the ambition is to identify whether patterns and perspectives established in previous lessons continue to be drawn upon in current teaching.

The wider view on didactic classroom studies

The empirical essays illustrate the complexities of our knowledge about classroom teaching and learning. In Osbeck and Ingerman's essay on potential research directions, the eight are categorised according to their aim, theoretical framework, empirical design, didactical research tradition, knowledge claims, and implications, and considered for their future potential in didactic classroom studies, while also singling out the factors that may carry this research direction forward. Finally, Klette concludes with an international perspective on didactic classroom studies, with brief comments on each of the empirical essays and a discussion of their contribution as a whole to the international field.

The Swedish context

In didactic classroom studies the specific context is of large importance. Most of the classrooms are embedded in a Swedish school system which may not be familiar to the reader, so a brief introduction is in order. Since 1842, Sweden has had compulsory education for all children, and today most children go to preschool, all children have nine years of obligatory schooling, and most young people continue for another three years at an upper-secondary school. The Swedish school system is broadly similar to the other Nordic countries, especially when it comes to its religious and political background (historically, Lutheranism and social democracy have dominated). In the 1960s there was school reform similar to many anglophone countries, and the school system changed from one with several different tracks to an elementary school which all pupils attended for the full nine years. However, in the 1990s so-called free schools (*fristående skolor*) were permitted, and today there is a debate as to whether this has opened up for a new kind of segregation. There are also international influences at work, for example from the OECD, which affect how teaching and learning are regarded. The notion of accountability has also recently been stressed in the Scandinavian countries (Skarre Aasebo et al. 2017). These wider processes affect teaching and learning in individual classrooms, and are thus evident in our results even though they are not the specific research focus of these studies.

With this introduction, we as editors invite you to enjoy each individual study and reflect on the contribution of classroom studies as a potential research direction in the field of didactics.

References

Biesta, G. (2009), 'Good education in an age of measurement: On the need to reconnect with the question of purpose in education', *Educational Assessment, Evaluation & Accountability*, 21/1, 33–46.

Bronäs, A. & N. Runebou (2010), *Ämnesdidaktik: En undervisningskonst* (Stockholm: Norstedt).

Duit, R., H. Gropengieber, U. Kattmann, M. Komorek & I. Parchmann (2012), 'The model of educational reconstruction: A framework for improving teaching and learning science', in D. Jorde & J. Dillon (eds.), *Science education research and practice in Europe* (Rotterdam: Sense).

Fensham, P. J. (2004), *Defining identity: The evolution of science education as a field of research* (Dordrecht: Kluwer Academic).

Fenstermacher, G. D., R. D. Osguthorpe & M. N. Sanger (2009), 'Teaching Morally and Teaching Morality', *Teacher Education Quarterly*, 36/3, 7–19.

Fredricks, J. A., P. C. Blumenfeld & A. H. Paris (2004), 'School engagement: Potential of the concept, state of the evidence', *Review of Educational Research*, 74/1, 59–109.

Gundem, B. B. (2011), *Europeisk didaktikk: Tenkning og viten* (Oslo: Universitetsforlaget).

Hopmann, S. (2007), 'Restrained teaching: The common core of didaktik', *European Educational Research Journal*, 6/2, 109.

Hudson, B. (2007), 'Comparing Different Traditions of Teaching and Learning: What can we learn about teaching and learning?' *European Educational Research Journal*, 6/2, 135–46.

Ingerman, Å. & P. O. Wickman (2015), 'Towards a teachers' professional discipline: Shared responsibility for didactic models in research and practice', in P. Burnard, B. M. Apelgren & N. Cabaroglu (eds.), *Transformative teacher research: theory and practice for the C21st* (Rotterdam: Sense).

Jackson, P. W. (1968), *Life in the classroom* (New York: Holt, Rinehart & Winston).

Jank, W. & H. Meyer (1997), 'Nyttan av kunskaper i didaktisk teori', in M. Uljens (ed.), *Didaktik: Teori, reflektion och praktik* (Lund: Studentlitteratur).

Kindenberg, B. & P. O. Wickman (2018), 'Dags för didaktiken att bli egen vetenskap', *Pedagogiska Magasinet*, 2, 14–17.

Klafki, W. (1995), 'Didactic analysis as the core of preparation of instruction (Didaktische Analyse als Kern der Unterrichtsvorbereitung)', *Journal of Curriculum Studies*, 27/1, 13–30.

Klette, K. (2007), 'Trends in Research on Teaching and Learning in Schools: Didactics meets classroom studies', *European Educational Research Journal*, 6/2, 147–60.

Kroksmark, T. (1989), *Didaktiska strövtåg: Didaktiska idéer från Comenius till fenomenografisk didaktik* (Gothenburg: Daidalos).

Künzli, R. (2000), 'German Didaktik: Models of re-presentation, of intercourse, and of experience', in I. Westbury, S. Hopmann & K. Riquarts (eds.), *Teaching as a reflective practice: The German Didaktik tradition* (Mahwah, NJ: Lawrence Erlbaum).

Ongstad, S. (2006), 'Fag i endring: Om didaktisering av kunskap', in id. (ed.), *Fag og fagdidaktikk i lærerutdanning: Kunnskap i grenseland* (Oslo: Universitetsforlaget).

Oettingen, A. von (2016), *Almen dannelse: Dannelsesstandarder og fag* (Copenhagen: Hans Reitzels).

Pickering, A. (1993). 'The mangle of practice: Agency and emergence in the sociology of science', *American journal of sociology*, 99/3, 559-589.

Riquarts, K. & S. Hopmann (1995), 'Starting a dialogue: Issues in a beginning conversation between Didaktik and the curriculum traditions', *Journal of Curriculum Studies*, 27/1, 3–12.

19

Roberts, D. A. (2007), 'Scientific literacy/science literacy', in S. K. Abell & N. G. Lederman (eds.), *Handbook of research on science education* (Mahwah, NJ: Lawrence Erlbaum).

Ruthven, K., C. Laborde, J. Leach & A. Tiberghien (2009), 'Design tools in didactical research: Instrumenting the epistemological and cognitive aspects of the design of teaching sequences', *Educational Researcher*, 38, 329–42.

Seel, H. (1999), 'Didaktik as the professional science of teachers', *TNTEE Publications*, 2, 85–93.

Skarre Aasebo, T., J. Midsundstad & I. Willbergh (2017), 'Teaching in the age of accountability: restrained by school culture?' *Journal of Curriculum Studies*, 49/3.

Straesser, R. (2007), 'Didactics of mathematics: More than mathematics and school', *ZDM* 39/1, 165–71. doi: 10.1007/s11858-006-0016-x

Uljens, M. (2004), *School didactics and learning: A school didactic model framing an analysis of pedagogical implications of learning theory.* (Hove: Taylor & Francis).

Werler, T., D. L. Cameron & N. Birkeland (eds.) (2012), *When Education Meets the Care Paradigm* (Münster: Waxmann).

—— S. Claesson & O. Strandler (2016), 'Sweden', in H. Döbert, W. Hörner, B. von Kopp & L. Reuter (eds.), *Die Bildungssysteme Europas* (Baltmannsweiler: Schneider Verlag Hohengehren).

Wickman, P. O., K. Hamza & I. Lundegård (2018), 'Didactics and didactic models in science education', *Nordic Studies in Science Education*, 14/3, 239–49.

Young, M. (2013), 'Overcoming the crisis in curriculum theory: A knowledge-based approach', *Journal of Curriculum Studies*, 45/2, 101–118.

Abstract

This essay reports findings from a project in social studies, especially religious education (RE), with three Year 6 classes in Sweden. In the project, the social studies classes were observed for one academic year and pre– and post-tests in RE were also used, which indicated differences in both results and development between the classes. In this essay, the two classes that showed the largest differences in test results between themselves are the focus. Transcriptions of two similar pairs of lesson observations—one an introduction to RE and one a lesson centred on a news quiz—are analysed, focusing on the communication patterns in the two classes that may contribute to an understanding of the differences in achievement and development. A socio-cultural perspective is used, where knowledge and subject-matter knowledge is understood as language that is developed in contextual negotiations. The findings show that questions, both from teachers and from pupils, were more frequent in the class with the better test results. The speech genre used in this class was more analytical and varied, less information dominated, and the content was clearly broader in one of the lessons. The teacher position was also more pupil-oriented and problematising, while what it meant to be a competent pupil in this class was to be talkative and curious.

CHAPTER 2

Questions and speech genres in social studies classrooms

Comparisons of communication patterns

Christina Osbeck

In this essay, observed communication patterns in two social studies classes in a Swedish middle school are analysed. Social studies is an interdisciplinary subject area consisting of religion, history, geography, and civics. The two classes of 12-year-old pupils, here termed A and C, are part of a research project where previous analyses have shown that the classes' average results and development in a knowledge test in religious education (RE) (*religionskunskap*) conducted at the beginning and end of the academic year 2011–2012, showed statistically significant differences. The research question of this essay concerns the kinds of communication patterns in the two classes that may contribute to an understanding of the identified differences in achievement and development, as defined in the RE test.

It is known from previous studies that the particular class being taught says a great deal about any differences in achievement. A recent Swedish study shows, for example, that about 25 per cent of the variance in the results of a national science test could be explained by looking at the pupil group (Bach et al. 2015). There are certain characteristics in teaching that are known to affect differences in achievement (for example, Nordenbo et al. 2008; Hattie 2009). One way to describe this is used by Hattie in his comparison of expert teachers and experienced teachers (2003). The experts distinguish themselves from experienced teachers with their deep and multi-faceted understanding of the subject, which can mean problematising current themes and linking themes to previous teaching. Expert teachers are also more alert to classroom climate and relations, which can mean adapting their teaching to specific pupil groups, caring for and having high expectations of the pupils, and creating an atmosphere where they are not afraid to make mistakes. A focus on goals and working processes is also characteristic of expert teachers, which can mean being explicit about goals and expectations, focusing on what the pupils know and gaps in their knowledge, giving relevant feedback, and formulating challenging tasks.

Another way of summarising research on what enhances pupils' learning is, like Hattie (2009), to stress the importance of making learning visible, creating a joint focus for teachers and pupils concerning what to learn, pupils' current knowledge, and necessary steps to take. Questions asked by both teachers and pupils therefore matter since they show not only the direction for learning but also the current knowledge position to work from. Small-scale qualitative studies are a valuable way to examine the potential uses of teacher–pupil communication, and what in certain situations hinders and facilitates informative interaction. Such studies in mathematics and science education have shown that teachers' questions tend to be more topical and procedural than conceptual, which means that they are more focused on facts and acts than deeper understanding (Emanuelsson 2001). Moreover, questions have been shown to be an important tool for teachers when helping their pupils translate their questions from everyday language into a scientific idiom in order to develop their understanding (Lundin 2007).

The research project and context of the study

This essay is based on a Swedish project in which three Year 6 classes—located in different towns—were observed. About 80 lessons were audio recorded and transcribed. An RE test was designed according to the requirements of the Swedish curriculum, in which RE has since the 1960s been described as a neutral and plural subject. It is compulsory and includes four core content areas: 'Religions and other outlooks on life', 'Religion and society', 'Identity and life issues' and 'Ethics' (Skolverket 2011, 178–80).

The first empirical article from the project focuses on teachers' perspectives (as described in interviews) and pupils' perspective (as expressed in the RE pre-tests). These perspectives were examined as conditions for teaching and learning (Osbeck 2014). The study shows that the pupils' perspectives at the beginning of the year were far removed from the intentions of the curriculum. For instance, the pupils' statements concerning religion as a phenomenon were vague—some even confused 'religion' and 'region'—and their interpretations of religious symbols are therefore hard for them to use in further analyses. A problem for the teachers was that they lacked knowledge about pupils' difficulties in RE, which affected their ability to direct teaching. One teacher, Hans, was an exception: he noticed that pupils had difficulties with comparing, finding connections, and thinking of life in an abstract way, and therefore used classroom communication so that the pupils had the opportunity to develop by encountering such perspectives expressed by others. Furthermore, the teachers' intentions—their RE goals in relation to the curriculum—were rather general, and primarily related to fostering fundamental values.

The second article focuses on the relation between the pre- and post-tests (Osbeck 2017). The findings show that a progression in test results between autumn and spring can be identified in all three classes, and that there were differences between the classes both in achievement levels and development. This is interpreted as an indication of the variation in the ways of facilitating RE learning in the classroom. In addition to this, the test also provided information about pupils' communication patterns both in and outside school, and about their general school experience, making it possible to examine whether this related to their RE test scores. Of these factors, 'asking questions' when one is curious or does not understand appears to be important. The largest achievement differences were between classes A and C, and the test also shows statistically significant differences between classes in the pupils' willingness to ask questions during whole-class activities: the pupils in Class A, where both the achievement level and development were lower, were less interested in doing so. The essay's findings led to the current study, which examines what more can be said about the communication patterns in classes A and C, which may contribute to an understanding of the differences in achievement.

The broader RE research context of the study

Empirical studies concerning the relationship between teaching and learning are rare when it comes to RE, the didactical subject matter of this study. One quantitative study in which about 2,500 pupils in Year 5 participated shows that it is harder to explain achievements in RE than it is in mathematics and Greek. The study also suggests that individual factors—such as previous knowledge, sex, and socioeconomic status—explain more variance than do classroom factors. Nevertheless, the study emphasizes that ways of structuring teaching and asking questions—not only their frequency, but also their focus, quality, and timing—are of importance (Kyriakides & Creemers 2008).

There have been some qualitative classrooms studies, although their interests differ from the current study. A few have looked at how communication patterns create specific understandings of religions as a phenomenon (for example, Afdal 2015; Kittelmann Flensner 2015; Lippe 2011; Osbeck & Lied 2012), and have demonstrated the influence of a plural and secular society. Others have focused on identity politics, subject formation, and the construction of societal hierarchies that take place in RE, where pupils are labelled and anyone who is religious tends to be constructed as 'the other' (Buchardt 2008; Karlsson 2015; Nicolaisen 2013). A couple of these studies can also be said to examine what kind of school subject—what kind of RE subject—is being constructed (for example, Karlsson 2015; Kittelmann Flensner 2015). The study that can be said to be closest to the current one, because it examines teachers' strategies and meaning-making in classroom interaction, is Liljestrand (2002);

however, as Liljestrand focuses on the discussions in RE and civics in upper-secondary school that centre on controversial societal issues and looks at the potential of these discussions in educating democratic citizens, neither his study nor RE didactic classroom studies as a whole provide the current study with much to draw on.

Task, theory, and tools

The research question to be examined here is what communication patterns in Class A and Class C may contribute to the differences noted in achievement and development, as defined in an RE test. This task requires a description of what is meant by knowledge, subject-matter knowledge, and learning in the context of this study. Knowledge, then, is understood as intimately linked to language, and learning is understood to be linked to the development of language. Such a perspective is stressed in a socio-cultural approach to learning, where language, according to Vygotsky, is the tool of tools that mediates our being in the world (for example, Säljö 2005, 81). Subject-matter knowledge can be understood as the language of certain spheres of reality (for example, Postman 1998; Skogar 2000) and RE knowledge, given its dual aim of learning *about* and *from* religions (Grimmitt 1987), as both a 'language of religions' and a 'language of life' (Osbeck 2009). Well-developed language makes it possible to think, speak, and act in a richer and more nuanced way. However, language is not something that one has or does not have, but rather it is used and developed in practices that privilege various kinds of languages (Wertsch 1991, 14; Tappan 1992).

The varied contexts where we participate and develop linguistically are discursive practices. A school class can, in an overarching sense, be understood as one discursive practice, but can also on closer examination be understood as consisting of many discursive practices, linked to different tasks. Speech genres are specific ways of speaking in these practices that also regulate content, since form and content are interrelated (Bakhtin 1986, 60). The negotiation of a hegemonic speech genre is the negotiation of content and content learning that is made possible (cf. Lundin 2007). Speech genres that become hegemonic in a practice are related to the social ideals of these practices—in other words, interpretations of what it means to be a competent actor, since such competences include mastering hegemonic speech genres. Thus learning can to a large extent be understood as appropriating a practice and becoming a competent actor in that practice (Säljö 2005, 140). However, in a discursive practice, there are different positions such as teacher or pupil, and consequently learning takes different directions depending on one's position (Säljö 2005, 87–8; Foucault 1989).

In a previous study of textbooks as part of this project, communicative activities (Englund 2000, 44) were interpreted as links between discursive practices and hegemonic speech genres. I suggested, on the basis of an analysis of RE curricula in Swedish compulsory school from 1962 on, that there are central kinds of communicative activities in RE, and I distinguished between the informing, analysing, interpreting, existential-interpreting, and narrative activities in RE (Osbeck 2013). However, the distinction between communicative activities and speech genres is hard to maintain. Communicative activities can also be understood as Bakhtian speech genres of sorts. Informing activities were defined as those that 'address certain facts as part of established knowledge', analysing activities as those involving 'two or more perspectives that are being related to each other' (Osbeck 2013). Interpretative activities also refer to two or more perspectives, but where 'one of the perspectives is related to the learners' experience'. An existential-interpretative activity is one where 'questions about meanings in relation to one's own life and one's purpose in life are raised' and narrative activities were self-explanatory (155). The division shows similarities with Bloom's taxonomy of educational objectives (see, for example, Krathwohl 2002).

In the following examination of communication patterns, the concepts of speech genres, discursive practices, positions, and competent actors are central. The first step focuses on teacher questions (not all teacher statements) and pupil questions and comments, and analyses frequency, unanswered teacher questions, whether questions were open or closed (cf. Liljestrand 2002), and the form and content of the speech genres. It should be stressed that speech genre here, for analytical reasons, is studied first from the perspective of form and only thereafter from the perspective of content, but as already noted speech genre must be understood as an intertwined phenomenon in this respect. The second step interprets these analyses with a focus on how positions are performed and competent actors are highlighted in the two discursive practices (A and C), and what it may mean to learn and appropriate these discursive practices as wholes.

In order to compare the communication patterns in the two classes, lessons that were as similar as possible in focus have been chosen so that the differences are as visible as possible. Two introductory lessons about the study of religion and two lessons where the classes worked with a news quiz have been analysed. Due to the limitations of space, the quiz analyses are represented primarily as summaries, focusing on whether the patterns identified from the RE lessons are confirmed or called into question by the findings from the news quiz.

The classes and teachers

Class A, which has 33 pupils, is taught by Christer and Elisabeth, who every year teach new classes of Year 6 pupils in order to make the transition from middle school to lower-secondary school smoother. This particular class was made up of pupils who had been in two separate classes the previous year. The teachers use a flexible system of grouping the pupils, which is why there are two teachers for 33 pupils, rather than having two groups with one teacher each. Generally, they start with the whole group and then continue with individual work. The teachers describe the school district as a mixture of two housing areas: one dominated by homeowners, the other by rental accommodation. 74 per cent of the pupils' parents had a post-upper secondary education (Skolverket 2015).

In Class C, Hans teaches 16 pupils. He has been their class teacher for two years and also taught them RE the year before that. The school is located in a small dormitory town where more than 50 per cent of its inhabitants commute. The area is dominated by detached houses and 65 per cent of the school's parents had post-upper secondary education (ibid.).

The lessons

In Class A, the introductory RE lesson was Year 6's first social studies lesson to focus on religion. It lasted about 40 minutes. Class C,
meanwhile, had had a revision lesson before the introductory one in
which they had recapitulated the RE teaching from previous years,
which had focused on how Christianity arrived and developed in
Sweden. Now in the introductory lesson to the Year 6 RE, they are
to 'focus on what it's like in the rest of the world', as Hans says in his
introduction to the 60-minute lesson (see Table 2.1).

There are clear similarities between the two lessons given to classes
A and C. Hans and Elisabeth, whose colleague Christer remains
passive during this lesson, focus on the spread of different religions
in different regions of the world and use the same introductory film.
Both lessons can be divided into four sequences. Elisabeth starts by
defining religion and reading the national goals for RE that have
been printed out and stuck on a cupboard. In the second sequence,
the spread of religions is in focus, and Elisabeth informs her pupils
about this orally and with the help of two maps: a world map available in the classroom and another that she has drawn in order to
show the spread of religions. The third sequence is when the film is
shown (20 minutes—not analysed here) and in the fourth sequence,
Elisabeth concludes by stressing similarities between religions, such
as the Golden Rule and a belief in life after death. In Class C, Hans
starts by going over the previous revision lesson for a pupil who
had been absent. In the second sequence, he focuses on the spread
of the religions by getting the pupils to read a textbook (including
maps) and by using the map of the world. He continues, thirdly,
with small-group discussions about the pupils' knowledge of world
religions (20 minutes—not analysed) and the film constitutes the
final sequence (again, not analysed here).

In the two classes' work with the same news quiz there are two main
sequences. Firstly, the pupils are supposed to answer the questions
individually; secondly the correct answers are called out. The analysis
here focuses on the teachers' and pupils' comments and questions
rather than the actual quiz. While the pupils read the questions in

	Class A; 40 min (20 min film – not analysed)	Class C; 60 min (20 min group discussions + 20 min film – not analysed)
Questions teacher	10	12
Questions/comments pupils	2 (1 question + 1 comment)	9
Unanswered questions teacher	3	0
Open questions teacher	4	5
Closed questions teacher	6	7
Open questions pupils	0	5
Closed questions pupils	1	4
Speech-genre form of the questions/comments		
Informing	8 (7 teacher + 1 pupil)	7 (4 teacher + 3 pupil)
Analysing	2 (1 teacher + 1 pupil)	8 (4 teacher + 4 pupil)
Interpreting	2 (teacher)	6 (4 teacher + 2 pupil)
Existential-interpreting	0	0
Narrative	0	0
Speech-genre content of the questions/comments		
Geography/Religion	6 (teacher)	13 (7 teacher + 6 pupil)
Learning and thinking processes	1 (teacher)	4 (3 teacher + 1 pupil)
Churches	0	1 (pupil)
Archaeology/History of religions	3 (2 teacher + 1 pupil)	0
Phenomenology of religions	1 (teacher)	0
Source criticism	1 (pupil)	0
Concepts	2 (teacher – included above)	3 (2 teacher + 1 pupil)

Table 2.1. Communicative patterns during the two lessons "Introduction to the study of religions" in Classes A and C.

the first sequence in Class C, Christer reads the questions to the pupils in Class A (see Table. 2.2). The quiz takes slightly longer than 30 minutes in Class C, and just less than 20 minutes in Class A.

Teacher questions and pupil questions/comments

In the introductory RE lessons, the numbers of teacher questions in the two classes are almost the same, with a slight predominance of closed questions in both. However, the number of pupil-initiated questions and comments is much higher in Class C (9 versus 2). In Class A, Elisabeth also has difficulties getting answers to her questions in almost half of her attempts. On one of these occasions, she manages to get a

	Class A (20 minutes)	Class C (30 minutes)
Questions/comments teacher	11 (6 questions + 5 com-ments)	24 (12 qu + 11 co + 1-mixed)
Questions/comments-pupils	4 (comments)	19 (9 questions + 10-comments)
Unanswered questions-teacher	1	2
Open questions teacher	2	6
Closed questions teacher	4	6
Open questions pupils	0 (only comments)	2
Closed questions pupils	0 (only comments)	7
Speech genre form of the questions/comments		
Informing	15 (11 teacher + 4 pupil)	31 (18 teacher + 13-pupil)
Analysing	0	3 (teacher)
Interpreting	0	3 (teacher)
Existential interpreting	0	0
Narrative	0	6 (pupil)
Speech genre content of the questions/comments		
Political science	4 (teacher)	8 (3 teacher + 5 pupil)
Task-solving processes	5 (teacher)	12 (7 teacher + 5 pupil)
Words, pronunciation,-abbreviations	2 (teacher)	6 (5 teacher+ 1 pupil)
Jokes	4 (pupil)	1 (pupil)
Links, contexts	0	5 (4 teacher + 1 pupil)
Geography/map	0	4 (1 teacher + 3 pupil)
Society and culture generally	0	7 (4 teacher + 3 pupil)

Table 2.2. Communicative patterns during the two lessons "The news quiz" in Classes A and C.

reply by guiding the process and giving clues, but is not satisfied with the answer and instead gives the answer she had in mind.

In the other situations, her questions remain unanswered and instead are answered by Elisabeth herself, as in the following example where she refers to the seen film:

> E: Religion… Does any one of you remember… caught what religion means… [None of the pupil respond] That it was an intertwinement of people and a higher power…

Hers is a very broad question, both fundamental and multifaceted, while the answer that she seems to expect and later gives is quite specific, but also abstract and hard to understand. In addition, it differs from two other definitions given earlier. The pupils do not respond to the question and the content. While there are no unanswered questions in Class C, it seems from Elisabeth's comments that she is used to unanswered questions. She expresses negative expectations on a couple of occasions in the formulation of her questions: 'Anyone who has an idea?' Unsuccessful communication and failed subject-matter exchanges are not unexpected.

When the analyses of the two news-quiz lessons are added, another difference becomes apparent, since here too the teacher questions/comments are more common in Class C than in Class A. In line with previous findings, the frequency of the pupils' questions and comments are more numerous in Class C, while there is no clear difference between the number of closed and open questions in the two classes. In both classes there are unanswered teacher questions, but they seem to surprise Hans and his pupils more than they do Elisabeth and her pupils.

It is worth stressing that all four pupils comments in Class A are sarcastic remarks or jokes about difficulties with the quiz and incorrect answers. When, for example, Christer reads the response options to the question about which fairy tale was written by the Danish author Hans Christian Andersen and one of the alternatives is *Mio, My Son*, the title is repeated by some of the pupils in an artificial, almost shocked but amused way. Such comments go unchallenged in Class A, while both the teacher and one of the pupils in Class C react to a similar comment:

> 6: Åland Islands belongs to a Nordic country, which one? 1 Denmark, 2 Norway, or 3 Finland?
> 10: That was difficult… [sarcastically]

H: Sh!!

8: Well, I have no idea…

The teacher rejects the comment by hushing the pupil and is immediately backed up by another pupil, who draws attention to not only the oddness of the first pupil's behaviour but also the possibility of admitting ignorance in the classroom.

Speech genre forms

The speech genres also differ between the two classes. While Class A is heavily dominated by an informing genre, the distribution between informing, analytical, and interpreting forms is more equal in Class C and therefore more varied.

An example of an informing speech genre is the question about the religion 'which is the most common where we live… Is there anyone who knows what religion I'm looking for?' (Elisabeth). The expected answer is one word: Christianity. Elisabeth also uses the map as a tool that might facilitate the informing practice and help answer the questions.

> E: These religions are spread out in different places in the world. We have made a map where we have drawn…. Here you can see that one religion is very big and very widespread, and it is represented, not in all parts of the world, but in almost all parts of the world… which one is it?

Since the information obtained from analysing the map is the same as the information given in the question itself (that the religion is large and represented in most parts of the world), the map can hardly be taken to be an analysing tool.

In Class C, they also work with maps, but here Hans formulates the questions so that the answers require more information gatheing and analysis.

[After one of the pupils has read out a text about Judaism from the textbook.]
H: Judaism emerged in Israel, fine, but where is that? Where is Israel? Can someone come forward and point out where it is located?

The map is here used as a tool to clarify the information given in the textbook; the practice of doing an additional analysis to broaden the knowledge given is encouraged. The pupils in Hans's class also ask analytical and critical questions. One pupil, for instance, examines the map in the textbook, notices what he considers to be an inadequate drawing, and asks 'Isn't Buddhism in India, too?' Hans reacts encouragingly and eagerly, and invites him to continue reading the text to obtain more information: 'Well actually it is… It is, actually…! Read!' The practice of reading in order to evaluate one's knowledge, here concerning the spread of Buddhism, is stressed as important.

The fact that analysing comments and questions are more frequent in Hans's lesson does not mean that they do not exist in Elisabeth's. A problematising and analytical comment is made by one of the pupils, for instance. In the final sequence of the lesson, Elisabeth reads out a letter that she announces as 'the world's oldest love letter', using it to show how old the phenomenon of religion is, and how the presence of a religious worldview can also be found in this particular letter. One of her pupils reacts to the description 'the world's oldest love letter', and comments by adding 'the world's oldest *known* love letter'—which may be understood as a relevant source-critical remark. The teacher's reply is another source-critical reflection—'mm… *surviving* love letter…'—followed by a change of subject. The teacher's comment has the character of a reprimand: it is meant to top the pupil's comment, although it is not certain that it does. There could of course have been older letters that do not survive, but this does not mean that there are no older letters as yet unfound. The analytical, problematising, and critical speech genre that the pupil uses can be understood as having been made less appropriate by the utterances of the teacher.

The analyses of the news-quiz lessons show that all questions and comments in Class A were of an informative speech genre. This genre also dominates in Class C, but here there are also analysing and interpreting examples, and several of the pupils' contributions are of a narrative character, since they refer to their own and others' related experiences, holidays, and news.

Speech genre content

Elisabeth's class demonstrates the broadest repertoire of speech genre content in the RE introductory lessons, even if this is to a large extent due to single utterances. Most of the content in both classes concerns the relation between religion and geography. In both classes, there are also questions and comments that are about learning and thinking processes. These utterances are most common in Hans's class. In Elisabeth's classroom, there are in addition examples of discussions about source criticism, the meaning of religion as a phenomenon, and the history of religion. In Hans's class, one pupil brings up the appearance of a church, based on a reflection from the film. In both classrooms, certain concepts are stressed and made into objects of learning to a greater or lesser extent. In Class C, the concepts are monotheism, prejudice (which Hans introduces), and *bindis* (the decorative marks worn on the forehead that are often associated with Hindu women), which one of the pupils brings up. In Class A, the concepts introduced by the teacher are monotheism and archaeology.

The analyses of the news-quiz lessons differ from the pattern identified in the introductory lessons. Here, it is Class C that clearly has the broadest speech genre content, which both teachers' and pupils' utterances contribute to. In both classes, the questions and comments often concern political science, but also task-solving processes, as well as words and pronunciation. However, the kinds of task-solving processes differ between the classes.

In Class A, some comments related to task-solving are introducing the theme and encouraging the pupils, but the majority of the comments are achievement-directed. When the correct responses are presented Elisabeth says, 'Is there anyone who has nine correct answers so far? [Some people say 'Yes!'] We have some here with the chance at getting ten...' (Elisabeth). In Class A, task-solving comments that have an encouraging character are more frequent: 'And then comes the third... I reckon you'll be able to solve it. You never know, but...'. Comments of a strategy-building character are highlighted in Class C. One example is how Hans, when he calls out the correct answers, shows how to use the map as a thinking tool.

> H: Next question! ...was about the Åland Islands... if you look at the map, it isn't so hard, right...? [Rolls down the map]. You can see the Åland Islands... But what is that red line there? What might the red line indicate? 11?
>
> 11: It's a border...
>
> H: A border, yes, and what... what... how can you figure out, then, which country it belongs to? Now I couldn't hear what 11 said.
>
> 11: You look for which [country] is closest.
>
> H: Exactly... So why can't it belong to Sweden, then, if you look at the map?
>
> 11: Because the border is there...
>
> H: There it goes, between Sweden and the Åland Islands, so it should belong to which [country]? 2!
>
> 2: Finland!
>
> H: That's right!

The example also shows how it is through the pupils' comments that Hans develops his message and makes it distinct. The incomplete comment from Pupil 11 (about looking for the country closest to the island when deciding which country it belongs to) makes Hans take a step back, and use a question to stress the meaning of the red line as a border that decides the issue, so showing what should have been added to Pupil 11's answer to make it complete.

Other speech genre content that contributes to the broader repertoire in Class C concerns geography, society, and culture generally, and themes that link the current subject matter to shared experiences.

Teacher positions and competent pupils

When interpreting the findings from the RE lesson analyses by focusing on how the teacher positions and the competent pupil positions are performed in the two discursive practices, A and C, teaching tools seem to be important.

In Class A, Elisabeth is the main source of information, while Hans teaches from the textbook, from which the pupils read aloud. This difference seems to give Hans a position from which he can comment on and problematise the content. Hans's position is reminiscent of an older and more competent peer who is also being presented with new information, and on this basis reflects, scrutinises, and formulates possible conclusions. The different teacher positions also facilitate different reactions and interactions in class. Elisabeth, who herself is the main source of content in her lessons, is almost offended when a pupil makes a critical comment about the content, while Hans is delighted in a similar situation and participates in the critical analysis of the textbook, which here is the source of content.

In Hans's classroom, the negotiated understanding of a competent pupil seems to be a person who is active—who discusses and analyses. In Elisabeth's classroom, the collective norms are to a larger degree related to being reserved and quiet. These different positions seem to characterise the discursive practices as a whole.

The interpretations of the analyses of the news-quiz lessons show a similar pattern. In addition, it becomes clear that Hans's peer-like position should not be mistaken for one that is less careful with regard to the planning of the lesson. The news-quiz task is given a clear purpose and has a learning-centred character. When one of the pupils wants to fill in the quiz by herself instead of discussing in class, Hans explains:

> H: …there are a lot of complicated words here, and there are many comments to make about it all… not least, you have so much to say, things and stuff, about those questions, so it isn't just what's in the questions, but we learn a lot of other stuff, too.

Here, broadened repertoires of knowledge emerge as the central aim of the news-quiz work. In contrast, this work seems to be more of an interlude in Class A. Elisabeth and Christer introduce the work by saying that they might have forgotten the quiz if the pupils had not reminded them, and the task ends with Elisabeth saying 'Now, you can get to work'.

Concluding discussion

So, what differences in communication patterns have been identified that contribute to an understanding of why the achievements and development in the RE test were found to be stronger in Class C than in Class A—an achievement pattern that also occurred in the national tests in the core subjects for these two classes (Skolverket 2015)? A part of the answer may be that questions, from both teachers and pupils, are generally more frequent in Class C, which also means that teacher intentions, pupils' knowledge, and learning processes are more visible here (for example, Hattie 2009). It is possible for the teacher to draw on the information obtained from these questions when planning and teaching. Simultaneously, the pupils may understand from the teacher's questions what he or she considers to be central knowledge.

In Class C, the speech genres used are more analytical and varied, while they are mostly informative in A (cf. Emanuelsson 2001). One reason for this discrepancy may be that Hans avoids being the sole source of information, and instead takes a position from which he can analyse and problematise the content. It is seldom pointed out that the use of textbooks can create this advantage. Hans's problematising work also seems to encourage his pupils to do the same. When the teacher is the sole source of information, as in Class A, pupils' questioning of the content can be interpreted as a criticism of the teacher, which in turn may curb pupils' interest in further problematisations.

The repertoire concerning content of the speech genres in both RE classes is limited and concerns mainly the spread of religions over different regions in the world. It is worth remembering that some pupils actually mixed up 'religion' and 'region' in the tests (Osbeck 2014). The RE content in these lessons, of course, provides only a narrow perspective, focusing on a very limited part of the curriculum, and many of Smart's dimensions of religion (1997) are absent. The well-known domination of learning-about perspectives in RE in relation to learning-from perspectives is obvious (for example, Osbeck & Pettersson 2009). It is important to bear in mind that these were introductory lessons, but nevertheless the findings can be read in relation to existing research patterns showing the heavy influence of geography on social studies in middle school (Kristiansson 2014; Stolare 2014). Even if Class A tackles a somewhat broader theme in this lesson, including the meaning of the phenomenon religion, the issue is brought up in such a superficial way that the theme also seems to be difficult for the teacher. This recalls the findings from the initial interviews, where the teachers' RE aims were found to be of a rather vague, general character, relating primarily to fundamental values (Osbeck 2014). In relation to research findings that stress the importance of teachers' deep understanding of the subject, their ability to problematise the themes being dealt with (for example, Hattie 2003), and to translate between different language games such as science and everyday language games (for example, Lundin 2007; Ongstad 2006), the findings from these observations seem problematic. However, the observations also show how Hans introduces a task with the purpose of mapping out his pupils' understandings, which is in line with the findings from the initial interview, where he had ideas about pupils' difficulties in RE in relation to the goals of curriculum. In the task, Hans shows an interest in examining how best to direct his teaching in future.

In the news-quiz lessons, it was clearer how the communication patterns in Class C offered a comparatively broader repertoire of speech genres, and how a broad use of speech genres is related to a broad body of shared experience that can be used as a link between different subjects and that constitutes a resource to draw on. The fact that the pupils in Class C and their teacher have worked together for a long time may in this sense be an advantage that is lacking in Class A. In relation to previous research, showing work with news in school to be frequent but also time-consuming, isolated, fragmentary, and weakly connected to the goals of the curriculum (for example, Kristiansson 2014; Olsson 2016), the current study stresses how different this kind of work can be, and that detailed analyses of how certain work it is conducted and communicated are needed in order to evaluate such work.

The examples have also shown how the teachers' position appears different in the two discursive practices. Hans's reflexive and analytical position, where he creates a distance between himself and the content and appears as a more competent peer, could perhaps also make his modelling ability as a learner stronger.

Similarly, pupil positions and what it means to be a competent pupil differ. In Class C, the position includes an active, curious, rather carefree, and talkative way of being, where one shares experiences without feeling inhibited, while almost the opposite is true for Class A. Whether these patterns can be related to the fact that there are almost twice as many pupils in Class A as in Class C, that the pupils and teachers in Class C have worked together for a long time, and that the pupils in Class C have a habit of working collectively, are questions of further interest. However, the Class A's discursive practice appears rather controlled and restricted, whereas Class C's comes across as permissive and creative—a practice where knowledge is explored and problematised.

Despite the similarities in the classes' lessons, the study shows the differences in the communicative patterns, which can contribute to an understanding of the comparatively advantageous development in Class C, indicated by the RE tests (Osbeck 2017). Communicative patterns in a classroom are not, however, something that the teacher alone determines. As we have seen, it is something that is negotiated collectively.

The didactical consequences

Unfortunately, there is not much previous research in the field of RE didactic classroom studies with which to compare. While it adds to the novelty value of the study, it is hard to know how best to direct such a study in order to contribute with findings that challenge or confirm the knowledge field. However, since this study is partly theory-driven it is possible to chart the logic of the theoretical perspectives on a general level, and to contribute by demonstrating how these perspectives can appear in the complex reality of RE and social studies classrooms. In this essay, a couple of useful studies from other fields of subject-matter didactics are noted, indicating that another state of the art—one constructed across subject-matter didactical fields—might have been beneficial. However, the discussion here shows how RE research, with its connections to the wider field of social studies, can contribute to the current study with valuable perspectives for interpreting and understanding the findings.

'Didactical consequences' can be understood as the implicit focus of this empirical study. One can say that it is the potential didactical consequences of certain communication patterns, discursive practices, and speech genres that are explored and discussed here. The concept grasps the focus of this didactical RE classroom study where the complex interactional processes between pupils and teachers concerning specific content are highlighted—with an emphasis on the teacher's positions and opportunities. Didactical consequences thus describe the performances that take place in the classroom thanks to that communication.

But what further didactical consequences might this study have for RE practice beyond the empirical cases examined? The findings raise awareness of the importance of communication patterns, how speech genres in classroom may vary and how teachers through their way of initiating and responding to questions influence these patterns. The findings may contribute with an awareness of the intertwining of form and content in teaching and learning, and an understanding of teaching and learning as linked to the discursive classroom practice as a whole, including its specific teacher and pupil positions. More specifically, didactical consequences of this study may be an understanding of how both pupil and teacher questions are important in order to make knowledge and learning visible, of how analytical and problematising speech genres become central in learning processes and seem to create curiosity. An insight about how a pupil-oriented teacher position where the teacher becomes a role model while acting as one of the learners, albeit a more experienced and skilled learner, is a central implication of the current study—perhaps hinting at the potential benefit in avoiding being the sole source of information. The didactical consequences of this study might be new collegial conversations about the actions to take in order to encourage pupils to be more talkative, curious, and linguistically advanced, practising both the languages of religion and the languages of life.

References

Afdal, G. (2015), 'Modes of learning in religious education', *British Journal of Religious Education*, 37/3, 256–72.

Bach, F., B. Frändberg, M. Hagman, E. West & A. Zetterqvist (2015), 'De nationella proven i NO åk 6: Skillnader i resultat mellan olika grupper', *Educare* 2, 48–70.

Bakhtin, M. (1986), *Speech genres and other late essays* (Austin: University of Texas Press).

Buchardt, M. (2008), *Identitetspolitik i klasserummet: 'Religion' og 'kultur' som viden og social klassifikation: Studier i et praktiseret skolefag* (Copenhagen: Københavns universitet).

Emanuelsson, J. (2001), *En fråga om frågor: Hur lärares frågor i klassrummet gör det möjligt att få reda på elevernas sätt att förstå det som undervisningen behandlar i matematik och naturvetenskap* (Gothenburg: Göteborgs universitet).

Englund, T. (2000) 'Kommunikation och meningsskapande i fokus: Ett sociopolitiskt perspektiv på det vi kallar undervisning och lärande', in C. A. Säfström and P. O. Svedner (eds.), *Didaktik* (Lund, Studentlitteratur).

Foucault, M. (1989). *The archaeology of knowledge.* (London: Routledge).

Grimmitt, M. (1987), *Religious education and human development* (Great Wakering: McCrimmon).

Hattie, J. (2003), 'Teachers Make a Difference: What is the research evidence?' paper presented to the ACER, Melbourne Australia, 19–21 October, http://research.acer.edu.au/research_conference_2003/4.

—— (2009), *Visible learning: A synthesis of over 800 meta-analyses relating to achievement* (London: Routledge).

Lippe, M. von der (2011), *Youth, Religion and Diversity: A qualitative study of young people's talk about religion in a secular and plural society: A Norwegian case* (Stavanger: University of Stavanger).

Karlsson, A. (2015), V*ilket religionskunskapsämne? Ämneskonstruktioner i* *religionskunskap på gymnasiet med samtalsförhandlingar i centrum* (Karlstad: Karlstads Universitet).

Kittelmann Flensner, K. (2015), *Religious education in contemporary pluralistic Sweden* (diss., Gothenburg: Göteborgs universitet).

Kristiansson, M. (2014), 'Samhällskunskapsämnet och dess ämnesmarkörer på svenskt mellanstadium: Ett osynligt eget ämne som bistår andra ämnen', *Nordidactica—Journal of Humanities & Social Science Education*, 1, 212–33.

Kyriakides, L. & B. Creemers (2008), 'Using a Multidimensional Approach to Measure the Impact of Classroom-Level Factors upon Student Achievement: A Study Testing the Validity of the Dynamic Model', *School Effectiveness & School Improvement*, 19/2, 183–205.

Krathwohl, D. R. (2002) 'A Revision of Bloom's Taxonomy: An Overview', *Theory into Practice*, 41/4, 212–18.

Liljestrand, J. (2002), *Klassrummet som diskussionsarena* (Örebro: Örebro universitet).

Lundin, M. (2007), 'Questions as a tool for bridging science and everyday language games', *Cultural Studies of Science Education*, 2, 265–79.

Nicolaisen, T. (2013), *Hindubarn i grunnskolens religions- og livssynsundervisning: Egengjøring, andregjøring og normalitet* (Oslo: Universitetet i Oslo).

Nordenbo, S. E., Søgaard Larsen, M., Tiftikçi, N., Wendt, R. E. & Østergaard, S. (2008), *Teacher Competences and Pupil Achievement in Pre-school and School: A Systematic Review Carried Out for the Ministry of Education and Research, Oslo* (Copenhagen: Danish Clearinghouse for Educational Research, School of Education, University of Aarhus).

Olsson, R. (2016), *Samhällskunskap som ämnesförståelse och undervisningsämne: Prioriteringar och nyhetsanvändning hos fyra gymnasielärare* (Karlstad: Karlstads Universitet).

Ongstad, S. (2006), 'Fag i endring: Om didaktisering av kunskap', in id. (ed.), *Fag og fagdidaktikk i lærerutdanning: Kunnskap i grenseland* (Oslo: Universitetsforlaget).

Osbeck, C. (2009), *Att förstå livet: Religionsdidaktik och lärande i diskursiva praktiker* (Uppsala: Svenska kyrkan).

—— & Pettersson, P. (2009), 'Non-confessional and confessional education: Religious education in public schools and in the Church of Sweden', in U. Riegel & H.-G. Ziebertz (eds.), *How Teachers in Europe Teach Religion: An International Empirical Study in 16 Countries* (Münster: LIT-Verlag).

—— & Lied, S. (2012), 'Hegemonic speech genres of classrooms and their importance for RE learning', *British Journal of Religious Education*, 34/2, 155–68.

—— (2013) 'Social Studies: One Context in which Central RE Knowledge in Sweden is Constructed', in G. Skeie, J. Everington, I. ter Avest & S. Miedema (eds.), *Exploring Context in Religious Education Research: Empirical, Methodological and Theoretical Perspectives* (Münster: Waxmann).

—— (2014), 'Conditions for Teaching and Learning in Religious Education (RE): Perspectives of Teachers and Students at the Beginning of the 6th Grade in Sweden', *Nordidactica: Journal of Humanities & Social Science Education*, 2, 76–96.

—— (2017), 'Knowledge Development of Tweens in RE: The Importance of School Class and Communication', *British Journal of Religious Education*, 1–14.

Postman, N. (1998), *När skolans klocka klämtar: Om behovet av meningsskapande berättelser* (Gothenburg: Daidalos).

Skogar, B. (2000), 'Religionsdidaktikens kärnproblem', in M. Linnarud (ed.), *På spaning efter ämnets kärna: didaktiska tankar kring några skolämnen* (Karlstad: Universitetstryckeriet).

Skolverket (Swedish National Agency for Education) (2011), *Curriculum for the Compulsory School, Preschool Class and the leisure-time Centre 2011.* (Stockholm: Fritzes).

—— (2015), *SiRiS: Kvalitet och resultat i skolan [database]*, [WWW dokument]. URL http:// siris.skolverket.se/siris/f?p=SIRIS:33:0 (2015-05-22). See also https://www.skolverket.se/skolutveckling/statistik

Smart, N. (1997), *Dimensions of the sacred: An anatomy of the world's beliefs* (London: Fontana Press).

Stolare, M. (2014), 'På tal om historieundervisning: Perspektiv på undervisning i historia på mellanstadiet', *Acta Didactica Norge—Tidsskrift for Fagdidaktisk Forsknings– og Utviklingsarbeid i Norge*, 8/1, 1.

Säljö, R. (2005), *Lärande och kulturella redskap: Om lärprocesser och det kollektiva minnet* (Stockholm: Norstedts).

Tappan, M. B. (1992), 'Texts and contexts: Language, culture, and the development of moral functioning', in L. T. Winegar & J. Valsiner (ed.), *Children's development within social context*, i: *Metatheory and theory* (Hillsdale: Lawrence Erlbaum).

Wertsch, J. V. (1991), *Voices of the mind: A Sociocultural approach to mediated action* (Cambridge, MA: Harvard University Press).

Abstract

Mathematics teaching in Swedish compulsory school uses tasks and examples from which pupils can generalise. Studies have shown that which examples are chosen and how they are sequenced are of significance, since it can impede or enhance pupils' learning. It has been suggested that a systematic variation within and between sets of examples is more likely to result in progress than unstructured sets. In this essay, we report on two studies in which systematic variation was built into examples used in two lessons about multiplication in Year 4 and two lessons about multiplication and division in Year 7. The aim is to describe how teachers in the two studies used systematic variation in and between examples. We show that in the first study, the variation used in the examples sheds light on mathematical strategies and structure, whereas in the second study, the variation illuminates conceptual understanding and mathematical structure. The implications for pupils' learning of the implementation of systematic variation in and between sets of examples are discussed, and compared to the implications of teaching using sets of examples that have little systematic variation. It is argued that the use of systematic variation in and between carefully chosen sets of examples may provide pupils with greater opportunities for learning.

CHAPTER 3

Systematic variation in examples in mathematics teaching

Angelika Kullberg & Christina Skodras

Teachers face many challenging and important decisions when planning their teaching. In discussing the issues, this essay will go into considerable detail. Imagine that you are going to teach subtraction with regrouping to Year 1 pupils. What do you use as your first example? On what basis do you select the example? Which example should you use next? In a lesson study in Japan, a group of teachers spent a considerable amount of time discussing what would be a good example to start with when teaching subtraction with regrouping in Year 1 (Fernandez & Yoshida 2004). The team of teachers came to the conclusion that some examples showed better than others what they wanted their pupils to learn (strategies for decomposing the subtrahend—the number being subtracted). For example, $12-7$ focused on the decomposition of the subtrahend (here 7) in a better way. The team argued that $12-9$ would not be a good choice since 9 is so close to 10 that the pupils would not use the strategy that the teachers wanted to focus on—in other words, the pupils would decompose the number 12 into 10 and 2 to proceed with the calculation instead of decomposing the number 9 into 2 and 7. One teacher suggested $12-4$, but this example was also rejected because 4 was too easy to decompose $(2+2)$ and the team reasoned it would not bring about the intended learning outcome. This suggests that the teachers were aware that the examples they choose are important for what is made salient for learners.

Several studies indicate that what examples are chosen and how they are sequenced are of decisive importance for pupils' learning (for example, Kullberg & Runesson 2015; Rowland et al. 2003; Watson & Mason 2006). A study of novice teachers' selection of examples found that examples were selected randomly (Rowland et al. 2003). In another study of more experienced teachers, they claimed that they had never talked about their use of examples with colleagues: 'All five teachers whom we observed claimed that they had never articulated how to select and generate examples—not throughout their years of preservice and inservice education nor with colleagues or other forms of professional communications' (Zodik & Zaslavsky 2008, 173). These findings may indicate that teachers are not always aware of the choices they make regarding examples or the implications that these choices may have for pupils' learning. Furthermore, Kullberg and Runesson (2015) found that teachers used single examples or only a few examples to illustrate a procedure or mathematical principle. Dienes (1963) argues that single examples are insufficient to generalise from, since several examples are needed to get a sense of a concept.

We would argue that teachers need strategies and tools that can help them plan what examples to use or to decide how to exemplify something in the heat of the moment. The aim of this essay is to illustrate how teachers used systematic variation in and between examples. Two studies, one about multiplicative structure in Year 4 (Skodras 2015), and one about multiplication and division with numbers between 0 and 1 in Year 7 (Kullberg et al. 2014) are used to show how variation highlights the critical aspects of mathematical topics. In both studies, variation theory (Marton 2015; Marton & Booth 1997) was used in the analysis of the lessons.

Variation theory

Variation theory is the theoretical framework used in the two studies on which this essay is based. The theory emanates from more than thirty years of research in the phenomenographic research tradition (Marton 1981) and is based on the idea that the experience of variation is a prerequisite for learning (Marton 2015; Marton & Booth 1997). If everything varies, it is not possible to discern differences, since only what varies against an invariant background is likely to be noticed. According to the variation theory of learning, the learner needs to discern critical aspects of the object of learning. A critical aspect is what the learner needs to discern or distinguish between in order to learn. What those critical aspects might be cannot be known in advance, since it depends on the learners. Variation in regard to critical aspects is essential in order to be able to notice an aspect, and to see similarities and differences in relation to other aspects.

Ideas about the discernment of differences through variation are not new and are discussed by several scholars (Dienes 1960; Gibson & Gibson 1955). Dewey (1916) in *Democracy and Education* addressed the question of learning as differentiation. He wrote that the way in which something (for example, a chair) differs from something else with regard to its specific features is of significance for learning. It is not the qualities in themselves that are of greatest importance, but instead how they differ from other qualities. 'We do not really know a chair or have an idea of it by inventorying and enumerating its various isolated qualities, but only by bringing these qualities in connection with something else—the purpose which makes it a chair and not a table: or its difference from the kind of chair we are accustomed to, or the 'period' which it represents, and so on' (168).

For teachers, variation theory can be used to plan and analyse teaching and learning. In Chinese pedagogy, teaching with 'variation' (*bianshi*) is a well-known practice (Huang et al. 2006) that also emphasises variation in regard to instruction. Sun (2011) identifies three ways that bianshi is used in mathematics teaching: in the first way, 'one problem, multiple solutions', the teacher varies the solutions and allows the pupils to discern differences between them; in the second way, 'one problem, multiple changes', the teacher varies conditions and conclusions in the mathematical problem, and in the third way, 'multiple problems, one solution', the teacher varies the presentation of problems that could be solved in the same way. In each category, there is a pattern of variation and invariance.

Previous studies have demonstrated that mathematics examples used in a lesson could be described in terms of patterns of variation and invariance (Bartolini Bussi et al. 2013; Watson & Mason 2006). When sets of examples are presented (by the teacher or in a textbook), certain things vary while others remain invariant. As Watson and Mason (2006) argue, 'Constructing tasks that use variation and change optimally is a design project in which reflection about learner response leads to further refinement and precision of example choice and sequence' (100).

In this essay, we discuss the use of examples in mathematics teaching by reporting sections of two published studies in which variation was used in sets of examples to accomplish pupil learning. The rationale for selecting these studies was that they show two different ways that variation in examples can benefit pupils in their learning of mathematical strategies (Study 1), and of conceptual understanding (Study 2). We do not report the full analysis presented in these studies, and we do not enlarge on the existing, published analysis. Detailed information about the method and process of analysis are found in the studies (Kullberg et al. 2014; Skodras 2015).

Examples used for mathematics teaching

According to Rowland (2008), the examples teachers use and what they choose to focus on are important. As already noted, it has been argued that single examples may have little effect on pupil learning (Dienes 1960; Mason & Pimm 1984). For instance, if a teacher only uses the example 0.3×2 to show that multipliers between 0 and 1 make a 'smaller' product, this may not be sufficient to understand that all multiplication with numbers between 0 and 1 makes the product 'smaller'. It might be that the teacher is presenting one single example with the intention of its being an example of a generality. By just giving one example, the pupils may not experience the example as an instance of a generality (Mason & Pimm 1984). Furthermore, examples should be selected in a way that invites pupils to think and reason mathematically (Simon & Tzur 2004). Several researchers indicate (for example, Watson & Mason 2002) that it is important 'for pupils to have several examples from which to get a general sense of what is being taught' (378). Teachers should choose 'generic examples' that promote the general aspect and not the specific aspect of the example (Mason & Pimm 1984). Examples should help pupils to move from the specific to the general by making it possible to see relationships and generalisations (Simon & Tzur 2004; Watson & Mason 2002, 2006; Zazkis & Chernoff 2008), and the teacher needs to help pupils not just to 'learn' the example, but to see the generality in sets of examples (Mason & Pimm 1984). One way to discern relationships in and between examples is through systematic variation.

Variation in examples used for mathematics teaching is considered an essential component for pupil learning. Dienes (1960) suggests four principles for mathematics learning, of which two concern variation: the mathematical variability principle, and the perceptual variability principle. Influenced by Wertheimer (1945), Dienes suggested that certain variation is more effective for concept growth.

> With the concept of a parallelogram we can vary the shape by varying the angles and the length of the opposite sides; we can vary the position, as long as we keep the opposite sides parallel. Clearly a set of congruent parallelograms placed in the same position would not be a suitable set of experiences for the growth of the concept. We might formulate this by saying that as many variables as possible should vary so as to provide optimum experience in concept growth. (Dienes 1960, 43)

By giving the pupils the opportunity to see parallelograms in several examples, as Dienes suggests, the pupils are offered the chance to identify key mathematical ideas. Dienes highlights that it is not enough to provide several examples of the same type, such as ones where all parallelograms are placed in the same position. If pupils only experience the same type of examples, it will not support them in gaining a thorough understanding of the concept. In Dienes's example with the parallelogram, two critical aspects for pupils' experiences of parallelograms are mentioned, shape and position. Sun (2011) argues that looking at 'one-thing-at-a-time' gives fewer opportunities to link the examples to one another than looking at several aspects simultaneously. If the example only focuses on 'one-thing-at-a-time', the pupils may have greater difficulty in discerning the critical aspects.

Study 1, teaching multiplicative structure

Study 1 reports on findings from a BA dissertation which illustrates how variation is used in classroom teaching in enacted sets of examples in multiplication (Skodras 2015). The data was generated from lessons about multiplication taught in Year 4 with fifteen pupils. The study examined how examples in multiplication taken from the teaching material *Muffles' Truffles* (Cameron & Fosnot 2007) are constructed and what aspects it was made possible to discern for pupils in the classroom when the teacher used the material. The teacher (the second author) had sixteen years of experience of teaching in elementary school. The pupils, who participated voluntarily and had written consent to participate, had previously experienced multiplication as repeated addition, an additive structure (for example, 4×3=3+3+3+3).

In the study, the teacher uses arrays to illustrate the multiplicative structure for the pupils. The examples used during the lessons are from a teaching guide that is part of the *Muffles' Truffles* material. This guide differs from many other teaching guides in mathematics since it has 'strings' of examples that are intended for the teacher to use in class. A string is a set of related examples with systematic variation in and between the examples. When teaching one string, the examples are presented one after the other. In that way the pupils have the opportunity to see all the examples separately but can also relate them to the other examples in the string. The study reported

The second string	The third string
2 x 5	2 x 5
1 x 5	4 x 5
3 x 5	4 x 10
5 x 4	10 x 4
4 x 5	10 x 6
5 x 5	6 x 10
	10 x 12
	10 x 18

Fig. 3.1.

on an analysis of five lessons with five strings (sets of examples) in multiplication. Skodras (2015) analysed how the examples varied and what was possible for pupils to discern from the examples. In this essay, we present the analysis of the second and the third string, and hence the variation in and between the examples (Fig. 3.1).

In the implementation of the second string, the teacher shows an array to illustrate the multiplication for each example. The first factor in each multiplication represents rows (for example, 2 in 2×5) whereas the second factor in each multiplication represents columns in the array (for example, 5 in 2×5) (Fig. 3.2). The first example (2×5) in both of these strings is familiar to the pupils as they have previously worked with a '2×5 box equals 10' in a context about truffles. The example, 2×5, was represented by the teacher (Fig. 3.2). A key issue is that the teacher shows the arrays very briefly so that pupils do

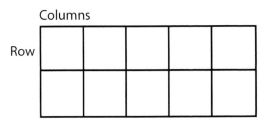

Fig. 3.2.

not have time to count each square in the array. In the third string, the teacher only writes the example on the board and the pupils are supposed to come up with an array of their own.

Lesson 1, the second string

This string has six examples that are related to one another with a certain variation in order to highlight critical aspects concerning mathematical strategies and structure. This gives the pupils the opportunity to discern some important mathematical ideas such as the distributive law and the commutative law (Fig. 3.3).

The variation of the first factor in the three examples (2×5, 1×5, and 3×5), and the fact that the examples are presented as a set and not as one example, gives the pupils the chance to compare the examples and look at relationships (for example, Simon & Tzur 2004; Watson & Mason 2002). If the teacher just gave the example 3×5, it is not certain that the pupils would be able to notice that 3×5 is a combination of 2×5+1×5 and the distributive law may not come to the fore. The next pair within the set, 5×4 and 4×5, varies in another way, by switching the order of the factors 4 and 5. When the order of the factors is switched, it becomes possible to distinguish a new critical aspect of multiplication, namely the *commutative law*. The analysis of what the pupils say in their discussion of the examples 5×4 and 4×5 shows that the pupils see that 5×4=4×5, and reflect on the ways the multiplication can be illustrated with an array (two 2×5 units or two 5×2 units combined in different ways, horizontally or vertically). This indicates that the examples 5×4 and 4×5 in combination with an array invite pupils to think and reason mathematically (Simon & Tzur 2004). In this part of the lesson, the pupils reason mathematically about what the first and the second factor stand for, and about the relationship between 5×4 and 5×2+5×2. Even in this example, where the focus is on the commutative law, the pupils are forced to use the distributive law (5×4=5×2+5×2 and 4×5=2×5+2×5) to explain how they should illustrate the multiplication using arrays.

Through the systematic variation in the second string, pupils are

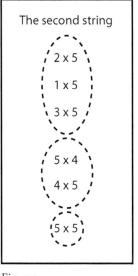

Fig. 3.3.

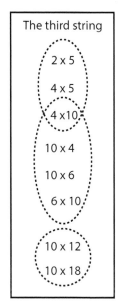

Fig. 3.4.

given an opportunity to solve the last example (5×5) by combining arrays, two 2×5 arrays and one 1×5 array arranged vertically. By comparing the different examples in the string, the pupils are able to discern that this last is another example for them to solve with a focus on the distributive law. In this string, the variation in the set of examples highlights different critical aspects concerning mathematical strategies and laws.

Lesson 2, the third string

In Lesson 2 when the next string is implemented the teacher does not show images of the arrays. Instead, the teacher writes the examples on the whiteboard one at a time. The pupils are prompted to figure out how the multiplication could be illustrated as an array. The string contains eight examples that vary systematically. The examples in this string do not vary in the same way as in the first string.

In the first set (Fig. 3.4), in the examples 2×5=10, 4×5=20, 4×10=40 the first or second factor is varied by being doubled. This highlights

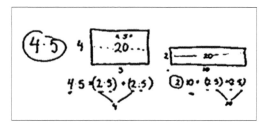

Fig. 3.5.

what happens to the product when one of the factors is doubled. A critical aspect that is highlighted in this set of examples is that it does not matter *which* factor you double, the product will still be doubled. Furthermore, the examples highlight the difficulties of combining two 2×5-units into 4×5 or two 4×5-units into 4×10. Pupils have different images of 4×5, which the teacher also highlights in the discussion.

The teacher compares what varied and what is invariant when the pupils combine 2×5 in two different ways (Fig. 3.5). She asks the pupils why 4×5 and 2×10 are equal. Both the pupils and the teacher talk about what varies and what is invariant. In this way, the associative law is introduced (for example, 2×(2×5)=(2×2)×5). However, neither the teacher nor the pupils mention the double/half aspect (that when one factor is doubled the other halves) (4×5 and 2×10) in their discussion of 2×(2×5)=(2×2)×5.

The examples in the second set (4×10, 10×4 and 6×10, 10×6) vary by shifting the position of the factors. It seems that the pupils have discerned the commutative law aspect. One pupil explains that he just 'rotated his paper' 90 degrees and then he had the other array (6×10 and 10×6). The pupils had previously encountered examples with the same mathematical idea in the first string. We assume that one reason for the construction of the strings is to help the pupils to move from the specific to the general by verbalising relationships and by comparing the examples (for example, Watson & Mason 2006; Zazkis & Chernoff 2008) both within and between the strings.

The last set of examples (10×12 and 10×18) gives the pupil the opportunity to discern the distributive law and a power of 10 (10×10) by splitting 10×12=(10×10)+(10×2)=100+20=120. The pupils solved the item in three different ways. It is likely that the pupils looked at this example and tried to apply some of the ideas from the previous examples. One of their strategies was doubling 10×6 to get 10×12 (10×6+10×6). The second strategy involved repeating the 2×5-unit 12 times and the third strategy made use of the distributive law, taking the 10×10 unit and combining it with a 10×2 unit as follows: (10×10)+(10×2). Hence, we can see that the variation in multiplication of two two-digit numbers gives rise to different strategies. This last set of examples shows how pupils benefited from the string. The string invited the pupils to reflect on and reason about how to solve two two-digit multiplications. The examples allowed the pupils to think and communicate about whether they could represent 10×12 in these three ways. Is 10×12 the same as 10×6+10×6 and the same as 10×10+10×2?

We suggest that the examples used in the lessons had a pivotal role in how the pupils were given opportunities to experience the content. The analysis shows that the way in which the examples were presented allowed the pupils to develop their own mathematical strategies. A relevant factor in the first lesson was the images of multiplication that the teacher showed very briefly. We suggest that these images might have helped the pupils take the step from seeing multiplication as an additive structure to seeing it as a multiplicative structure.

Study 2, teaching multiplication and division with denominators between 0 and 1

The second study illustrates variation in sets of examples about multiplication and division (Kullberg et al. 2014). The data in the study was generated from a type of theory-driven lesson study (a learning study) about division in Year 7, in which the teachers wanted their pupils to learn that when the denominator is a number between 0 and 1, the quotient becomes larger than the numerator. A learning study (Huang et al. 2016; Marton & Pang 2006) shares many common features with a lesson study (Fernandez &

Yoshida 2004; Lewis et al. 2009), in which a team of teachers work in collaboration in a cyclical process to plan, teach, and revise a single lesson. In a learning study, the teachers revise the lesson two or three times, and they use a learning theory (variation theory) as a tool to plan and analyse the lessons.[2] Four teachers and one researcher worked together for almost a full term. The teachers were experienced mathematics teachers, with about ten years' teaching in lower-secondary school. The teachers collaboratively designed the examples used in the lesson, in contrast to Study 1 in which the examples were designed by the authors of the teaching guide. The aim with a learning study is primarily to identify critical aspects of an object of learning and try to implement the identified critical aspects in the lessons in order to promote pupil learning. During the process of the learning study, the teachers also refined the enactment of sets of examples used in the lessons, and also made changes to the sets. What the teachers pointed out in regard to the examples was mainly what they believed were critical aspects for learning division and multiplication. It is known that pupils often make generalisations from previous experience of operations with whole numbers, for instance pupils may believe that multiplication always 'makes things bigger' whereas division always 'makes things smaller' (Vamvakoussi & Vosniadou 2004; Verschaffel et al. 2007). The teachers were aware of this, and in the second and third lessons in the cycle it was identified as critical for pupils to see the difference between when division makes a bigger quotient than the numerator and when it does not.

In the learning study, the teachers designed and implemented tasks that they discussed with their pupils. One task (Fig. 3.4) played a major role in the lesson in terms of the amount of time spent on it. Analysis of the pattern of variation and invariance in the set of examples shows that the operations vary in the two columns (multiplication and division), and hence it is possible to notice the difference between the operations. The number 100 is invariant in all examples. We can see that the numbers in the examples in each horizontal row are invariant (100×20 and $100\div20$). In each column, the numbers vary, from multiplication and division with larger

100 x 20 = 2,000	$\frac{100}{20} = 5$
100 x 4 = 400	$\frac{100}{4} = 25$
100 x 2 = 200	$\frac{100}{2} = 50$
100 x 1 = 100	$\frac{100}{1} = 100$
100 x 0,5 = 50	$\frac{100}{0,5} = 200$
100 x ,01 = 10	$\frac{100}{0,1} = 1,000$

Fig. 3.6.

numbers (100÷20), to multiplication and division with smaller numbers (100÷0.5). The last two examples in each column have numbers between 0 and 1 (0.5 and 0.1), as the denominator or one of the factors. The numbers in the whole set were deliberately chosen to make it possible for pupils to experience what happens with the product and the quotient when multiplying or dividing by a number between 0 and 1.

The examples in the set were designed to draw attention to critical aspects for pupils' learning of why the quotient is sometimes bigger than the numerator (Fig. 3.6). The critical aspects identified by the teachers before the first lesson were (*i*) the relationship between the numerator, denominator, and quotient; (*ii*) the two forms of division (partition and measurement); (*iii*) the positioning system for numbers; (*iv*) differences between multiplication and division; and (*v*) what a number between 0 and 1 is. However, the teachers' understanding of what these critical aspects entailed had deepened by the end of the study (for detail, see Mårtensson 2015). In the following section, a description is given of how the teachers enacted the set of examples in the first two lessons in the learning study.

Lesson 1

Teacher A, who taught Lesson 1 (L1) in the learning-study cycle enacted the examples in the set one at a time, starting with the two multiplication items on the left-hand side and then followed by the two division items on the right-hand side. After that, the following four multiplication items were solved and then the four division items. In L1, none of the critical aspects were addressed through the worked set of examples, even though the set of examples was designed to address division and multiplication with numbers between 0 and 1. One feature that was brought up by the L1 teacher was the inverse relationship between multiplication and division (for example, 20×5=100 and 100÷20=5); however, this aspect was not identified by the teaching team as being critical for pupils when it came to the intended object of learning (which was why the quotient sometimes becomes bigger than the numerator). In the post-lesson meeting, the teachers realised that 'why the quotient sometimes becomes bigger than the numerator' and the critical aspects associated with this needed to be focused on more explicitly, as the variation in the set of examples does not automatically reveal the critical aspects.

Lesson 2

In Lesson 2 (L2), a revised lesson implemented in another class, Teacher B worked through the items one by one together with the pupils, starting with the examples of multiplication and then continuing with division. Afterwards, the teacher asked whether the pupils could see any patterns in or between the columns. The teacher summarised the patterns identified as 'The numbers get smaller the further down the column you go', and 'The smaller the number multiplied by is, the smaller the product and the smaller the number divided by is, the larger the quotient'. The teacher pointed at 100÷20=5 and 100÷4=25, and said 'Here the quotient is a smaller number than the numerator; is it always like that?'. In the discussion, one pupil said that after 0 there was a difference and another pupil said that after 1 the quotient became larger than the numerator. At this point, one of the critical aspects was brought up by means of the examples, namely the relationship between the numerator, denominator, and quotient. In order to make the 'turning point' explicit, the teacher drew a line under items with 1 in the denominator or one of the factors. The teacher then continued, saying that 'When the denominator is smaller than one, the quotient [points to the quotient 200, in $100 \div 0.5 = 200$] is larger than the numerator [points to 100, in $100 \div 0.5 = 200$]'. The teacher directed the pupils' attention to the multiplication column when he said 'What happens with the multiplication item then?' By comparing what happened in the multiplication column with the division column, it was made possible to discern that the quotient became larger than 100, and the product smaller.

After L2, the team discussed the set of examples and restricted the variation in the examples even more in L3. They changed the numbers in the examples in the multiplication and division columns (for example, 100×50, 100×5, 100×1, and 100×0.5 and 100×0.1) in order to further direct pupils' attention towards the critical aspects, rather than calculations, by trying to ensure that the pupils were able to solve the items more easily in their heads. Thus, the examples used in the first two lessons were primarily designed and enacted to highlight the critical aspects initially identified for learning in relation to conceptual understanding of the topic taught. However, in L1, the teachers could not agree about how they should direct pupils' attention. Even though there was a pattern of variation and invariance in the task, the teacher did not address any of the critical aspects for the object of learning. However, in the post-lesson analysis of L1, the teachers agreed that the relationship between the numerator, denominator, and the quotient needed to be addressed in order to see why the quotient sometimes becomes smaller than the numerator.

Final remarks—didactical consequences for teaching and learning in the classroom

This essay reports two didactic classroom studies in which the variation of examples played a significant role. The specific aim of this essay was to illustrate how teachers used systematic variation in and between sets of examples in mathematics lessons. Our study contributes to knowledge about the role of sequence in the use of examples. We suggest that the enacted examples illustrated in the two studies show that what examples are used and how they are sequenced are of significance. Carefully chosen examples sequenced in a particular order can make it possible for learners to discern certain things; however, the teacher needs to direct the pupils' attention towards what the examples are intended to elucidate. We therefore agree with Rowland (2008), who suggests that single examples or randomly chosen sets of examples may impede pupils' learning (Rowland 2008; Rowland et al. 2003). Single examples, we would argue, limit pupils' opportunities to generalise from the example (Dienes 1960).

This essay highlights the use of sets of examples and what it is possible for pupils to discern from them. We have reported on two studies, and claim that the variation in and between sets of examples seems to play a significant role for learning by helping pupils to see mathematical structure and relationships. In comparison to the use of single examples, systematic variation within and between carefully chosen sets of examples, we suggest, may provide pupils with greater opportunities for learning. Hence, the variation in and between examples has subject-didactical implications in the classroom, since it illustrates what teachers can do in order to provide a more powerful learning situation for their pupils.

Lately, variation as a principle in the teaching of mathematics has gained a lot of attention, particularly in western teaching (Drury 2018; Huang 2017). The way teachers use variation in China, for example, 'one problem multiple solutions', is being used as a model by, for example, British teachers in order to accomplish better teaching and learning in the UK (Drury 2018). 'One problem multiple solutions' is variation on a larger-grained scale than the variation analysed in this essay (referred to by some researchers as procedural variation) (Drury 2018). However, variation can successfully be used in the classroom more or less systematically to a greater or lesser extent. In this essay we argue, along with others (for example, Marton 2015), that *what is varied* and *how* matters for learners' opportunities to discern what is intended. If teachers are not aware of what they vary or keep invariant, and why they do it, it is not likely to improve pupils' learning. Therefore, we suggest teachers need time to reflect on what variation may benefit learning in regard to the specific topic and group of learners.

In this essay, we have focused on systematic variation in regard to the examples used in two mathematics classrooms. We are aware that variation is not the only factor when teaching, since the complexity of classrooms also involves other important factors, some of which are discussed elsewhere in this volume. Nevertheless, variation as a teaching principle goes beyond the teaching and learning of mathematics, and hence can also be used in the teaching of other subjects. However, the question of which variation is the most powerful in order to enhance pupils' learning is one that needs further investigation. Systematic variation, we believe, can be used as a tool for teachers and researchers to plan and analyse lessons in order to enhance pupils' learning.

Notes

1 In this study, the term *critical aspects* primarily refers to the aspects that it is assumed to be necessary to discern in relation to the content and do not stem from how pupils experience the content.

2 For more details on the learning study and the learning study cycle, see Kullberg (2010).

References

Bartolini Bussi, M. G., X. Sun & A. Ramploud (2013), 'A dialogue between cultures about task design for primary school', in C. Margolinas (ed.), *Proceedings of ICMI Study 22: Task Design in Mathematics Education* (Oxford: ICMI).

Cameron, A. & C. Fosnot (2007), *New York Muffles' Truffles: Multiplication and division with the array* (Portsmouth: Heinemann).

Dewey, J. (1916), *Democracy and education* (New York: Macmillan).

Dienes, Z. (1960), *Building up mathematics* (London: Hutchinson Educational).

—— (1963), *An experimental study of mathematics-learning* (London: Hutchinson).

Drury, H. (2018), *Oxford teaching guides. How to Teach Mathematics For Mastery. Second school edition* (Oxford: Oxford University Press).

Fernandez, C. & M. Yoshida (2004), *Lesson study: A Japanese approach to improving mathematics teaching and learning* (Mahwah, NJ: Lawrence Erlbaum).

Gibson, J. J. & E. J. Gibson (1955), 'Perceptual learning: Differentiation or enrichment?' *Psychological Review*, 62/1, 32–41.

Huang, R., Mok, I. & Leung, F. (2006), 'Repetition or variation: Practising in the mathematics classrooms in China', in D. Clarke, C. Keitel & Y. Shimizu (eds.), *Mathematics classrooms in twelve countries: The Insider's Perspective* (Rotterdam: Sense).

Huang, R., Z. Gong & X. Han (2016), 'Implementing mathematics teaching that promotes students' understanding through theory-driven lesson study', *ZDM Mathematics Education*, 48/4, 425–39.

—— & Li, Y. (2017), *Teaching and learning mathematics through variation: Confucian heritage meets Western theories* (Rotterdam: Sense).

Kullberg, A. (2010), *What is taught and what is learned: Professional insights gained and shared by teachers of mathematics* (Gothenburg: Acta Universitatis Gothoburgensis).

—— & U. Runesson (2015), 'Examples with variation. Teachers' choice and use of mathematical examples.' Paper, presented at the European Association of Learning and Instruction biennial conference, Limassol, Cyprus, 25–29 August.

—— U. Runesson & P. Mårtensson (2014), 'Different possibilities to learn from the same task', *PNA*, 8/4, 139–50.

Lewis, C., R. Perry & J. Hurd (2009), 'Improving mathematics instruction through lesson study: A theoretical model and North American case', *Journal of Mathematics Teacher Education*, 12/4, 285–304.

Marton, F. (1981), 'Phenomenography—Describing conceptions of the world around us', *Instructional Science*, 10/2, 177–200.

—— & S. Booth (1997), *Learning and awareness* (Mahwah, NJ: Lawrence Erlbaum).

—— & M. F. Pang (2006), 'On some necessary conditions of learning', *Journal of the Learning Sciences*, 15/2, 193–220.

Marton, F. (2015), *Necessary conditions of learning* (New York: Routledge).

Mason, J. & D. Pimm (1984), 'Generic examples: Seeing the general in the particular', *Educational Studies in Mathematics*, 15/3, 227–89.

Mårtensson, P. (2015), *Att få syn på avgörande skillnader: Lärares kunskap om lärandeobjektet* (Jönköping: School of Education and Communication, Jönköping University).

Rowland, T. (2008), 'The purpose, design and use of examples in the teaching of elementary mathematics', *Educational Studies in Mathematics*, 69/2, 149–63.

Rowland, T., A. Thwaites & P. Huckstep (2003), 'Novices' choice of examples in the teaching of elementary mathematics', paper presented at the Mathematics Education into the 21st Century Project, at the conference The Decidable and the Undecidable in Mathematics Education, Brno, Czech Republic, 19–25 Sept.

Simon, M. A. & R. Tzur (2004), 'Explicating the role of mathematical tasks in conceptual learning: An elaboration of the hypothetical learning trajectory', *Mathematical Thinking and Learning*, 6/2, 91–104.

Skodras, C. (2015), Undervisning i multiplikation genom systematiskt varierade exempel (magisteruppsats/BA dissertation) [Teaching multiplication through systematic variation of examples]. (Gothenburg: Göteborgs universitet).

Sun, X. (2011), '"Variation problems" and their roles in the topic of fraction division in Chinese mathematics textbook examples', *Educational Studies in Mathematics*, 76/1, 65–85.

Vamvakoussi, X. & S. Vosniadou (2004), 'Understanding the structure of the set of rational numbers: A conceptual change approach', *Learning & Instruction*, 14, 453–67.

Verschaffel, L., B. Greer & E. De Corte (2007), 'Whole number concepts and operations', in F. K. J. Lester (ed.), *Second handbook of research on mathematics teaching and learning*, ii (Charlotte, NC: Information Age).

Watson, A. & J. Mason (2002), 'Student-generated examples in the learning of mathematics', *Canadian Journal of Science, Mathematics & Technology Education*, 2/2, 237–49.

Watson, A. & J. Mason (2006), 'Seeing an exercise as a single mathematical object: Using variation to structure sense-making', *Mathematical Thinking & Learning*, 8/2, 91–111.

Wertheimer, M. (1945), *Productive thinking* (New York: Harper).

Zazkis, R. & E. J. Chernoff (2008), 'What makes a counter example exemplary?' *Educational Studies in Mathematics*, 68(3), 195–208.

Zodik, I. & O. Zaslavsky (2008), 'Characteristics of teachers' choice of examples in and for mathematics', *Educational Studies in Mathematics*, 69/2, 165–82.

Abstract

This essay describes part of a study intended to develop an analytical understanding of learning in small groups within the research paradigm of phenomenography and the variation theory of learning, here paying specific attention to the role of the tutor in a small-group tutorial situation. The empirical study we are drawing on concerns small groups of first-year university physics students working on a problem in Newtonian mechanics on the behaviour of relevant forces when an ox pulls a box along the ground. We characterise the role of the tutor who intervenes at intervals as engaging with the space of meaning that is forming and reforming as the group discussion progresses. What is discussed is characterised using the identification of five objects of discussion, and in turn a number of dimensions of variation for each object of discussion. These are used to investigate how a space of meaning is constituted in the students' conversation, which can have different qualities, depending on the patterns in which dimensions of variation are handled in discussion. From this analysis, in terms of these patterns and objects of discussion, we posit a proto-model for tutor intervention: preparation, interaction, and exit.

CHAPTER 4

Engaging with a group's space of meaning
The tutor's role in small-group didactics

Åke Ingerman & Shirley Booth

A common feature of classrooms is that students are expected to work in groups, both for the expedient reasons of space, time, and resources, and didactic assumptions that talking to one another, articulating problems, and engaging with ideas will support students in their learning (see Freeman et al. 2014). Small groups are common features of the learning and teaching modes at all educational institutions, from pre-school to higher education. While lectures are the main feature of physics courses at university, which form the background to this essay, there are nevertheless small groups in traditional tutorial problem-solving classes and laboratory work, as well as in pedagogical trends such as problem-based learning, the flipped classroom, and other forms of interactive engagement (see Hinko et al. 2016, Hake 1998). And while lectures proceed on the assumption that knowledge can be transmitted from the lecturer to the learner using such resources as language, representations, and demonstrations, working in small groups assumes that engagement with the knowledge by students working together is at least complementary to lectures, and at best improves learning (see Larson 2010). The lecturer now takes the role of designer of the situation and tutor or mentor for the groups as they work. It is this didactic role that is the focus of this essay.

The aim of the study we draw on here has been to develop an analytical understanding of learning in small groups within the research paradigm of phenomenography and the variation theory of learning (Marton & Booth 1997; Marton & Tsui 2004; Marton 2015; Rovio-Johansson & Ingerman 2016). This approach enables us to address questions related to what constitutes the quality of a group discussion in terms of what is discussed, the character of the discussion, and the appropriate, effective didactical framing of group discussions. In particular, we ask what different approaches employed by tutors can support or hinder different groups in their discussions. In short, we ask three questions. What is the variation in what is discussed in the groups? What is the variation in how the students in the discussion attend to what is discussed? And what distinct tutor intervention approaches can be identified that can have bearing on the results with respect to the what and how of group discussions?

Whereas the archetypal phenomenographic study aims to describe learners' ways of experiencing a particular phenomenon they encounter in their education, generally with semi-structured interviews to generate data, here we take the variation theory of learning as our framework, in which observations of tutorials are appropriate sources of data. We do not ask how students experience their discussions in the group, or how they experience the tutor's interventions, but rather we draw on the theoretical development to address the issues of how the students together create a space in which meaning-making can take place, and by the end of the essay we will be able to address the question of what it takes for the tutor to be able to engage with that space in order to support the students' productive exploration of it.

The research approach adopted in this essay seeks to maintain the complex relationship between learners, teachers, and content matter, in the tradition of European didactics. The unifying concept is the space of meaning that the students form in their discussions around a simple but unusual problem in mechanics. The teacher, here a tutor who interacts with the groups, is able to engage with this space in one way or another, and that is the focus of the analysis offered here. In line with the relational view of knowledge and knowledge production that phenomenography espouses, we too take a relational view of the didactical triangle of learners, teachers, and content matter. All three nodes of the didactic triangle play a role in our study, and we return to them in our analysis.

Empirical design

The empirical data is taken from a study of seven groups of first-year students at a Swedish university, from one of two programmes—engineering physics or bioengineering—both of which have an equivalent physics course, partly with the same lecturer. The data has been analysed from various perspectives: gender (Berge & Danielsson 2013), problem-solving (Berge et al. 2012), group dynamics (Berge & Weilenmann 2014), and group work (Berge 2011; Berge et al. 2009).

Self-selected groups of three or four students were asked to solve a problem in Newtonian mechanics while being video- and audio-recorded in an otherwise naturalistic setting, in as much as a tutor known to the students dropped in a couple of times during the session to offer help and advice. The size of the groups was chosen to maximise the potential for both interesting group dynamics and engagement with the problem. The discussion was limited to 60 minutes, during which time the students were seen to be at ease during the discussions while retaining a clear focus on the physics problem-solving and discussions. Subsequent analysis relies on detailed transcriptions and the students' notes as well as the original recordings, the audio recordings being supported by video in order to distinguish speakers and follow gestures.

The physics problem the students were asked to work with concerned an ox dragging a box along the ground, and was intended to support the development of the conceptual understanding of force and friction in Newtonian mechanics while at the same time encouraging the students to talk and interact with one another. The intention of developing conceptual understanding was realised through presenting the students with two open questions: Which forces are acting on the ox and the box, and how are they related to

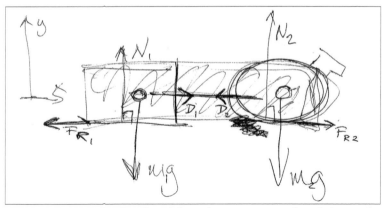

Figure 4.1. Example of students' force diagram. It was altered during the discussion from one to two systems. Note the correction of the friction force to be directed forwards.

one another? And which of these forces affect the movement of the ox and the box? The second intention, of encouraging discussion, was met by the deliberate exclusion of any numerical or mathematical features. Students might at first think, partly for this reason, that the problem is simple, but it comes with several well-known conceptual difficulties.

An acceptable answer to the first part of the problem is to draw the system—the ox and the box—with arrows to show the forces that affect it, and are of external origin, as that shown in Fig. 4.1. This is the force diagram of the system, one of the first things to be taught in the routine of solving such a problem (see Heckler 2010). Here, the relevant forces in the horizontal direction are the friction force acting on the ox's hooves and the friction force acting on the box. The vertical forces are the gravitational forces and the normal forces on the box and the ox. If the system moves with constant velocity, then Newton's second law tells us that in the direction of motion the total forces in opposite directions are equal in size—they balance one another. The Newtonian approach to understanding force is a major difficulty for students in grasping mechanics, as has been described in detail (see, for example, Trowbridge & McDermott 1981; Clement 1982; Johansson et al.

1985; Bowden et al. 1992; McDermott 1997; Palmer 1997). The widely used Force Concept Inventory (Hestenes et al. 1992) is grounds for the research-based, systematic development of forms of teaching (see, for example, Redish 2003), clearly indicating that 'active engagement' is thought to be very important, without clearly explaining what it means (see Hinko et al. 2016).

The key conceptual difficulty in this particular problem is to realize that balancing the friction force acting backwards on the box there is a friction force *forwards* on the ox's hooves, which is counter-intuitive (see, for example, Besson et al. 2007 for a discussion of the conceptual challenges associated with friction). Tutors in such a situation have a difficult task, for they need to engage with the ongoing discussion, interact in what is thought to be an appropriate way, and wind up the interaction in such a way that the group can continue, before they move on to another group. Their time is limited—in the case of this study, the tutor spent between 2 and 8 minutes with each group—and on entry they have no detailed insight into the direction and progress of the discussion. They have to engage with the meaning-making that the groups have embarked on and develop an approach that supports the group in exploring it productively.

Analysing group discussions

Before moving on to the work of the tutor, we will look at the ways in which the groups were found to discuss the problem and create spaces of meaning of differing quality. Our approach to the analysis characterises the students as constituting and experiencing a shared space of meaning, related to the pedagogical situation, primarily in terms of the design of the task and the group discussion format, taking variation as the basic mechanism for learning. We draw heavily on variation theory as the lens through which to inspect the group discussions, using tools that originate in the phenomenographic research tradition—for example, experience and learning (Marton & Booth 1997), dimensions of variation (Booth & Hultén 2003), the variation theory of learning (Marton & Tsui 2004), and threads of learning (Ingerman et al. 2009b). But in contrast to phenomenographic and variation theory studies of classrooms, where the teacher is thought to be the agent for learning, in our study the groups have their own agency.

The key concepts in variation theory concern the object of learning and the aspects of it that are critical for learning or understanding it in a particular way. In previous work on individual learning in group discussions we have characterised the process in relation to the variation around critical aspects of the object of learning as constituted in the course of the discussion (Booth & Hultén 2003; Ingerman et al. 2009a; Ingerman et al. 2009b). In this analysis, rather than focusing on individual learning, we are interested in portraying collaborative meaning-making, as manifest in the quality of the unfolding conversation and the space that is thereby being formed in which the meaning of the Newtonian concepts relating to friction and the problem can be explored. This leads to our first two research questions in analysing the qualitative variation between different discussions—what variation is to be seen, the ways the object of learning is handled, and what characterises the differences between discussions that handle the object of learning with varying degrees of sophistication?

Objects of discussion

One feature of the phenomenographic studies that inform the present work is to make an analytical separation between *what* is being learnt and *how* it is being learnt. Of the first, we could ask 'What phenomenon are the students learning about?' or 'What is the object of learning that is being handled?', thus drawing on phenomenography or variation theory respectively. Here we investigate the space of shared meaning that is constituted in the groups' discussions, which we hold to be a series of episodes, each of which addresses a specific feature of the problem, involving a complex of related phenomena. It is possible to determine a small number of distinct categories of episode in a thematic analysis, each focusing on a distinct complex of phenomena with respect to the problem. Doing so results in five categories, which we are calling *objects of discussion* (Fig. 4.2).

- the system/systems to be used to identify external forces
- the relationship between force and motion
- the characteristics of friction forces
- recontextualisation of the problem in other settings for comparison
- recontextualisation of the discussion in formal mathematical and symbolic terms

Figure 4.2. The five categories of episodes with the object of discussion.

The first three objects of discussion concern the specific problem, while the last two reflect more generic problem-solving tactics. They are related to three principal phenomena: Newton's first law of motion (that in an inertial frame of reference an object either remains at rest or continues to move at a constant velocity, unless acted upon by a force), friction (whether static or kinetic), and mathematics. When the 'what' of the discussions is analysed, episodes concerning these five themes occur repeatedly, whether in a single group of students or from group to group, in different patterns that are complicated by shifts in focus: the problem in question is focused yet open, and students move from phenomenon to phenomenon, topic to topic, theme to theme. One could analyse the discussions from a normative perspective of physics, but that would not tell us much about our students as learners or what they are learning. To progress in our didactical thinking, it is important to identify the *meaning* that emerges, and to do that from the perspective of the students. This may still be underpinned by a normative goal of understanding the physics of the problem. One of phenomenography's main aims is to capture the students' perspectives on a specific phenomenon. This work differs from the mainstream by having complexes of phenomena in each identified episode.

Next in our general analysis, we identify and analyse the objects of discussion where the *same* object of discussion was seen to be in focus. Taking our cue from phenomenographic studies (for example, Johansson et al. 1985), as well as relevant studies using other methods (for example, Trowbridge & McDermott 1981; McDermott 1997) we can expect the students to assume qualitatively different ways of understanding features in the discussion, and hence an object of discussion can also be expected to show a qualitative variation. And in the body of this essay it is the third of the objects of discussion, the characteristics of friction forces, that we focus on.

Focusing on one object of discussion

Here we draw on the theory derived from phenomenographic studies, that a phenomenon is experientially constituted of a number of dimensions of variation, and we studied the objects of discussion to see that they too can be thus expressed. That is to say that an object of discussion can consist of a small number of dimensions and different values for these can account for the overall variation. This amounts to the core of the discussion, giving meaning to what the object of discussion is, and is not, in the variation of the discussants' experience of the world—here Newton's first and second laws and the concepts involved in the problem of the box and the ox. In this phenomenographic analytical framework, learning requires that the learner comes to discern new dimensions of variation, thereby developing the capability of experiencing the phenomenon in qualitatively different, more complex and powerful ways (Marton & Booth 1997). Even in the case of discussions in a group, dimensions of variation will be opened and scrutinised by the participants in the group, thereby creating and developing the shared space of meaning and the potential to experience the objects of discussion in qualitatively new ways.

In this phase of analysis, four dimensions of variation concerning the characteristics of friction forces were identified in the empirical material as being distinctly different, meaningful, and relevant (Fig. 4.3). First, friction as *a distinct kind of force* is primarily related to the fact that a friction force is a response to the movement of the system through its interaction with what is external to it (in accordance with Newton's third law). Second, the *point of the application of friction* is that friction is not a force internal to a system, but it acts at system borders, in accordance with which system borders are to be considered. Third, the *magnitude of a friction force* is

Friction: a distinct kind of force
Friction: its point of application
Friction: its magnitude
Friction: its situation dependency

Figure 4.3. The four dimensions that are the object of discussion about 'the characteristics of friction forces'.

dependent on the specific features of, on the one hand, the system border, and, on the other hand, the kind of movement of the system. For example, the friction on a cartwheel is different in magnitude from the friction on a box that is being pulled, and it is different in magnitude if pulled on ice or on gravel. Fourthly, friction forces *depend on the situation* for they may have different behaviour and dependencies in different situations; for example, friction may be kinetic or static when something is pulled, or if the movement is fast then air resistance may appear as a friction force. Identifying these dimensions relied on an analysis of the students' articulation of different ways of understanding friction during their discussions. Now we are able to track the dimensions of variation concerning the characteristics of friction that were opened during and between episodes, singling out episodes where one or other of the dimensions was being treated in the discussion.

Constituting the space of meaning

When the students study the problem at hand, they pick up on specific points and articulate them, they respond to one another, they change the force diagram in front of them, they sigh and joke. All the time, a space of meaning is forming and reforming, and the potential for learning is created because a new dimension of variation is opened, or because one value in a dimension of variation is compared and contrasted with another (Booth & Hultén 2003). The formation of a space of meaning can have different qualities, depending on the patterns in which dimensions of variation are handled in the discussion. The least valuable pattern occurs when (A) the group members talk outside the dimensions related to the characteristics of friction—talking about the likeness of different students' drawings to an actual ox for example, or why an ox should pull a box anyway.

Then there are two engaged forms of discussion (B) where a single dimension of variation is held open and different potential ways of seeing that variation are articulated; and (C) where more than one dimension of variation comes into focus and they are put into relation with one another. While (A) has its social uses in the group dynamic, (B) leads into a deeper understanding of some aspect—in this case, an aspect of the characteristics of friction—and (C) leads to a deeper understanding of friction forces in the problem of the ox pulling the box. Patterns (B) and (C) can be seen as lending structure in the space of meaning that is forming, (B) in a linear manner and (C) in a multi-dimensional manner.

The tutor interacts with the group

Now we turn to the tutor who meets a group, which is busy creating the space of meaning, following one of the three patterns described above, with a variation in understanding of the concepts involved, here primarily friction forces. The tutor who meets the students during the session, for only a few moments, needs to be aware of potential conceptual and representational difficulties in the problem, and to be able to interpret what students tell her about their progress or lack of progress. At the same time, the tutor needs to take the learning goal of the problem into account, in the context of the course goals as a whole, when leading students towards a productive line of reasoning. And ideally, the tutor needs to be appraised of the variation in behaviours of problem-solving groups that we have shown here when devising tactics for support.

What might constitute didactical strategies to achieve a productive meeting between a tutor and a group? We will look more closely at two examples of how the tutor in this study met two small groups of students, both of which were stuck in the initial stages of reasoning on the problem, and we see first how the meetings differ and second what the didactical consequences might be. Thus the first example comes when the tutor enters the room where one group is meeting.[1]

The tutor enters the room as the students Leo, Mary, and Noah are completing their force diagram, a few minutes after the session started. She inspects it, confirms that they are on the right track, and asks a question about a force that had been entered as acting on the ox in the direction of motion: 'What might that be, in the horizontal direction, what could that be?'

The students pause, Noah confirming it was a good question! Mary starts to reason, 'But it must be that he sets his feet down on the ground... so that ...' The tutor encourages this with a nod and Noah adds, 'I was also thinking of some sort of friction force ... between the ground and ... yes ...'

More encouraging sounds from the tutor lead Leo to add, 'because if it is a smooth surface, then it's hard to move forward'. To which Noah responds: 'then it would slip, of course ... it wouldn't get anywhere'.

Leo sums it up with 'so it is optimal for the ox if there is a certain degree of friction' with which the tutor agrees. 'There has to be a certain friction force, yes?' she says, and Leo agrees too.

Now the tutor puts the question, 'How does that act on the ox?' followed by a lengthy pause.

Leo starts by reasoning about balance of forces. 'I suppose it should be the same as that on the box, or ... if it isn't so, except on each foot'. The tutor doesn't interrupt and Noah takes up the argument—'but the friction between the ground and his hooves must be quite great since he doesn't slip'.

Leo and Mary agree, thoughtful, and Noah says 'So it must be greater than... Well I don't know' he sighs.

The tutor now leads on by saying: 'Yes, right, he doesn't slip and that is the important thing'.

The discussion continues for a moment in this vein, and the tutor patiently lets it continue before asking another question: 'How great is the static friction on the ox then, the force of friction at rest? Can you draw it on your diagram?' she asks. This amounts to getting the students to see the main point she wants them to see, that the friction is acting in a forward direction when the ox is in motion.

Noah starts this time with 'the question is if...' Mary breaks the silence that ensues, saying 'the static friction, it should stand still then shouldn't it?'. The tutor now brings motion into the argument: 'then, the ox, when it moves then, there is no friction between, at the surface there is no movement then, it does not move.'

Leo sees an apparent contradiction and says 'No, it [the friction force in the diagram] should be backwards', to which Noah agrees, and Leo continues, 'or ... because it must be in the x-direction' which is echoed by the tutor: 'It must be in the x-direction'.

The group, where Mary now also takes part, turn their attention to the way in which the ox moves, how it puts its feet down and bends its legs, and what the consequences would be if the leg bent forward. Leo points out, 'no, it must be the other way around, because otherwise it would slip backwards if it were to bend in that direction ... 'cos they press down'

Mary and Leo start to discuss the ways in which feet enter into walking, Mary starting with 'But if it puts its foot forward, or when you put a foot forward, you have static friction that pushes you, against you, for otherwise the leg would' and Leo completes it, 'slip forwards'. And the tutor confirms that, but continues, 'Yes, but when you put it down, but when you push yourself forwards' and Mary breaks off 'Aha! So then [the force] is acting backwards', to which Noah agrees.

The tutor asks, 'Which force is acting backwards?' and Mary replies, 'The friction force isn't.'

Leo brings this to a head: 'So then the ground must push back at me.' Noah agrees, and the tutor brings it into physics terms: 'According to Newton's third'.

The tutor stays a moment or two, listening to the ensuing discussion, and quietly moves on.

Here we can see that the tutor engages in a process of drawing out the fact that the friction force, acting on the feet of the ox in a forward x-direction when the ox is at rest, is responsible for the motion of the ox pulling the box. She does not directly contradict the assertion that the friction must act in the opposite direction, but challenges the students to consider different scenarios.

Here is another extract when the same tutor enters a room where another group of students—Harry, Ingrid, John and Kathy—are working on the same problem, experiencing similar issues with how to account for the force on the ox and the box in the x-direction. They are in a similar space of meaning as the previous group, but observe what the tutor takes up with them:

> The tutor enters the room and her greeting is met with a nervous laugh. Kathy starts the conversation with 'Well, I don't know' and Ingrid follows with 'You realise now how little you know about these things.' The tutor says sympathetically, 'It looks so innocently simple, doesn't it?' to which the students agree.
>
> Kathy explains 'Well, we know there should be a force that acts on the box, don't we', to which Harry and Ingrid add, talking over each other, 'The tension in the rope should certainly be the same… the same in both directions… yes, but, er, driving force, shouldn't that mean that the ox has more friction than the box has?' and they immediately disagree with themselves, 'No!' at which everyone laughs, and some joking banter follows.
>
> Now the tutor starts a new thread. 'If we start with the rope, why is the force the same in both directions? We don't always talk about that, we just state it—have you thought about it?' There follows a discussion among the students on this new issue, putting forward aspects of the tension in the rope—admitting that they could not explain it even though they understood it to be so.
>
> The tutor persists. 'Have you even thought about the tension?' John puts it clearly, 'Well, I also have a feeling that they must be the same; it is one rope after all, it has to be the same force'. Both Kathy and John claim 'they oppose one another', to which Ingrid responds, 'If it had been a spring it wouldn't have needed to be so, because then one part can be more extended than the other', and the students discuss briefly what that would imply.
>
> Now the tutor starts to explain. 'You generally consider a little piece of the rope in the middle, and consider the forces on it; you have a force to the right from one part of the rope and a force to the left from the other part of the rope and those forces oppose one

another', interspersed with 'mmm' from the students. She continues, 'And that little bit of rope in the middle weighs nothing of course, that's the way it is in such an example'. But here Kathy breaks in 'No!' and they laugh, but Ingrid returns to the point—'It has zero mass'—and the tutor finishes: 'So there wouldn't be a net force on it even if it accelerates, therefore the forces must be equal.'

In the first example, we saw the tutor pick up on the students' current state of confusion, entering their space of meaning-making, and with her knowledge that friction, whether static or kinetic, is problematically counter-intuitive, she engages in a process of drawing out a fruitful understanding in the context of the problem. She does not directly contradict the assertion that the friction must act in the opposite direction, but challenges the students to consider different scenarios. With them she maintains both a focus on the characteristics of friction and explores friction in and across the dimensions of variation. First, she concentrates on drawing out the presence and importance of friction in resolving the problem, the first dimension of variation (see Figure 4.3), friction as a distinct kind of force, then she relates friction to the ox, the second dimension of variation, friction at the point of application. The third dimension of variation, friction's magnitude, enters immediately afterwards when the specific aspect of the problem—that the ox is pulling the box with a constant velocity—implies that the forces in the x-direction are in balance. This leads to introducing the fourth dimension of variation, the situational dependency, when Mary and Leo make the observation that the force on the ox is forwards when it pushes against the ground. This episode sees the tutor engaging with the problem and the students so that they work in the multi-dimensional mode of pattern C, as described earlier.

In the second example, where the students are grappling with the same issues as those in the first example, she appears to ignore the cause of confusion when they agree that they 'know nothing'. When Kathy says 'Well, we know there should be a force that acts on the box, don't we,' the tutor leads the group into a basic discussion of one of the forces that is acting on the box, namely the force exerted in the rope. Rather than entering their tentative space of meaning, she leads them into a different space; rather than taking up the concept of friction which is mentioned by Harry and Ingrid, an understanding of which is central to the goal of the problem, the tutor proceeds to show from first principles that the force on the ox caused by the rope is equal and opposite to the force on the box, maintaining a single focus divorced from friction. The transfer of force from the ox to the box is brought into focus, but not the origin of that force—not the friction that acts on the ox's hooves as it moves forward. While the characteristics of friction are one of the learning goals of the problem, on this occasion the tutor has turned the group's attention to quite a different aspect of the system and created a new space of meaning for them.

We can introduce the notion of *critical* variation, which implies that the discernment of new values in dimensions of variation in what is being discussed amounts to a change in meaning, in contrast to *non-critical* variation, which does not amount to such change in meaning. In relation to the problem given to the students, one example of critical variation is different possible ways of delimiting the system, another is whether the sum of forces equals zero or not. Examples of non-critical variation are the colour of the ox and the time of day. With respect to friction, in the first example above, the tutor takes up and enhances the critical variation in and across relevant dimensions, while in the second example, the tutor rather brings out variation with respect to the problem or the course aims in general, which is hardly critical in the context of the ongoing discussion.

Two possible explanations for this particular tutor's two different patterns of intervention approach come to mind. First, maybe she is so familiar with the two groups that she understands their patterns of behaviour. We can speculate that the first group is known to grapple, or is seen to be grappling, with a problem in a disjointed manner, and that a carefully crafted discussion with them is necessary to keep the goal of understanding friction to the fore. Conceivably, the second group is known to handle problem-solving as an effective team, with a structured manner of type C, and with them the tutor feels free to delve into an unconsidered feature of the mechanical properties of the problem, in the expectation that they will cope well with their own solution tactics. These two didactical strategies, hypothetical strategies in this case, would be justified given experience of the students involved and an understanding of the potential consequences.

However, the second possible explanation is more directly in line with what we consider to be the didactic consequence of our argument. While in the first episode the tutor clearly enters and engages with the students' ongoing space of meaning-making, in the second she instead initiates her own track of thought and diverges from the students' concerns. In order to ensure a didactically viable intervention the tutor needs, in the first instance, an enquiring approach in order to rapidly gauge the students' object of discussion, and then to relate it to the salient features of the problem at hand through the relevant dimensions and critical variation. This implies that while we can say that the first example is in all likelihood going to take the students along a line of reasoning that illuminates the forces of friction that are involved in the problem, whatever the state of the group's interaction, the second example would be liable to add to the confusion of a less coherent problem-solving group. The tutor needs to know or intuit her students as learners and the group as a problem-solving team if an appropriate intervention approach is to be employed.

Three pointers we can deduce from these examples to productive tutor intervention are preparation, interaction, and exit, a proto-model for tutor intervention. In preparation, the tutor needs to be aware of the learning goals of the session, potential difficulties students are likely to encounter, and the variation in what they might understand of the subject matter involved, as well as how they might be going about their discussions. In interacting with the groups, it is clear that entering their space of meaning is important for leading them in a productive direction, as well as modelling a clear focus on the dimensions of variation, both individually and as interrelated. The exit from the group should ensure that they continue in a meaningful direction, with the promise of further intervention if necessary, although a subtle departure is appropriate if all is well.

Conclusion

We referred earlier to the relational nature of the didactic triangle relating learners, teachers and content matter, and different relations are seen in the phases of the discussion and our analysis. The content matter, or knowledge, that is inherent in the problem is at the centre of, first, the students' discussions as challenged by the (absent) tutor. Then, the content matter is at the centre of the students' discussions among themselves. Thirdly, and central to our argument here, the content matter is at the centre of the meeting between students and tutor, as the tutor intervenes to interact with the on-going discussions.

The conclusion we are able to draw from this study and analysis is that, not only do groups of students display a variation in ways of going about problem-solving, with varying degrees of success, but also that tutors charged with advising intermittently also display variations in their approaches. Thus, we would suggest that a discussion of high quality can in some cases depend simply on the students involved, working with a relevant and well-designed task. To systematically support the most articulate patterns of discussion in all groups, however, is a non-trivial didactical challenge, as it also includes handling factors such as the allocation of time, timely support, and balancing group discussions with teaching more generally. This essay has contributed by articulating some of these dilemmas and by offering a model of the reasoning that can support tutors in their complex task.

Note

1 The dialogues given here use pseudonyms and are somewhat simplified from the detailed transcriptions that have been analysed, to aid clarity.

References

Berge, M. (2011), *Group work and physics: Characteristics, learning possibilities and patterns of interaction* (diss., Gothenburg: Chalmers University of Technology).

—— A. T. Danielsson & Å. Ingerman (2012), 'Different stories of group work: Exploring problem-solving in engineering education', *Nordic Studies in Science Education*, 8/1, 3–16.

——— & A. Weilenmann (2014), 'Learning about friction: Group dynamics in engineering students' work with free body diagrams', *European Journal of Engineering Education,* 39/6, 601–616.

Besson, U., L. Borghi, A. De Ambrosis & P. Mascheretti (2007), 'How to teach friction: Experiments and models', *American Journal of Physics,* 75/12, 1106–13.

Booth, S. & M. Hultén (2003), 'Opening dimensions of variation: An empirical study of learning in a web-based discussion', *Instructional Science,* 31/1–2, 65–86.

——— & Å. Ingerman (2015), 'The Pedagogical Potential of Phenomenography for Teacher Practice and Teacher Research', in P. Burnard, B.-M. Apelgren & N. Cabaroglu (eds.), *Transformative Teacher Research: Theory and Practice for the C21st* (Rotterdam: Sense).

Borrego, M. & J. Bernhard, J. (2011), The Emergence of Engineering Education Research as an Internationally Connected Field of Inquiry. Journal of Engineering Education, 100/1, 14–47.

Bowden, J., G. Dall'Alba, E. Martin, G. Masters, D. Laurillard, F. Marton et al. (1992), 'Displacement, velocity, and frames of reference: Phenomenographic studies of students' understanding and some implications for teaching and assessment', *American Journal of Physics,* 60, 262–8.

Clement, J. (1982), 'Students' preconceptions in introductory mechanics', *American Journal of Physics,* 50/1, 66–71.

Freeman, S., S. L. Eddy, M. McDonough, M. K. Smith, N. Okoroafor, H. Jordt & M. P. Wenderoth (2014), 'Active learning increases student performance in science, engineering, and mathematics', *Proceedings of the National Academy of Sciences,* 111/23, 8410–15.

Hake, R. (1998), 'Interactive–Engagement vs Traditional Methods: A Six-Thousand Student Survey of Mechanics Test Data for Introductory Physics Courses', *American Journal of Physics,* 66/1, 64–74.

Heckler, A. F. (2010), 'Some consequences of prompting novice physics students to construct force diagrams', *International Journal of Science Education,* 32(14), 1829–51.

Hestenes, D., G. Wells & G. Swackhamer, (1992), 'Force Concept Inventory', *Physics Teacher,* 30, 141–53.

Hinko, K., P. Madigan, E. Miller & N. Finkelstein (2016), 'Characterizing pedagogical practices of university physics students in informal learning environments', *Physical Review Physics Education Research,* 12/1.

Ingerman, Å., M. Berge & S. Booth (2009a), 'Physics group work in a phenomenographic perspective on learning dynamics as the experience of variation and relevance', *European Journal of Engineering Education,* 34/4, 349–58.

——— Linder, C. & Marshall, D. (2009b), 'The learners' experience of variation: Following students' threads of learning physics in computer simulation sessions', *Instructional Science,* 37/3, 273–92.

Johansson, B., F. Marton & L. Svensson (1985), 'An approach to describing learning as a change between qualitatively different conceptions', in L. H. T. West & A. L. Pines (eds.), *Cognitive structure and conceptual change* (New York: Academic Press).

Larson, J. (2010), *In search of synergy in small group performance* (New York: Taylor & Francis).

Marton, F. & S. Booth (1997), *Learning and awareness* (Mahwah, NJ: Lawrence Erlbaum).

—— & A. B. M. Tsui (2004), *Classroom Discourse and the Space of Learning* (Mahwah, NJ: Lawrence Erlbaum).

McDermott, L. C. (1997), 'Students' conceptions and problem-solving in mechanics', in A. Tiberghien, E. L. Jossem & J. Borojas (eds.), *Connecting research in physics education with teacher education* (Vandoeuvre-les-Nancy: ICPE).

Palmer, D. (1997) 'The effect of context on students' reasoning about forces', *International Journal of Science Education*, 19/6, 681–96. doi: 10.1080/0950069970190605

Redish, E. F. (2003), *Teaching physics with the physics suite*, i (Hoboken, NJ: John Wiley).

Rovio-Johansson, A. & Å. Ingerman (2016), 'Continuity and development in the phenomenography and variation theory tradition', *Scandinavian Journal of Educational Research*, 60/3, 257–71.

Trowbridge, D. E. & L. C. McDermott (1981), 'Investigation of Student Understanding of the Concept of Acceleration in One Dimension', *American Journal of Physics*, 49/3, 242–53.

Abstract

This essay addresses the socio-technological changes in the early literacy classroom and the significance of digital mediation and multimodal text design for pupils' understanding of content, as well as the role the teacher's instructional scaffolding may have. In particular, the study described here investigates how 8-year-old pupils make meaning from multimodal digital texts, and what motivates their semiotic focus. What are their modal preferences and how does the text design influence their reading? The study confirms the complexity of making meaning from digitally mediated multimodal texts, which requires an understanding of the semiotic and digital potential of texts. The analysis demonstrates that in the hybridity of the multimodal digital text, the young pupils predominantly interact with the visual meanings. Their literacy strategies are influenced by their prior experience as novice readers of the written word, as well as the semiotic meanings of the text. The teacher's redirection of the pupils' semiotic attention played a significant role for the processing of meaning. For classroom practice, this implies the significance of developing multimodal and digital pedagogies to support understanding of both the production and the reception of the multimodal design of digital texts.

CHAPTER 5

'You're meant to read the writing?'

Young pupils negotiating meaning from digitally mediated multimodal texts

Sylvana Sofkova Hashemi

The socio-technological changes in the communication and representation of meaning provide opportunities for more hybrid, intertextual, and creative texts, which go beyond traditional modes, conventions, and genres. In this ever more media-saturated construction of texts, digital literacies and multimodality play an important part in our print-based past (Palmeri 2012). Although as Jason Palmeri (2012) rightly points out, 'Composition Has Always Already Been Multimodal' (21) and 'All Media Were Once New' (85), pupils and teachers are nowadays expected to encounter and handle curricular content of a multimodal and interactive character, such as moving images, film, animations, slide shows, sound recordings, and digital games. Pupils learn to 'read' images and other modes of communication as well as print, and to 'write' non-print texts (Pennington 2014; Kress & Van Leeuwen 2006). The incremental integration of digital technologies in schools expands classroom's print-based practices with digital mediation, which enables the organising of ideas and meaning-processing using a broad range and combinations of modes and media (Kress 2003). This access to multiple semiotic systems in the representation of meaning requires the development of literacy strategies to design and understand texts based on the communicative potential of semiotic content and affordances in the technology used (Jewitt & Kress 2003; Cope & Kalantzis 2000). This also entails identifying pedagogies and educational tools to support an informed, explicit teaching of multimodal design of digital texts (New London Group 1996; Merchant 2008; Walsh 2008; Bezemer & Kress 2016; Kalantzis et al. 2016).

This essay addresses didactics from an empirical perspective, exploring the significance of digital mediation and multimodal text design for pupils' understanding of specific content, and with it the role that teacher's scaffolding may have in such a modified learning environment with access to digital technologies. In particular, the study described here observes how 8-year-old pupils make meaning from an instructional text composed by peers on computers, about making a bunny out of gloves. Designed as a classroom study, the goal was to analyse what in the text design draws the pupils' attention, how they collaborate and negotiate the meaning and what literacy strategies they apply when interacting with and making meaning from the screen-based text: what are the pupils' modal preferences, how does the text design influence their reading, what modal and digital strategies do they apply, and what is the role of the teacher's scaffolding for their understanding. The study's didactical value lies in the understanding of the socio-technological changes in early literacy learning and instruction in the young pupils' and their teacher's technology-mediated constructs of the world explored.

Digital design of texts and teaching

Today it is problematic to argue that speech and writing are the primary representations of knowledge. Increased digitalisation, with more texts and more multimodal texts where you can easily combine images, audio, and writing in the same format, requires readers to be able to make meaning of and understand this diversity of expression. Meanings are shaped in new formats, which means that it is necessary to be alert to the hybridization and intertextuality of texts (New London Group 1996, 81–2), with its blending of traditional texts and genres into multimodal products, as a way to connect to youth culture (Ware & Warschauer 2005).

Here I give an overview of what the previous research demonstrates in regard to pupils' multimodal reading and composition, as well as the research findings from classroom studies of teaching and instruction.

Pupils' multimodal meaning-making on-screen

Previous studies indicate that children aged 3–4 already demonstrate an understanding of multimodal text composition. For instance, in a study by Marsh (2006), 3– and 4-year-old children created animated films, and in a study by Merchant (2005), children experimented with font colour and content in text design. Shanahan (2013) demonstrates that pupils have a tacit knowledge in being able to combine semiotic signs into multimodal compositions. According to Warschauer, many pupils develop 'sophisticated artistic and compositional skills' (2008, 62) with which to explore multimodal genres such as movie trailers, poster advertisements and digital stories. This digital designing of texts is understood as being a more individualised, 'just-in-time' learning, where pupils interpret meaning across domains (Kress 2003; Warschauer 2008; Iedema 2003). Some scholars claim that digital composition enhances pupils' perception and conceptual understanding (for example, Schiller & Tillett 2004; Tomlinson 2013). Pupils are certainly able to combine visual and linguistic modes in creative ways (Mills 2011; Walsh 2008), beyond what is taught in the classroom (Shanahan 2013; Björkvall & Engblom 2010). The fact that pupils are motivated to combine semiotic resources digitally, however, does not imply that they are equipped with or naturally develop strategies for conveying meaning on-screen. On the contrary, Shanahan (2013) indicates in her study that pupils lack the meta-textual knowledge and strategies to design texts, and use the separate modes more strategically and in a way that is based on the communicative potential of semiotic content. Gilje (2010) also has examples of film-making practices where pupils were unable to transform meaning across modes. Digital, multimodal composition on-screen is more about 'discovering the possibilities and limitations of sign-making systems' and the 'search for commonalities across different modes', and requires the development of generative thinking and problem-solving strategies (Mills 2011, 64).

The presence of multiple semiotic systems in the representation of meaning requires readers not only to decode verbal language, but also to apply the strategies that mean they can understand for example, visual images, animations, music, and the combination of those modes (Serafini 2012; Hull & Nelson 2005). Such literacy practices require a broader awareness of the potential of digital mediation in the construction of meaning (Kress & Van Leeuwen 2006; Cope & Kalantzis 2000), as well as reading strategies to navigate and interpret multimodal designs (Serafini 2012). Multimodality as an aspect of literacy, and the role it plays in classroom practice expands what it means to be literate (Walsh 2008). In research, the semiotic perspective on reading is explored in the visual and verbal dimensions of picture books (Sipe 1998) and the interpretative practices of children and young people (for example, Arizpe & Styles 2003; Jimenez & Meyer 2016). Moving beyond the standard reading strategies for print texts, Serafini (2012) expands the role of the reader of multimodal texts to that of 'reader–viewer', who engages in social practices to perceive and navigate the multimodal designs and simultaneously interpret and design the text being read.[1] Digital reading also involves the auditory and tactile dimensions of multimodal texts, and increases the degree of interactivity and participation on the reader's part (Al-Yaqout & Nikolajeva 2015).

Multimodal meaning-making and instruction

In school, pupils need to develop strategies for communicating meaning based on the affordances offered by the various modes of the various media (Hull & Nelson 2005). Through the interpretation of content, and the transfer of content into other contexts and formats, the pupils can make use of different semiotic resources as tools for thinking, learning to be critical of the use of different forms of semiotic representation (Mills 2011; Sofkova Hashemi

2014). Previous research on the composition of multimodal digital texts in the context of early literacy education suggests a need for a common discourse to address meta-awareness of the potential of digital mediation, here in meaning-making practices in school in regard to the teachers' content knowledge and assessment (for example, Bearne 2009; Unsworth 2006).

The incorporation of digital, multimodal meaning-making into classroom practice requires the development of communicative competences, and an awareness of the role that different technology and semiotic representations play in conveying meaning. Multimodality as the interrelation of two or more modes requires an understanding of the contribution which images, words, spatial layout, and other semiotic resources make to the construction of meaning (Jewitt & Kress 2003). Previous research indicates not only a lack of meta-textual and digital awareness in the classroom, but also strategies with which to design texts based on the communicative potential of semiotic content and affordances in the technology used (for example, Unsworth 2006; Towndrow, Nelson & Yusuf 2013; Sofkova Hashemi 2014; Godhe & Lindström 2014; Lyngfelt et al. 2017). Although teachers and pupils use digital media in the classroom to represent meaning multi-modally on-screen (by combining signs such as images, sound effects, music, and animations), teaching and assessment practice usually focuses on the written or spoken message, disregarding the other modal resources (Godhe & Lindström 2014; Öman & Sofkova Hashemi 2015; Cederlund & Sofkova Hashemi 2018). The traditions of teaching and subject cultures have been shown to influence the ways and extent to which digital technology and media are embedded in classroom practice (for example, Karaseva et al. 2013). In the social science subjects—history, religion, geography, civics—films and images are often used during instruction to complement reading and support the pupils visually. Written texts and printed books have a prominent place in Swedish as a school subject (Erixon 2010). Merchant (2008, 757) describes such classroom practices as *separating* literacy from 'technologies of literacy' instead of making it part of the subject (see also Sofkova Hashemi & Cederlund 2017).

Data, theory and methodology

In addition to the context, theoretical perspective, and the design of the present study, I will consider here the analytical instruments I used to explore where the pupils direct their semiotic attention when making meaning from multimodal digital texts.

Empirical setting and study design

The multimodal digital text that the pupils in this study make meaning of was composed by their peers in the context of a collaborative cross-class assignment. The assignment was conducted within the frame of a longitudinal project, 'Digital Arenas in Literacy Practices in Early Primary School' (DILS), which involved 82 pupils and 4 teachers at three state schools in Sweden with existing one-to-one investment in technology, where each pupil was equipped with a laptop or tablet computer.[2]

The teachers in the project collaborated on planning this cross-class assignment during one of a series of workshops in the DILS project, together with the researchers. Grounded in the overarching, long-term goal to engage the 8-year-old pupils in digital encounters in order to promote literacy development, the teachers decided to work on instructional texts, a text genre that is part of the syllabus for the subject of Swedish. The task was to become acquainted with instructional texts and both compose and interpret instructions in order to develop an understanding of this particular text genre. The teachers planned for both local work in their classes and cross-class tasks in collaboration with peers from the other schools. They arrived at a three-stage plan of work, which combined real instructions in diverse formats and the design of pupils' own instructional text, an exchange of texts with peers in the collaborating class and the inter-pretation of instructions, and finally a redesign of the instructional text in accordance with their peers' response. There were thus three stages to the assignment of the Design–Interpretation–Redesign of instructional texts (Fig. 5.1).

After a period of local work in class on the characteristic features

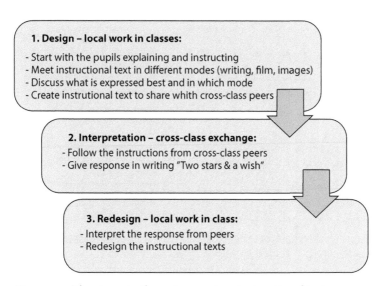

Figure 5.1. The stages to the assignment on instructional texts.

and formats of instructional texts (Stage 1)—cooking spaghetti, baking cakes, peeling apples, playing games, and other work that comes with instructions—the pupils created their own instructional texts in pairs on computers to share with peers in the collaborating class. They composed instructional texts for baking cakes and making sweets, making paper boats and paper-folding projects, making hand puppets from gloves, performing the 'Cup Song' (an a cappella song where the singers use plastic beakers as percussion),[3] and soccer rules and indoor or outdoor games. When it came to the distribution of design choices by twelve pairs of pupils who were creating these texts (Table 5.1), the compositions varied from written texts that used drawings or digital images to give the writing greater information value (four pairs), that combined writing with video (six pairs), or that used video alone (two pairs).[4]

In order to explore the pupils' semiotic focus as they followed the instructional text composed by their peers, the analytical objective in this study is the interpretation phase in the cross-class exchange of instructional texts (Stage 2). One pair of the pupils (here anonymised as Nelly and Erik) follow and interpret an instructional text on making a glove bunny, which was of the kind with both written

Choice of design	No. of texts	Instructional text
Written instructions with images	4	• recipe for chocolate sweets • recipe for sponge cake • recipe for chocolate muffins • rules for outdoor game "King"
Filmed instructions	2	• folding a paper bunny • performing the Cup Song
Written and filmed instructions	6	• making a glove bunny • folding a paper boat • making a hair bow • recipe for fruit with coconut • rules for blinking game • rules for football

Table 5.1. Overview of types of instructions and designs used for composing the texts.

and filmed parts (see Table 5.1). I also discuss their work on peer response in regard to semiotic attention when the pupils apply the 'two stars and a wish' method, a peer-response strategy for formative assessment that involves pupils in a reflective, active practice (Black & William 1998, 2012), giving constructive feedback limited to two positive points about their peer's successful achievement, followed by a comment about development and improvement (Webb & Jones 2009). Although peer feedback may not achieve the same quality as teacher feedback, pupils are quite capable of identifying strengths and weaknesses, and give concrete ideas on how to improve one another's work. This assessment technique is also considered to be self-assessing, because it ensures pupils' participation in the assessment of their own learning (Gardner 2012).

Methods

In regard to classroom research, the focus of this study is the pupils' specific practices when making meaning of multimodal digital texts, which situates literacy in the context of social practices in the classroom. Applying this practice-based ethnography, the data was collected in accordance with Heath and Street's (2008) ways of relating educational issues to ethnography in education. The cross-class work was followed in each of the three classes on two separate occasions, with pupils making meaning from the instructional texts created by their peers and preparing and sharing their response to the text, applying the 'two stars and a wish' method. Data were gathered through ethnographic techniques examining the specific practices at macro– and micro-levels (Walford 2008). One stationary camera was placed to capture the whole-class activities at macro-level, and two to three researchers took field notes and photographs and made close-up video-recordings of the pupils' work in pairs. Semi-structured follow-up interviews were conducted with the teachers and pupils, and the pupils' work—the text compositions and peer responses—were collected (Kawulich 2005).

Analytical instruments

The study is informed by the theoretical perspectives of social semiotics (Bezemer & Kress 2016; Kress & Van Leeuwen 2006), where meaning-making is understood as a material, social, and textual practice. Moving beyond the linguistics and linearity of texts towards the communication of meaning in multiple modes requiring multiple aspects of literacy, or multiliteracies (New London Group 1996), the emphasis in this framework is placed on the design, production and presentation of a broad range of semiotic resources (or elements of design): linguistic, visual, spatial, gestural, and auditory (Cope & Kalantzis 2000). This is a revised view of the construction of meaning, understood as a transformation of available resources (available designs) into a new design by means of recreation and reproduction (redesign). In this, pupils are regarded as sign-makers who use signs (or modes), which are elements in which meaning and form are brought together in a relationship motivated by the interest and the intentions of the sign-maker (Bezemer & Kress 2008). The process of meaning-making is always subject to the situated practice and the availability of semiotic resources, meaning the observable actions and objects used for communication. In other words, it is a question of how different semiotic resources contribute to the construction of meaning in the context in which the pupils are situated. The selected semiotic resources are then set in relation to the communicative means available to the pupils.

With the aim of exploring the semiotic focus of 8-year-old pupils when making meaning from and responding to peers' instructional text, I use social semiotic theory and the grammar of visual design to examine the overt purposes and intentions (the semiotic functions) of the instructional text, and what in the meaning of the text captures their attention. Based on functional grammar and Halliday's (1994) three types of linguistic meanings or metafunctions of texts (ideational, interpersonal, and textual), Kress and Van Leeuwen (2006) defined a grammar of the visual design of representational, interactional, and compositional meanings when analysing multimodal texts. When dealing with the representational metafunction, such an analysis reveals which participants and events (people, things, places, ideas) are present and which of them constitute meaning (Van Leeuwen 2005, 76–7). The interactional function concerns communicative interaction between these represented participants and the reader-viewer of the text by visual means such as direction of the gaze, distance, or angle of the camera. An analysis of the compositional meaning thus aims to demonstrate the configuration and layout of selected resources in texts. This can be signalled by the information value (for example, the placement of elements in the centre or margin of pages), salience (size, colour, overlap) or framing (lines, spaces, contrasts) (see also Machin 2007; Bateman 2008).

Results

Nelly and Erik follow instructions from their peers in the collaborating class on how to make a hand puppet that resembles a bunny from a pair of gloves. Focusing on the two pupils' and their meaning-making from this multimodal digital text, the analysis of the overt purpose and intention of the instructional text is first presented, revealing the semiotic functions of the text. This is followed by an analysis of the pupils' semiotic focus during the process of following the instructions and making the glove bunny, revealing what available resources in the design of the text receive their attention.

Purpose and intention of the instructional text

The peers' instructional text on making a glove bunny combines written and filmed versions of the instructions in a digital slideshow presentation. The pupils' peers had utilised the affordances of the digital tool composing a text that combined visual, auditory, and linguistic resources such as personal photographs, animations, colour, music, speech, writing, and film, giving the text a close personal distance to the reader-viewer.[5] They used a photograph in black and white on the front page of the two pupils sitting close to each other, smiling, with two fingers over their heads symbolising the bunny, followed by the title 'Glove bunny', also in black, and the names of the pupils as authors below the picture in pink (Table 5.2. slide 1). Then come the written instructions on the next slide, which begin with animated effects of three small black-and-white photographs of the pupils smiling and making funny faces flying in one by one, accompanied by stardust in different colours (Table 5.2. slide 2). The written instructions, in pink and italics, bounce into the centre of the page, covering almost the whole slide. This central placement gives the written text a prominent information value on the page. The pink colour makes a contrast on the white and yellow background. Besides the italics, there are no other dynamics in the text such as variation in the size or typeface or how the writing is structured on the page. It is rather hard to read this text, which runs over the page without any new lines or paragraphs for the steps in the instructions. The written instructions start with a greeting and an explanation of what the instructions are for and what you need to make a glove bunny, followed immediately by what to do in numbered steps. The written instructions pass by quickly in the slideshow, lasting for only three seconds (Table 5.2. slide 2).

The filmed version of the instructions that follows is framed by loud, cheerful music at the start and end of the film (Table 5.2. slides 3 & 5). Calm music then plays in the background during the whole of the filmed instructions. One of the peer pupil demonstrates the making of the glove bunny, sitting down in the classroom in front of the camera with the gloves (Table 5.2. slide 4). The other pupil (not visible in the picture) records the film and gives verbal instructions. The pupils use direct gaze and gestures as well as distance as semiotic

Time	Slide No.	Slide	Content and design
00:00	1		**Background:** light blue **Image:** black-and-white photo of the two pupils with fingers over their heads symbolising a bunny, centred and placed in the upper part of the page. **Writing:** title in black, lower case; their names in pink, written in capitals: glove bunny: BY PUPIL1 AND PUPIL2!!!!!!!!!!
00:01	2		**Background:** light blue; three frames in white or yellow **Writing:** title in green Glove bunny **Transition effects:** three black-and-white photos of the pupils fly in one by one accompanied by stardust in different colours; written text in pink flies in
00:08	2		**Background:** light blue; three frames in white and yellow **Writing:** title in green Glove bunny **Image:** three black-and-white photos of the pupils **Writing:** pink text on white and yellow background: *Hi we will make a bunny from 1 pair of gloves. You need:* *1 pair of glove-pairs and your hands.* *1: Put one glove on the hand you are most used to or the other hand that you decide yourself.* *2: Take the other glove and push in the middle finger on the glove you do not have on the hand.* *3: then you Push in the middle finger in the middle finger that is on the glove **that you do not hold in the hand**.* *4: **then you have 6 fingers left up 4 fingers are empty** and you put down 2 empty fingers and then you have a bunny. Hope you are pleased with your bunny.* **Transition effect:** slide flies away

Table 5.2. Design of the instructional text for making a glove bunny.

00:10	3		**Transition effect:** loud music, picture appears and title flies in **Background:** light blue **Music:** loud volume **Image:** black-and-white photo of the two pupils with fingers over their heads symbolising a bunny, centred and placed in the upper part of the page. **Writing:** title in red on white background, lowercase bunny glove:
00:17	4		**Background:** light blue **Music:** calmer with lower volume **Gestures:** sits and looks at the camera, smiling; shows gloves and hands in front of the camera **Speech:** Hi, we will make a glove bunny. You need one pair of gloves and your hands. First put one glove on the hand you are most used to or the other hand, that you decide yourself. < **Transition effect: black-and-white picture of pupils appears with effects and dissolves**> Take the other glove and push in the middle finger on the glove that you do not have on the hand. < **Transition effect: black-and-white picture of pupils appears with effects and dissolves** > Then you put the middle finger in the other middle finger on the other glove. **Then you fold over the glove that is on the middle finger.** < **Transition effect: black-and-white picture of pupils appears with effects and dissolves**> **And then you pull down there on the glove that is on your hand and make sure that the thumb and forefinger are not visible.** Then you put down two of the fingers that do not have fingers in them. Then you have a bunny. Hope it went well! Bye!
01:56 02:09	5		**Transition effects:** loud music, pictures and names flying in **Background:** light blue **Music:** loud volume **Image:** colour and black-and-white photos of the two pupils, centred and placed in the upper part of the page; two half-clouds in light blue and pink with white text **Writing:** the names of pupils as authors in coloured half-clouds, centred. By Pupil1 By Pupil2

Table 5.2 continued.

99

resources, by zooming in on the presenting the pupil's hands and the gloves (Table 5.2. slide 4) and visually involving the reader-viewer, giving the text its interactional meaning. The steps of the filmed instructions for making the glove bunny are framed by visual transitions of the slideshow where the pupils again use animated effects and black-and-white photos of themselves. The filmed instructions are almost two minutes long (1:39 min). The instructional text ends with crescendoing music and, again, animations of colour and black-and-white photos flying in, accompanied by the pupils' names below the pictures in coloured clouds (Table 5.2. slide 5).

The written and filmed instructions render the same content to begin with, but gradually differences arise between the texts. Both versions signal the separate steps in the instructions, using numbers in the written version and animated transitions in the filmed version. Some parts of the steps are more developed in the writing and some are more developed in the filmed instructions (see Table 5.2.).

Making a glove bunny

Nelly's and Erik's process of making a glove bunny from the instructional text presented in the previous section is analysed here to explore which of the available resources in the text they focus their attention on and which literacy practices they engage in. The role of the teacher's instructional scaffolding during their meaning-making is discussed. Table 5.3 presents their semiotic focus and the literacy practices they engage in when making the glove bunny; the last row in the table indicates the decisions they make when shifting their attention.

Nelly and Erik spend almost the entire one-hour lesson (57 min) making the glove bunny, shifting between viewing and listening to the filmed part of the instructions and reading the written part. Nelly downloads the instructional text from their peers from the class Dropbox to the tablet computer and the pupils start to watch the slideshow. The written instructions pass by quickly and the pupils watch the filmed version. Silently they watch and listen to what is going on and Erik gets up and brings his black gloves and starts to make the bunny. The sound is weak and at some point Nelly comments: 'We can't hear what they say'. 'No, but we see what they do,'

Semiotic Focus	Film (13 min)	Writing (7 min)	Film (2 min)	Writing (13 min)	Film (22 min)
Literacy Practices	Download file Start presentation Watch and listen Adjust volume Rewind Start over Bring gloves Watch and listen E makes bunny	Call teacher Pause screen Read aloud E makes bunny Discuss	Lean to hear Watch and listen Discuss E makes bunny	Read step by step E makes bunny Count fingers	Scroll Compare Start over Watch and listen N and E each work on own bunny N finished N instructs
Shift in Focus	→ Agree they cannot hear or see clearly	→ Continue with film	→ Decide to look at writing	→ Think that they are finished	→ Finished

Table 5.3. Shifts in semiotic focus and literacy practices during meaning making.

encourages Erik and continues working on the bunny. They continue to play the slideshow and realise that they also have difficulties in seeing what is going on in parts of the filmed instructions, since the gloves that the peer pupil is working with in the film are not always visible in the picture. 'You could not see anything', says Erik.

After thirteen minutes of trying to make the glove bunny, they call over the teacher, who almost immediately draws their attention to reading the written instructions that swish by in the slideshow, lasting for only three seconds. Here is the excerpt from the conversation with the teacher after Erik starts the slideshow:

> Excerpt 1: Pupils call for the teacher's attention
> [Erik hits the play button to start the slideshow from the beginning]
> Teacher: Oh! Could you read it? [Exclaiming; referring to the written instructions that pass by quickly]
> Erik: No.
> Nelly: No.
> Teacher: What can you do then?
> Erik: Pause. [Pauses the screen]
> Teacher: Exactly. [Nods in assent]
> Nelly: *You're meant to read the text?* [Surprised; referring to the written instructions.]

Teacher: Perhaps it's good that you know what it says in any case, or what do you think?

Nelly: mm.

Teacher: What if the whole explanation was there?

[Nelly and Erik both sit down and follow the paused written instructions displayed on the screen. Nelly begins to read aloud. The teacher leans over the pupils and follows the pupils reading.]

Nelly: Hi we will make a bu– bunny from one pai– pair of gloves … [Reads slowly.]

Teacher: GOOD! [Loudly and clearly.] Now I'll leave you for a moment to read through it FIRST and then try, that's a tip. [Leaves the pupils.]

As the excerpt from the conversation with the teacher reveals, the pupils engaged in viewing and listening do not initially pay attention to the written instructions in the slideshow, and Nelly explicitly asks if they are even meant to. She then starts to read the instructions aloud. Erik stops her in the middle and they go over what they have understood so far and Erik makes the glove bunny. After seven minutes of reading, they abandon the written instructions and turn to the film again. The poor sound quality of the film is still an issue, so they lean in towards the tablet to hear. They make the glove bunny, but something is still not right, and Erik is frustrated that it is not working: 'Shouldn't you have it on your hand?' he wonders, and Nelly disagrees about his method: 'What about folding it again?' she asks. They decide to read the written instructions again, going through them step by step. After a while (13 min), they seem to have succeeded. However, the bunny does not look like the one made by their peers, and when they count the glove fingers they realise that something is not right. Now they examine the filmed instructions once more. Nelly fetches her own pair of gloves and they both try making the bunny. Fifteen minutes later (50 minutes in total) Nelly succeeds, and shows Erik how to make the bunny. They compare the results and proudly show their glove bunnies to their classmates and the teacher.

Although the instructional text as a whole invites interpretation of written, spoken, visual, and auditory designs, the meanings and

Figure 5.2. Distribution of semiotic focus over modes and time.

semiotic functions represented in the text and the pupils' focus on the speech and visual resources causes them primarily to view and listen, and to spend less time on making meaning from the written instructions. From their shifts of semiotic focus one sees the distribution by modality and time (Fig. 5.2). The visual and oral designs of the filmed part of the instructional text are central in the pupils' reading–viewing, who spend a total of more than half the time (37 min) on the filmed instructions and one-third (20 min) on the written instructions. The poor voice quality and not being able to see the activity of the peers in the video means that the pupils also engage in digital practices such as adjusting the volume, rewinding and scrolling the film, and shifting their attention to the written message. Furthermore, the conversation between the pupils signals their preference for keeping their attention on the film and that they can see what is going on even though the sound is poor. Here they signal their awareness of using several modes when making meaning from the filmed instructions—viewing and listening (Walsh 2008).

The pupils shift their semiotic focus between the modalities when they are faced with critical choices. Overall they engage more in making meaning from the oral and visual elements due to the text design that (unintentionally) gives writing a less prominent role. However, both the written and filmed instructions contributed to their understanding, and it is not until they avail themselves of all the semiotic resources of the text (written, visual, and spoken) that they finally succeed in following the instructions and making the glove bunny.

Semiotic focus in peer response

When Nelly and Erik put together their response to the peers, they start by comparing the design of their own instructional text with the peers' text, checking that the names of the peers are there. For the 'stars' they take inspiration from the class work on instructional texts, which is displayed as a list on the whiteboard in the

TWO STARS AND A WISH
to:

that you had a heading.

that you showed what was needed.

that you should have your hands a little further up because we did not really see what you did.

Figure 5.3. Semiotic focus in response to peers.

classroom—'Title, What you need, "Doing words", Clear order'. They choose to say to their peers that having a title for their instructions was a good thing to do, as was showing what was needed (Fig. 5.3). The use of the word 'show' in their response indicates that their semiotic focus on the filmed instructions and visual resources continued.

Regarding their constructive feedback to the peers (the 'wish'), Nelly first insisted on making their peers aware of the poor visual clarity of the filmed instructions, especially what to do with their hands, as the following excerpt from the conversation between Nelly and Erik shows:

> Excerpt 2: Pupils negotiating about the 'wish' in their peer response
> Nelly: They should have shown that.
> Erik: That you should hold up your hands.
> Nelly: We did not see how you did that.

For the wish element of the peer response, they continue to focus on the visual design and demonstrate their awareness of the compositional, interactional functions of the filmed instructions that affected their comprehension, whereas the design of the written instructions went unmentioned.

Discussion and conclusion

The hybridity of the instructional text in the blend of semiotic resources (writing, speaking, animations, photographs, film, music) designed as a multimodal product, affords the pupils a wide range of available designs. By focusing on the semiotic meanings of this multimodal digital text, this study reveals not only what semiotic resources capture pupils' attention when making meaning of the text, but also how the semiotic functions of the text influenced their understanding. Observations of the pupils' actions and negotiations further demonstrate the significance of the teacher's scaffolding in the pupils' shifts in semiotic attention.

As novice readers of the written word, the pupils concentrate on viewing and listening to the filmed instructions, and their desire to succeed is revealed in their conversation. Initially, none of the pupils notice, let alone use, the written version of the instructions to make meaning of the text—that is, until the teacher directs their attention towards the writing. Revealing the semiotic functions of the instructional text by means of the grammar of visual design (Kress & Van Leeuwen 2006) demonstrates that the pupils' semiotic focus is motivated by the representational, interactional, and compositional meanings of the text. Although the written instructions have a central information value in the composition of the slide in question, the three-second slot in the slide presentation and the composition as a running text make it less valuable for the pupils to notice. Instead they pay attention to the filmed instructions that are framed by animations and loud music, and which invite them to interact by means of the direct gaze and zooming in on the hands of the peers. In their peer feedback, they also refer to their experience of the visual design, and in a constructive way assess their own learning of the semiotic functions in that particular mode (Gardner 2012).

The pupils make meaning from a mix of genres (written text, film, slideshow), which implies the involvement of literacy strategies used with print-based texts and multimodal literacy strategies. They also engage in screen-based practices to adjust the volume, rewind, pause, and scroll through the digital text. The findings of this study thus clearly demonstrate the socio-technological changes in classroom practice when making meaning from digitally mediated multimodal texts, which often take this hybrid form and thus require an active engagement on the part of the reader if they are to understand the semiotic and digital potential of the text. This entails a knowledge of the meaning-making systems used in text production, and the ability to process multiple genres and combinations of modes (Kress 2010), as well as digital awareness and knowledge. The pupils' focus on the spoken and visual elements of the instructional text demonstrates the significance not only of a multimodal and digital understanding of texts, but also of the teacher scaffolding promoting shifts in modal focus and the use of digital literacy strategies. For classroom practice, this involves considering both the production and reception of texts, and a detailed understanding of the multimodal design of texts as well as the digital context (for example, Serafini 2012; Bearne 2009). The didactical consequences for early literacy education thus entail the development of multimodal and digital pedagogies to support an understanding of multimodal design of digital texts and the semiotic work that young pupils engage in when 'reading' print, film, music, and images. Informed teaching practice is needed to achieve understanding of text hybridity, how modes combine in multimodal ensembles, and the development of literacy and digital strategies to convey and make meaning of multimodal texts on-screen.

Notes

1 Serafini's reconceptualization (2012) expands the Freebody and Luke (2003) four resources model of the reader as code-breaker, text participant, text user, and text analyst.

2 The author wishes to thank the Marcus and Amalia Wallenberg Foundation for its support and particularly all the teachers and pupils for their participation in the research project 'Digital Arenas in Literacy Practices in Early Primary School' (2012–2015). dilsprojektet.wordpress.com

3 The 'Cup Song' originates from the Carter Family song 'When I'm Gone' from 1931 and became popular after Anna Kendrick covered it for the 2012 film Pitch Perfect.

4 The twelve texts were selected for observation based on the involvement of the pupils that were the focus of the DILS project, who were selected in joint consultation with their teachers.

5 Distance concerns the apparent social distance to the reader-viewer and relates to image cropping, whether face or head (intimate), at the waist (personal), full-length (social), or with several people (public) (Kress & Van Leeuwen 1996, 129–31).

References

Al-Yaqout, G. & Nikolajeva, M. (2015), 'Re-conceptualising picturebook theory in the digital age', *Barnelitterært Forskningstidsskrift/Nordic Journal of ChildLit Aesthetics*, doi: 10.3402/blft.v6.26971

Arizpe, E. & M. Styles (2003), *Children reading pictures: Interpreting visual texts* (New York: Routledge).

Bateman, J. A. (2008), *Multimodality and Genre: A foundation for the systematic analysis of multimodal documents* (New York: Palgrave Macmillan).

Bearne, E. (2009), 'Multimodality, literacy and texts: Developing a discourse', *Journal of Early Childhood Literacy*, 9/2, 156–87. doi: 10.1177/1468798409105585

Bezemer, J. & G. Kress (2008), 'Writing in Multimodal Texts: A Social Semiotic Account of Designs for Learning', *Written Communication*, 25, 166–95.

———— (2016), *Multimodality, learning and communication: A social semiotic frame* (London: Routledge).

Björkvall, A. & C. Engblom (2010), 'Young children's exploration of semiotic resources during unofficial computer activities in the classroom', *Journal of Early Childhood Literacy*, 10/3, 271–93. doi: 10.1177/1468798410372159

Black, P. & D. William (1998), 'Assessment and classroom learning', *Assessment in Education: Principles, Policy & Practice*, 5/1, 7–71.

———— (2012), 'Assessment for Learning in the Classroom', in J. Gardner (ed.), *Assessment and learning* (2nd edn, London: SAGE).

Cederlund, K. & S. Sofkova Hashemi (2018), 'Multimodala bedömningspraktiker och lärares lärande', *Educare* 1, 43–68.

Cope, B. & M. Kalantzis (2000), *Multiliteracies: Literacy learning and the design of social futures* (London: Routledge).

Erixon, P.-O. (2010), 'School subject paradigms and teaching practice in lower secondary Swedish schools influenced by ICT and media', *Computers & Education*, 54/4, 1212–21. doi: 10.1016/j.compedu.2009.11.007

Freebody, P. & A. Luke (2003), 'Literacy as engaging with new forms of life: The "four roles" model', in G. Bull & M. Anstey (eds.), *The literacy lexicon* (2nd edn, Frenchs Forest, NSW: Pearson Education).

Gardner, J. (2012), *Assessment and learning* (2nd edn, London: SAGE).

Gilje, O. (2010), 'Multimodal redesign in filmmaking practices: An inquiry of young filmmakers' deployment of semiotic tools in their filmmaking practice', *Written Communication*, 27/4, 494–522.

Godhe, A.-L. & B. Lindström(2014), 'Creating multimodal texts in language education: Negotiations at the boundary', *Research & Practice in Technology Enhanced Learning*, 9/1, 165–88.

Halliday, M. A. K. (1994), *An Introduction to Functional Grammar* (2nd edn, London: Edward Arnold)

Heath, S. B. & B. Street (2008), *On Ethnography: Approaches to language and literacy research* (New York: Teachers College Press).

Hull, G. A. & M. E. Nelson (2005), 'Locating the semiotic power of multimodality', *Written Communication*, 22/2, 224–61. doi: 10.1177/0741088304274170

Iedema, R. (2003), 'Multimodality, resemiotization: Extending the analysis of discourse as multi-semiotic practice', *Visual Communication*, 2/1, 29–57.

Jewitt, C. & G. Kress (2003), *Multimodal literacy* (New York: Peter Lang).

Jimenez, L. M. & C. K. Meyer (2016), 'First Impressions Matter: Navigating Graphic Novels Utilizing Linguistic, Visual, and Spatial Resources', *Journal of Literacy Research*, 48/4, 423–447 doi: 10.1177/1086296X16677955

Kalantzis, M., B. Cope, E. Chan & L. Dalley-Trim (2016), *Literacies* (2nd edn, Cambridge: CUP).

Karaseva, A., P. Pruulmann-Vengerfeldt & A. Siibak (2013), 'Comparison of Different Subject Cultures and Pedagogical Use of ICTs in Estonian Schools', *Nordic Journal of Digital Literacy*, 8/3, 157–71.

Kawulich, B. B. (2005), 'Participant Observation as a Data Collection Method', *Forum: Qualitative Social Research*, 6(2).

Kress, G. (2003), *Literacy in the new media age* (London: Routledge).

—— (2010), *Multimodality: A Social Semiotic Approach to Contemporary Communication* (London: Routledge).

—— & T. van Leeuwen (2006), *Reading images: The grammar of visual design* (London: Routledge) (first pub. 1996).

Lyngfelt, A., S. Sofkova Hashemi & P. Andersson (2017), 'Analys och textsamtal om multimodala digitala elevtexter', in K. Helgesson, H. Landqvist, A. Lyngfelt, A. Nord & Å. Wengelin (eds.), *Text och kontext: Perspektiv på textanalys* (Malmö: Gleerups).

Machin, D. (2007), *Introduction to multimodal analysis* (London: Hodder Arnold).

Marsh, J. (2006), 'Emergent media literacy: Digital animation in early childhood', *Language & Education*, 20/6, 493–506.

Merchant, G. (2005), 'Barbie meets Bob the Builder at the workstation: Learning to write on screen', in J. Marsh (ed.), *Popular Culture, New Media and Digital Literacy in Early Childhood* (London: Routledge).

Merchant, G. (2008), 'Digital writing in the early years', in J. Coiro, M. Knobel, C. Lankshear & D. J. Leu (eds.), *Handbook of research on new literacies* (New York: Lawrence Erlbaum).

Mills, K. A. (2011), '"I'm making it different to the book": Transmediation in young children's multimodal and digital texts', *Australasian Journal of Early Childhood*, 36/3, 56–65.

New London Group. (1996), 'A pedagogy of multiliteracies: Designing social futures', *Harvard Educational Review*, 66/1, 60–92.

Öman, A. & S. Sofkova Hashemi (2015), 'Design and redesign of a multimodal classroom task: Implications for teaching and learning', *Journal of Information Technology Education: Research*, 14, 139–59.

Palmeri, J. (2012), *Remixing Composition: A History of Multimodal Writing Pedagogy* (Carbondale: Southern Illinois University Press).

Pennington, M. C. (2014), 'Trends in Writing and Technology', *Writing & Pedagogy*, 5/2, 155–79. doi: 10.1558/wap.v5i2.155

Schiller, J. & B. Tillett (2004), 'Using digital images with young children: Challenges of integration', *Early Child Development and Care*, 174/4, 401–14.

Serafini, F. (2012), 'Expanding the four resources model: Reading visual and multi-modal texts', *Pedagogies: An International Journal*, 7/2, 150–64. doi: 1 0.1080/1554480X.2012.656347

Shanahan, L. E. (2013), 'Composing "Kid-Friendly" Multimodal Text: When Conversations, Instruction, and Signs Come Together', *Written Communication*, 30/2 194–227. doi: 10.1177/0741088313480328

Sipe, L. R. (1998), 'How picture books work: A semiotically framed theory of text–picture relationships', *Children's Literature in Education*, 29/2, 97–108.

Sofkova Hashemi, S. (2014), 'Meaning-making and Communication in Virtual Nordic Classrooms: Transmediation in cross-border understanding', *EDU-LEARN14 Proceedings, 6th International Conference on Education and New Learning Technologies*, 1820–30.

Sofkova Hashemi, S. & K. Cederlund (2017), 'Making room for the transformation of literacy instruction in the digital classroom', *Journal of Early Childhood Literacy*, 17/2, 221–53. doi: 10.1177/1468798416630779

Tomlinson, M. M. (2013), 'Literacy and Music in Early Childhood: Multimodal Learning and Design', *SAGE Open*, July–September, 1–10.

Towndrow, P. A., M. E. Nelson & W. F. B. M. Yusuf (2013), 'Squaring Literacy Assessment with Multimodal Design: An Analytic Case for Semiotic Awareness', *Journal of Literacy Research*, 45/4, 327–55. doi: 10.1177/1086296X13504155

Unsworth, L. (2006), 'Towards a metalanguage for multiliteracies education: Describing the meaning-making resources of language–image interactions, *English Teaching: Practice & Critique*, 5/1, 55–76.

Van Leeuwen, T. (2005), *Introducing social semiotics* (New York: Routledge).

Walford, G. (2008), *How to do Educational Ethnography* (London: Tufnell).

Walsh, M. (2008), 'Worlds have collided and modes have merged: Classroom evidence of changed literacy practices', *Literacy* 42, 101–108.

Ware, P. D. & M. Warschauer (2005), 'Hybrid literacy texts and practices in technology-intensive environments', *International Journal of Educational Research*, 43/7–8, 432–45.

Warschauer, M. (2008), 'Laptops and literacy: A multi-site case study', *Pedagogies*, 3/1, 52–67.

Webb, M. & J. Jones (2009), 'Exploring tensions in developing assessment for learning', *Assessment in Education: Principles, Policy & Practice*, 16/2, 165–184.

Abstract

All the essays in this volume are concerned with teaching and learning from different perspectives, as well as methods for studying these perspectives. In this essay, the classroom is in focus. I intend to present and discuss the teaching and learning activities that take place from the perspective of the classroom: what affordances (Kress 1993) are there in classroom design, and what implications might these affordances in design have for teaching and learning, with a focus on subject-specific language? These questions will be discussed using examples from classrooms I have worked in as teacher, from classrooms I have worked in as a researcher, and from other research on (class)rooms. I will discuss classroom design: how a school subject is understood from its design, what teaching and learning activities take place, and how participants interact. The analysis of interaction will focus on when, where, and how subject-specific language is used and what didactical consequences this has.

CHAPTER 6

A classroom is a classroom is a classroom?

A study of the affordance of classroom design for classroom interaction

Anna Maria Hipkiss

In secondary schools, some teachers are fortunate enough to have their own classroom to which different groups of pupils come. Some classes have their own so called 'home classrooms' to which different teachers come to teach. Yet other teachers and pupils move around during the school day, meeting different classrooms with every school subject. When I started researching how classroom design and artefacts interact in teaching for my thesis, I was reminded of a classroom I shared with a colleague and a class many years ago. It was a science classroom that the pupils had furnished according to their wishes. They had wanted curtains in front of the fume cupboards, so that when they were not doing chemistry, they could 'hide that subject'. It was an aesthetic as well as pedagogical choice on their part. As these pupils were used to having discussions together as a group since primary school, they also chose to have circular tables for four to five pupils instead of that school's traditional three-pupil laboratory benches. Following the design of the classroom, the teaching and learning that took place was based on the pupils' views and their experiences of how they learn best.

Background

Why is teaching and learning interesting from the perspective of classrooms? Some teachers might say that they could 'do the job' just as well regardless of the classroom, and I am sure they could. Belief in one's setting, i.e. the classroom, and how this is used influence the teaching and learning activities that take place (Woolner 2015). At the same time, classrooms are reflections of society, enforcing rules and norms relevant to life outside school, and artefacts and access to different spaces within the classroom regulate behaviour (see for example Dahlberg & Åsén 2012; Eriksson Bergström 2013; Hipkiss 2014 and Ravelli 2008). Furthermore, social rules and traditions for teachers as well as pupils are strong, so traditions around classroom designs are transferred to new classrooms when classes are moved to new buildings (Davidsson 2005), meaning that we do what we have always done and what we know works. At the same time, we must understand that how we read a classroom, a space, affects what we do with our language (Pennycook 2010). It is not so much the situation that affects what we say and do, but the space in which we interact that affects interaction, in Pennycook's view.

The design of a space affects how interaction evolves in teaching and learning (Kress & Sidiropoulou 2008, 112). The interpersonal meaning (Halliday & Matthiessen 2004)—how relations are created and maintained—consequently instantiates different pedagogic discourses (Bernstein 1999), depending on how furniture is arranged, what is visible on the walls, what is accessible, and how participants (are encouraged to) communicate (Björklid 2005; Hipkiss 2014 and Jewitt 2005). Along with how the space is arranged, how it is used affects pedagogic discourse and interpersonal relations (Lim 2011; Lim et al. 2012). Teachers who position themselves at the front of the classroom create a formal distance (built on tradition) from pupils, but by moving and changing positions, this distance can be reduced. Moving too much, however, might change their interpersonal relations. For example, when a teacher appears to be patrolling the classroom, pupils feel watched, and focus on the teacher's perceived expectations, even though the teacher's intention might merely have been to be available (Lim 2011). At the same time, how furniture is arranged in a classroom mirrors the teacher's ambitions and individual pedagogic discourse, for example, maintaining open social relations (Elm Fristorp 2012) or creating a supervisory space for teachers (Hipkiss 2014).

Along with affecting the pedagogic discourse, the design of a classroom affects pupils' abilities to acquire or learn the vertical discourse of the school (Jones 2008)—the subject-specific language use, in other words. This brings a second dimension to the study of classroom design: the language practices in the classroom. Interaction in the classroom between teachers and pupils entails cognitive and linguistic socialisation: pupils learn the subject disciplines and how they are realised linguistically in subject-specific language (also referred to as academic language) (Gibbons 2006). Subject-specific language is here characterised as subject-specific terminology, grammatical metaphors, and the passive voice. These characteristics are essential for acquiring both the concepts and the language of any subject (Gibbons 2006; Schleppegrell 2004). Studying interaction and its place in the classroom provides insights into how, when, and where pupils are invited or encouraged to use subject-specific language, and are consequently provided with affordances for meaning-making and knowledge-building. Subject-specific language is primarily realised as written texts (Christie 2005; Jones 2005). Interaction in the classroom must therefore allow pupils to develop their understanding of subject content and language in varying forms (Hipkiss 2014; Macnaught et al. 2013; Martin 2013; Maton 2014; Matruglio et al. 2013). Education should aim to provide opportunities for pupils to build knowledge cumulatively, as opposed to segmentally (Maton 2014). Cumulative knowledge-building entails new knowledge being added and integrated with existing knowledge, as can be seen from pupils' ability to contribute to discussions about content on an everyday basis, from their use of abstracted, generalised, subject-specific language, and their ability to see the connections temporally and spatially (Maton 2013).

In this essay, I discuss classroom design: how a school subject is understood from its design, what teaching and learning activities take place there, and how participants interact. The analysis of interaction will focus on when, where, and how subject-specific language is used.

Method

This essay is based on approximately 29 hours of observations and recordings of teaching in biology, chemistry, and home and consumer studies (HCS) in five classrooms in two lower secondary schools in Sweden. The recordings have been transcribed for linguistic analyses of the subject-specific language use, such as grammatical metaphors (Halliday & Matthiessen 1994), and the use of the passive voice in the teachers' and pupils' interaction in relation to artefacts and classroom design (Hipkiss 2014). The research project was ethically approved and participants either agreed to be filmed or agreed to have their communication audio-recorded.

Analysing classroom interaction

The recorded lessons were analysed using the framework of curriculum macrogenres (or curriculum units) derived from genre theory (Christie 1995; Jones 2005; Martin & Rose 2008), in order to identify teaching and learning activities. Curriculum macrogenres are staged, goal-oriented, and social processes (Christie 1995; Jones 2005) that consist of various steps and aim to achieve different educational goals, outlined in the curriculum and syllabus (Christie 2005, 22). Christie (ibid.) has described a prototypical linear curriculum macrogenre as being made up of three genres: curriculum initiation, which establishes the objectives of the lesson(s); curriculum collaboration, which often continues over several lessons, and involves independent work as well as group work or lectures; and curriculum closure, which finalises the work, for example as a presentation or a test.

Within the genres, there are clearly separated sections called stages (for example, orientation, repetition, follow-up). These are identified by their overarching purpose; for example, introducing a new subject, developing lab-work skills, or deepening pupils' understanding of

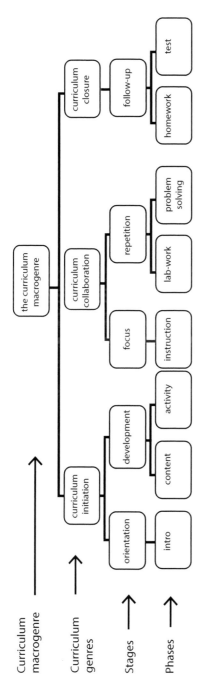

Figure 6.1. Part of the framework of curriculum macrogenres.

	A:1	B:2	B:2	C:2	D:2	E:2	Total
Classroom/school	A:1	B:2	B:2	C:2	D:2	E:2	
Subject	HCS	HCS	HCS	BI	BI	CH	
Curriculum macrogenre	Choices	Baking	Baking	Body	Body	Acids & bases	
Stages/Analysed phase	6:8	6:16	3:12	7:19	9:29	10:44	37:128
Communicative pattern							
Teacher monologue	4	8	7	13	9	23	64
Pupil monologue	1						1
Teacher IRF		5			14	10	29
Pupil IRF						2	2
Dialogue				1	1		2
Participatory exchange	1	3	4	4	4	9	25
Other			1	1	2		4

Table 6.1. Summary of data by classroom, subject (HCS=home & consumer studies, BI=biology, CH=chemistry), macrogenre, stage, phase, and communicative pattern (Hipkiss 2014).

the subject by reading on their own. These stages, in turn, consist of phases (for example, introduction, setting up, homework follow-up, lab work), which are identified by communicative patterns (Gibbons 2006) such as teacher monologue, teacher IRF (initiation, response, feedback), pupil IRF, participatory exchange, and dialogue (Fig. 6.1).

There are several similarities between the analytical process in this study and the analytical processes in studies by Rocksén and Kilhamn et al. (chapter 9 and 8 in this volume). In all three studies, interaction through participation and subject-specificity form the basis for coding the material, and our analyses move between parts and whole, although with different focuses. The analyses of the observed lessons, genres, stages, phases, and communicative patterns are thus summarised in Table 6.1. The analysis did not extend to temporal aspects, such as how long a phase is or how long a participant's turn lasts. Plainly, communication in the classrooms was for the most part controlled by the teachers. Of 128 phases, 93 were either teacher monologues or teacher IRF. Pupil-controlled communication occurred in 31 of the 128 phases (pupil IRF and participatory exchanges) and took place during work in kitchens, lab work, or work from the textbook. These communicative patterns corresponded to the design in the classrooms, which are presented in the sections below. A description is also given of where and how subject-specific language use occurred. Here, the use of the term subject-specific language is restricted to indicators such as grammatical metaphors and processes (Halliday & Matthiessen 2004). These lexicogrammatical resources are at the abstract end of the continuum of the school's vertical discourse and are strongly linked to textbooks, as already noted. However, for pupils to appropriate the vertical discourse they must meet it in other semiotic resources as well.

Analysing classroom space

When analysing the classrooms and their affordances for teaching and learning, I have used a framework taken from linguistics: systemic functional linguistics (Halliday 1978; Halliday & Matthiessen 1994). This framework has inspired much research in fields outside traditional linguistics, for example visual grammar in images and pictures (Kress & Van Leeuwen 2009) and three-dimensional grammar in statues and museums (O'Toole 1994; Stenglin 2008), while Sofkova Hashemi (chapter 5 in this volume) has shown how social semiotics can be used to gauge pupils' multimodal meaning-making on-screen.

The starting point for systemic functional linguistics theory is that meaning is communicated through three metafunctions: the ideational metafunction (ideas about what is communicated), the textual metafunction (the form of the communication, for example, written text or speech or dialogue), and the interpersonal metafunction (how relationships are created and maintained). In this essay, I have chosen to use only part of the analytical framework for these metafunctions (Table 6.2). The framework used here is built on the work of a number of researchers who apply systemic functional linguistics theory to the study of three-dimensional space (Kress & Van Leeuwen 2009; Van Leeuwen 2005; O'Toole 1994; Stenglin 2004; Ravelli 2008).

Classrooms typically foreground certain artefacts associated with the subject being taught. Fume cupboards and other visible science equipment communicate the ideational meaning of

Metafunction		
Ideational metafunction	Textual metafunction	Interpersonal metafunction
Analytical concept		
Literal & symbolic meaning (O'Toole 1994)		
Grounding (Kress & Van Leeuwen 2009)	Paths & venues (Stenglin 2004)	
Separation & access (Ravelli 2008)	Power & social distance (Ravelli 2008)	
Questions to the classrooms		
What is the literal idea of the classroom (presented in for example, activities and foregrounded artefacts)? What is the symbolic meaning of the classroom?	What flow or movements are possible in the space and do all participants have access to all spaces? What is the reading path? What venues (where activities take place) and paths (between these venues) are there?	What relationships between participants are created and maintained through how the space is designed and furnished?

Table 6.2. Analytical framework.

a science classroom (the literal meaning). Seating arrangements, for example around circular tables, add to the ideational meaning of a pupil-centred classroom (the symbolic meaning). The textual meaning involves the paths and venues of the classroom, and pupils' and teachers' access to these venues. Pupils might be free to move about and help themselves to equipment and books for their work, or equipment may be stored out of reach, which means different levels of separation or access. Furthermore, classrooms communicate meaning regarding how interaction is meant to take place. This is the interpersonal meaning—how relationships are created and maintained. Power relations can be displayed using a separate teacher platform or the way in which pupils' desks are arranged. Different affordances for how teaching and learning are realised follow from the different meanings communicated in the design.

Five classrooms were studied (Fig. 6.2). Two, classrooms A and B, were dedicated classrooms for home and consumer studies. Classroom B was shared by two teachers. Two classrooms were biology classrooms, C and D, and one classroom was a chemistry classroom, E. The classrooms were fairly similar. In the following sections, I will present my analysis of the classroom designs and the affordances

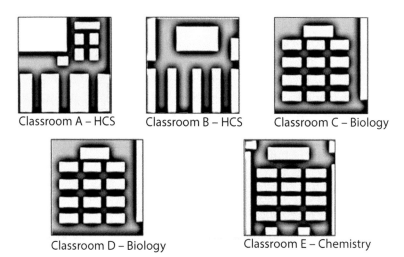

Classroom A – HCS   Classroom B – HCS   Classroom C – Biology

Classroom D – Biology   Classroom E – Chemistry

Figure 6.2. Schematics of the five classrooms studied.

for teaching and learning in these designs, based on observations of classrooms without participants, the use of the classrooms, and the occurrence of subject-specific language.

The ideational classroom

All of the studied classrooms had strong identities. Subject-specific artefacts such as fume cupboards, stuffed animals, or cookers were foregrounded. These literal meanings convey to the pupils, firstly, which subject is in focus and, secondly, what within the subject is prioritised, depending on the artefacts on display on the teacher's desk or side tables. The teachers would prepare equipment for experiments, talks, or cooking so that when the pupils arrived they might be met by a skeleton at the front of the classroom or a cart with solutions and equipment for a chemistry experiment. These artefacts constructed a literal ideational meaning that stressed the subject, the lesson's content, and what was expected of the pupils during lessons. In the cases of HCS and chemistry, the presence of the pupil kitchens and lab equipment constructs HCS and chemistry as practical subjects. Thus, when teachers chose not to use the kitchens for baking or

119

not to use the fume cupboards, they worked against the ideational meaning of the classrooms. All classrooms expressed activities such as scientific investigations and household activities as part of the ideational meaning, which is in alignment with the syllabuses.

As regards the symbolic meaning, one of the HCS classrooms (Classroom A) stood out in its ideational design. It made use of its wall space for posters and newspaper clippings that related to HCS work in the classroom, but with an everyday angle, which is also part of the syllabus. In addition, cookbooks in this classroom were both representations of HCS textbooks from past to present and coffee-table cookbooks from high-street bookshops. The symbolic meaning in Classroom A was interpreted as constructing a subject relevant to both home and school. In comparison, the other class-rooms were bare or minimalist; there were no permanent installations that showed, for example, how biology or chemistry were relevant to what goes on outside school.

In all classrooms, interaction was concerned with the subject in focus, as was the classroom design. However, Classroom A, by its symbolic ideational meaning, also invited input from the world outside school, from teachers and pupils alike. Pupils' own experi-ences were introduced by the pupils during whole-class sessions and during pupil work in kitchens. In the other classrooms, experiences from life outside school were introduced by the teachers. From the analytical perspective of the ideational metafunctions of a classroom, the language practices there were in harmony with both literal and symbolic ideational meanings. Communication centred on the sub-jects; both pupil and teacher interaction focused on either content or activities. Pupils knew when they walked into these classrooms what to expect of the lesson, and what was expected of them from the subject-specific and lesson-specific artefacts.

The textual classroom

The five classrooms all had two distinct venues where teaching and learning activities took place: the teacher venue at the front by the whiteboard or teacher's desk, and the pupil venue, where the

Example	Venue	Communicative pattern and examples
1	Teacher venue	Teacher IRF
		Okay. So what is this? 'Liquid ingredients'—it's a word, a term you use when baking. And when it says in the recipe that the liquid ingredients should be a certain temperature. What is it that needs to be a certain temperature?
2	Pupil kitchen venue	Participatory exchange
		S1: Hey, teacher. This is?
		T: Mm, has S2 felt it too?
		S2: What?
		T: Do this now [demonstrates] and keep your finger in it for a while. How does it feel?
		S2: A bit warm.

Table 6.3. Example of interaction 1: Home and consumer studies: Classroom B. Italics=subject specific concept (liquid ingredients) and 2: italics= reference to subject specific concept (e.g. pronouns).

pupils sat during whole-class activities led by the teacher. The HCS classrooms (A and B) had one additional venue, the pupil kitchen venue. Here pupils mainly cooked and at times also carried out other group work. These venues were all clearly defined, as were the activities. In Classroom B (HCS), the teacher venue was connected to the pupil venue, as there was no teacher's desk. However, there was an understood boundary between these venues, as the teacher alone had access to the whiteboard and the pupils left extra space for the teacher to put files and other paperwork on the shared table space. Throughout all the lessons, the teacher venue was a restricted space for pupils. They rarely entered it, and instead approached the teachers during activities when the teachers were in the pupil venues.

Pupils and teachers had access to the pupil venues and pupil kitchen venues during activities such as experiments and group work. During teacher-led activities such as lectures or homework follow-up, however, pupils were expected to stay in their seats, and access to other venues was restricted. These differences in access were also realised in language practices. Teacher–pupil interaction during teacher-led activities led from the teacher venue was characterised mainly by teacher monologues or teacher IRF and subject-specific language, in contrast to the context-embedded participatory exchanges during cooking and lab work. These differences can be explained by the change in physical distance between participants, as well as the change in location, for example, from the description of an activity on the whiteboard or in the book to its execution at the desk or in the kitchen.

The examples from the HCS classrooms illustrate the change in interaction between venues (Table 6.3). Example 1, from the teacher venue, demonstrates the use of subject-specific language. It introduces a central term and concept for baking with yeast: liquid ingredients. Example 2 shows how communication in the pupil venues regarding liquid ingredients was realised, and specifically how context and place make subject-specific language redundant. However, if a concept is an essential one, it should also be made part of the context-embedded language used between teachers and pupils.

One noteworthy difference between classrooms A and B was in the designs of the pupil kitchen venues. In Classroom B, the pupil kitchens were separated by a wall, making all kitchens into individual units with no visual outlook on the others, apart from one space where two groups of pupils could work back to back. This design emphasised the ideational meaning of the classroom as a school subject classroom, to the extent that it appeared like a test station where the teachers could observe all pupils from a distance. During the examination lesson, pupils could feel that they were being observed, but they did not know if the teacher was observing them or somebody else (the notion of the panopticon). The separated spaces also restricted communication to the designated partner, thus pupils did not share experiences or thoughts with pupils in other kitchens while they were cooking.

In the other HCS classroom, there was more openness. The pupil kitchens were open between the overhanging cupboards so pupils could see what someone else was doing without leaving their kitchen. This meant that there would always be between four and six pupils who could communicate about their progress, their experiences or questions. Furthermore, the teacher could not observe from a distance. The classroom space and furniture arrangement required the teacher to approach the pupil kitchen venue in order to follow and assess the pupils' work.

The interpersonal classroom

The classrooms studied here were unmistakable in their interpersonal meaning. From when they entered the classrooms, pupils knew how interaction should play out. Classroom A (HCS) had a pupil-centred arrangement in the pupil venue. Here, pupils were seated in groups of four, which was more reminiscent of seating arrangements at home or in restaurants. The two biology classrooms (C and D) had pupil desks arranged in pairs facing the teacher venue at the front. In Classroom C, the teacher led interaction from the front, not necessarily from behind the desk, but moving between the whiteboard to the desk and the first pair of pupil desks, from where the teacher asked questions and pupils responded or worked at the desks either individually or with their neighbour. In Classroom D, the desk arrangement did not quite fit the teacher–pupil interaction that actually took place. The teacher moved around in the front part of the classroom, making little use of the whiteboard, and instead making use of his own body and the bodies of pupils and the artefacts brought into the classroom. It was a very talkative class where the teacher spoke most, introducing the biology content and then exemplifying this using the pupils' own experiences. Similar to Example 2 given earlier, interaction was characterised mainly by context-embedded, biology-related content in everyday language, and very little subject-specific language was in evidence. As most communication was spoken, with the aid of illustrative artefacts, it would have made more sense if the classroom had been arranged with the desks in a circle so the teacher could more easily show the artefacts and move around, and so the pupils could see one another when they interacted.

The chemistry classroom (Classroom E) had a clear synthesis of design and communication. Communication was led by the teacher from the lectern, which was raised so that pupils on the back benches could see demonstrations of experiments and so on. During lab work, the communication was between pupils at their desks, in groups of two or three. The organisation of teaching and learning activities was clear to the pupils, as was who had control of the communication. Each lesson followed a distinct pattern, which also corresponded to

Example	Venue	Communicative pattern and examples
3	Teacher venue	Teacher IRF
		T: If a solution has pH2, is it an acid or a base or is it perhaps neutral? S3?
		S3: Acid
		T: It's an acid, yes. If the pH is 13 what solution is it then? Is it an acid, base, or neutral? Yes, S4.
		S4: A base.
		T: It is a base. And what is the pH value for neutrals?

Table 6.4. Example of interaction 3. Chemistry.

the ideational meaning of the classroom design: chemistry equals experiments. The interactional pattern when not experimenting was a traditional triad of teacher initiation, pupil response and teacher feedback (Table 6.4). IRF patterns of this type do not allow for pupils to formulate answers using subject-specific language; it is IRF with the purpose of checking up on homework or whether pupils understand concepts, instead of allowing linguistic socialisation.

The distinct venues in all the classrooms, with their corresponding interactional patterns, reflect the social relations created by designs that put teachers in power in the classrooms, particularly in the teacher venues. Also, when the teachers moved around in the pupil venues in order to help or supervise work, the social distance was maintained, as pupils were seated and teachers were walking or standing. On occasion, teachers would approach pupils on a more equal level, by bending down or crouching. These moves on the teachers' part resulted in more private interaction in which power was still with the teacher, but the social distance was reduced. In these exchanges (participatory exchanges) there was subject-specific language, while everyday language was used to explain or elaborate on pupils' questions. Similarly, interaction was context-embedded and social distance was reduced in the HCS Classroom A with the open pupil kitchens. Here pupils were near one another, and the design also encouraged or required the teacher to reduce social distance as well, in contrast to when pupils were seated in the HCS classrooms. The simple fact that everyone was standing up and communicating at eye level in the pupil kitchen venues served to reduce the teacher's power status.

Conclusion

School classrooms are versions of contemporary society, and norms and regulations are presented in their design and use. In the classroom, this is realised through artefacts that regulate behaviour and access, such as desks and chairs, signs, and locked or unlocked doors (see for example Dahlberg & Åsén 2012; Eriksson Bergström 2013; Hipkiss 2014; Ravelli 2008). Similarly, classrooms are coded for certain activities, and these codings affect how classrooms are defined (Dahlberg & Åsén 2012). In this study, all five classrooms have strong identities, due to subject-specific artefacts that are foregrounded in the classroom.

This study of the design of classrooms and interaction shows that classrooms have different affordances for teaching and learning activities. The classrooms create participating or listening pupils, depending on the venue in which interaction is lead—whether it is lead from the teacher venue or in the pupil venues. In addition, the designs influence pupils' opportunities for sharing experiences and knowledge. Lecture-like seating or seating that creates a distance between participants necessarily restricts pupils' opportunities for participation. The distance requires teachers to moderate their communication so that it is inclusive, inviting pupils in. As noted earlier (for example, Selander & Kress 2010, 42) and in the results from this classroom study, classroom designs affect social relations, and different designs provide different affordances. Classrooms create meaning for interaction and shared experiences. The five classrooms presented here are examples of classrooms that provide a range of affordances for sharing experiences and interacting. Ideational meanings that put the subject in focus are dominant in both design and content, and the ideational meaning of classrooms as rooms for activities such as lab work or cooking is also prevalent—and understood from the designs. Pupils are schooled into a teacher–pupil relationship that presents the teacher at the lectern as the one who controls interaction, as the desks face forwards in all but one classroom. A lecture hall has its given mode of communication: the lecturer speaks, the audience listens, and asks questions if invited to do so. A classroom with desks in pairs facing the whiteboard and the teacher's lectern tells us that focus is on the teacher, who thus controls communication, while pupils are limited to communicating with their desk partners or the teacher. In addition, the design affects the language practices on a local level, within the interactional patterns.

Communication is an essential part of teaching and learning. How this communication is best enacted can be explicit from the design of a classroom, as this essay has illustrated. Communication led from the teacher venue, by the teacher, was prominent (93/128 phases) and typically identified as teacher IRF or a teacher monologue. In order for pupils to develop their use of subject-specific language or the vertical discourse of the school and to build knowledge cumulatively, they need to be able to use subject-specific language in different situations. In the lessons studied here, interaction offered few opportunities for pupils to do this, as teachers and textbooks provided the subject-specific input.

What is *in* a classroom, how it is used and altered, affects the affordances for teaching and learning, as do the activities and communication (Hipkiss 2014). Kress et al. (2001) describe teaching and meaning-making as materialisations of motivated choices that pupils and teachers make with regard to different semiotic resources, such as artefacts and interaction in the classroom. Thus, how a classroom is designed and used ought to be part of what we include when preparing and planning for teaching and learning activities. A classroom is a space which 'is organized and given meaning in interaction with humans' (Pennycook 2010:7) and the language practices in the classroom are constructed and reconstructed as a result of the affordances of these spaces. This means that when planning activities, teachers have to consider the arrangement of furniture and pupils. If the purpose is to 'show and tell' and to include pupils in the activity, the language practice will, or should, move between the abstract subject-specific textbook terminology and actual, context-embedded pupil experiences and artefacts in the classroom, leaving language practices to oscillate between the everyday and the abstract (Hipkiss 2014; Maton 2014).

References

Bernstein, B. (1999), 'Vertical and Horizontal Discourse: An Essay', *British Journal of Sociology of Education*, 20/2, 157–73.

Björklid, P. (2005), *Lärande om fysisk miljö: En kunskapsöversikt om samspelet mellan lärande och fysisk miljö i förskola och skola* (Forskning i focus, 25; Stockholm: Myndigheten för skolutveckling).

Christie, F. (1995), 'Pedagogic Discourse in the Primary school', *Linguistics & Education*, 7/3, 221–42.

—— (2005), *Classroom Discourse Analysis: A Functional Perspective* (London: Continuum) (first pub. 2002).

Dahlberg, G. & G. Åsén (2012), 'Loris Malaguzzi och den pedagogiska filosofin i Reggio Emilia', in A. Forsell (ed.), *Boken om pedagogerna* (Stockholm: Liber).

Davidsson, B. (2005), 'Klassrum, lekrum och andra rum: Om rum för lärande i integrerade verksamheter', *Didaktisk tidskrift*, 15/1–2, 51–63.

Elm Fristorp, A. (2012), *Design för lärande: Barns meningsskapande i naturvetenskap* (diss., Stockholm: Stockholm University).

Eriksson Bergström, S. (2013), *Rum, barn och pedagoger: Om möjligheter och begränsningar i förskolans fysiska miljö* (diss., Umeå: Umeå University).

Gibbons, P. (2006), Bridging Discourses in the ESL classroom: Students, Teachers and Researchers (London: Continuum).

Granly, A. & E. Maagerø (2012), 'Multimodal Texts in Kindergarten Rooms', *Education Inquiry*, 3/3, 371–86.

Halliday, M.A.K. & C. Matthiessen (2004), 'An Introduction to Functional Grammar (3rd edn, London: Hodder Education).

Hipkiss, A. M. (2014), *The Semiotic Resources of the Classroom: An Applied Linguistics Perspective on the School Subjects Home and Consumer Studies, Biology and Chemistry* (diss., Umeå: Umeå University).

Jewitt, C. (2005), 'Classrooms and the Design of Pedagogic Discourse: A Multimodal Approach', *Culture & Psychology*, 11/3, 309–320.

Jones, P. (2008), 'The Interplay of Discourse, Place and Space in Pedagogic Relations', in Unsworth 2008.

Kilhamn, C., Rystedt, E., Nyman, R. & Holmberg, B. (2019), The contribution of video studies to classroom research: seeking hidden dimensions of teaching and learning in algebra. In Osbeck, C., Ingerman, Å. & Claesson, S. (eds.). *Didactic classroom studies: A potential research direction*. Lund: Nordic Academic Press.

Kress, G. (1993), 'Against Arbitrariness: The Social Production of the Sign as a Foundational Issue in Critical Discourse Analysis', *Discourse & Society*, 4/2, 169–91.

—— C. Jewitt, J. Ogbord & C. Tsatsarelis (2001), *Multimodal Teaching and*

Learning: The Rhetorics of the Science Classroom (London: Continuum).

—— & T. van Leeuwen (2006), *Reading Images: The Grammar of Visual Design* (London: Routledge) (first pub. 1996).

—— & C. Sidiropoulou (2008), 'Klassrumsdesign', in A.-L. Rostvall & S. Selander (eds.), *Design för lärande* (Stockholm: Norstedts Akademiska Förlag).

Lim, F. V. (2011), 'A Systemic Functional Multimodal Discourse Analysis Approach to Pedagogic Discourse' (diss., Singapore: University of Singapore).

—— K. L. O'Halloran & A. Podlasov (2012), 'Spatial Pedagogy: Mapping Meanings in the Use of Classroom Space', *Cambridge Journal of Education*, 42 /2, 235–51.

Macnaught, L., K. Maton, R. J. Martin & M. E. Matruglio (2013), 'Jointly constructing semantic waves: Implications for teacher training', *Linguistics & Education*, 24/1, 50–63.

Martin, J. (2013), 'Embedded literacy: Knowledge as meaning', *Linguistics & Education*, 24/1, 23–37.

Martin, J. R. & Rose, D. (2008), *Genre Relations* (London: Equinox).

Maton, K. (2013), Making semantic waves: A key to cumulative knowledge-building. *Linguistics and Education*. 24 (2013). 8-22.

Maton, K. (2014), *Knowledge and Knowers: Towards a Realist Sociology of Education* (London: Routledge).

Matruglio, E., K. Maton & J. R. Martin (2013)), 'Time travel: The role of temporality in enabling semantic waves in secondary education', *Linguistics & Education*, 24, 38–49.

O'Toole, M. (1994), *The Language of Displayed Art* (London: Leicester University Press).

Pennycook, A. (2010), *Language as A Local Practice* (London: Routledge).

Ravelli, L. J. (2008), 'Analysing Space: Adapting and Extending Multimodal Frameworks', in Unsworth 2008.

Schleppegrell, M. J. (2004), *The Language of Schooling: A Functional Linguistics Perspective* (Mahwah, NJ: Lawrence Erlbaum).

Selander, D. & G. Kress (2010), *Design för lärande: Ett multimodalt perspektiv* (Stockholm: Norstedts).

Stenglin, M. (2004), 'Packaging Curiosities: Towards a Grammar of Three-dimensional space' (diss., Sydney: University of Sydney).

Stenglin, M. (2008), 'Interpersonal Meaning in 3D space: How a Bonding Icon Gets Its "Charge"', in Unsworth 2008.

Unsworth, L. (ed.), *Multimodal Semiotics: Functional Analysis in Contexts of Education* (London: Continuum).

van Leeuwen, T. (2005), *Introducing Social Semiotics* (London: Routledge).

—— (2008), 'Space in Discourse', in Unsworth 2008.

Woolner, P. (2015), 'Introduction: A school environment to help, not hinder: Understanding the role of physical space in education', in P. Woolner (ed.), *School design together* (London: Routledge).

Abstract

There have been calls that Swedish classrooms should be silent and that pupils should comply more with their teachers. The response has been to claim that it is possible to achieve discipline in the classroom in a variety of ways, and that a more holistic view of teaching and learning is needed. We have revisited a number of classroom observations in order to find the patterns in the way teachers handle discipline in their everyday teaching. The aim of this essay is to answer the question of what teaching strategies are available, and which appear to be successful. Our study takes a hermeneutical and lifeworld phenomenological approach. The result shows three different teaching strategies: one where the teacher most of the time addresses individual pupils; one where the teacher is directed towards the whole class; and one where the teacher often and in relation to contextual aspects oscillates between the individual pupil and the class. When it comes to order and discipline, the third strategy appears to be the most successful. The didactical consequences are that order and discipline are embedded in everyday teaching. In the past, teachers had to be flexible about content and methods, but today they also need to be flexible towards their pupils.

CHAPTER 7

The importance of relationships in the classroom

Annika Lilja & Silwa Claesson

Silence is golden?

Swedish politicians and media have claimed that a classroom with order and discipline is a silent classroom, where each pupil works on their own tasks. These demands have been answered with claims that it is possible to achieve discipline in the classroom in a different way, and that what has been called a more holistic view on teaching and learning is needed. This essay seeks answers about what kind of solutions have been used earlier in history, but with the main focus on today's teaching when it comes to classroom discipline. Whether the pupils are interested in learning what is planned for the lesson or not, the teacher has the responsibility of keeping the classroom under control. What we mean by a lesson where there is order and discipline is not necessarily that all pupils work quietly on their own, but that the teacher and the pupils are directed towards the same object and that the pupils have the opportunity to expand their horizons, although there might, on and off, be a bit of hustle and bustle in the classroom. Even though the examples from four different classrooms described in this essay differ when it comes to subjects and the pupils' age, we have searched for and discovered some teaching patterns that go beyond these factors. This study is a contribution to an ongoing discussion in the field of *Allgemeine Didaktik* or general didactics.

In a study about order and discipline in the classroom it is useful to look at the historical background to the discussion of today's order and discipline in the classroom. When attendance at school became mandatory in Sweden in 1842, the so-called Lancaster model was recommended (Landahl 2011). This English model was based on Bell and Lancaster's principles of teaching, where up to 900 pupils were taught at the same time by one teacher. The pupils stood in groups under the guidance of an older or a particularly skilled pupil known as a monitor. The teachers were available in the classroom, but they were mainly silent. For different types of offences there were punishments—for example, the pupils were not allowed to be quiet. The sound was therefore mostly cacophonous (Larsson & Westberg 2014). During the late nineteenth century, several people, such as cultural figures and politicians, opposed the Lancaster system. In Sweden, a so-called 'Normal Plan' was introduced for the school, which meant that the classes were not as big as before, pupils were to sit on chairs with a bench in front of them. The pupils were now seated, facing their teacher, so it would be possible for the teacher to control them, and when the pupils wanted to talk they were supposed to raise their hands. Corporal punishment was applied at the teacher's discretion, and the Normal Plan also introduced homework. Landahl (2011) emphasizes that this was a new way to organise teaching—now the teachers spoke and moved around the room, not the pupils. In the late nineteenth and early twentieth centuries, many ideas about how schools could function in alternative ways were presented. Reforming educators such as John Dewey (1959), Rudolf Steiner (Nobel 1991), Maria Montessori (1967), and Ellen Key (Ambjörnsson 2013) published texts about learning environments that were based on humanist values, and they showed how teaching could be arranged so that every individual pupil could develop and learn in a more personal way. However, these famous educators who advocated new ways of teaching initially met with little interest in the Swedish community (Hartman 2005).

Order and discipline in school is a topic that has engaged both politicians and the public (Utbildningsdepartementet 2010). This means that whether teachers will succeed in maintaining discipline in the classroom is a constant concern to many social actors, and is of interest to almost everyone. However, as children's roles in society have changed, it seems reasonable to assume that the methods for accomplishing a good classroom climate also need to change (Wedin 2007).

We have looked at two different ways of viewing teachers' work with order in the classroom. The first perspective stresses how different methods affect pupils' behaviour in the classroom by using the key concept 'classroom management' (for example, Lewis et al. 2014; Montuoro & Lewis 2014; Simonsen et al. 2008). 'Classroom management' is generally speaking about strategies that help teachers to make lessons work as well as possible by responding to different actions of pupils in the classroom. The most common strategies are related to pupils' behaviour (Montuoro & Lewis 2014). The main line in classroom management is to prevent pupils from disturbing the teaching (Simonsen et al. 2008). The strategies that teachers are expected to use are often designed on a general level, and originate from evidence-based practice (Levinsson 2013). The purpose of these strategies is to allow teachers to deal with pupils successfully and to improve pupils' behaviour (Lewis et al. 2014).

The second perspective takes a relational approach to education. Relational pedagogy is often associated with philosophers such as Martin Buber (1990) and Otto Bollnow (1989). Both Buber and Bollnow are interested in how relations between people can be expressed. Buber (1990) proposed a third way for pedagogy, not an individualistic or collective one, but an interpersonal way, where the learning occurs in the gap between two people. Bollnow (1989) highlighted the importance of the teacher's belief in his or her pupils and therefore that the teacher's trust in the pupils should be a starting point, because children are shaped by the expectations they experience. If the teacher expects that the pupil is going to behave badly, it may mean that this is exactly what the pupil will do. Today, many researchers address the importance of relations for the quality of teaching and for pupils' ability to learn (for example, Biesta 2004 & 2009; Bingham & Sidorkin 2004). Biesta (2004) argues that education is not what the teacher says and does, nor is it the pupils' activities, but the interaction between the two—a theory of education is a theory about relationships. In Sweden, classroom studies have also been conducted that in various ways highlight the relationship between teacher and pupils (for example Aspelin 2015; Rinne 2015; Levinsson 2013; Lilja 2013a; Frelin 2010, 2012; Aspelin & Persson 2011; Claesson 2011). The main focus in all these studies is not discipline in school, but something they have in common is that they highlight a different role for today's pupils and what consequences this might have in various classroom contexts. Further, these studies show how a new role for the pupils has changed the role of the teacher. A teacher needs to earn the pupils' trust, interest and attention in a different way from fifty years ago (Bingham 2004), which implies that discipline in today's schools is maintained in a new way, where the relational aspects of teaching and learning are taken into account. This means that order and discipline in the classroom, from a relational perspective, is intertwined with the teaching.

Theory and method

The ways of viewing order in the classroom are changing. To investigate the effects of this, we have returned to our earlier studies, but now with a view to analysing how teachers maintain discipline in Swedish classrooms of today. The observations (Lilja 2013; Claesson 2011; Claesson 2005) were carried out with the purpose of capturing the relationships between teaching and learning and the relationships between teacher and pupils. To create an understanding, we have used a phenomenological-hermeneutic theory (for example, Lilja 2015; Bengtsson 2013; Lilja 2013; Claesson 2011; Claesson 2009; Berndtsson et al. 2007; Claesson 2004; Van Manen 1991; Van Manen 1991). In using a phenomenological approach, there is an ambition to intertwine life and world, and a central idea in this approach is that everyone is always directed towards something, which implies that this is an important component when teaching as well (Claesson 2008). A study in this tradition implies that the phenomenon—in this essay order and discipline—is presented in a broad and rich way. Van Manen (1991) uses the term 'tact' to describe the subtle and ethical nuances that are implied in teachers' daily life with their pupils: teachers have to be tactful in relation to their pupils. However, it is primarily the concept of the horizon that is used in this study in order to discern how discipline appears in today's classroom. Husserl (1970) introduced this concept, and Gadamer (2005) has developed it, but here it is above all inspired by Merleau-Ponty (2008), who suggests that we experience the world in a non-dualistic way—where body and soul are regarded as intertwined. Each person has an implicit horizon, which means that different directions and perspectives emerge (Van Manen 1991) and the horizon changes continuously (Berndtsson 2001). The concept of horizon can be used in order to see 'what it is possible for us to achieve' (horizon of opportunity), and it can also be used as a horizon of action: everyone is aware of their opportunities and choices and chooses to act according to them (ibid.). In a classroom, all pupils experience what happens from their own unique perspective, which means that it is a challenge for the teacher to reach all of them and make them choose to act according to the purpose of the lesson, instead of choosing activities that may interfere with what the teacher has planned. Since we view order and discipline in a classroom as a situation when teacher and pupils are directed towards the same object, we use the concept horizon in the field of didactics to elicit knowledge about how teachers assist their pupils to expand their horizons during a given lesson.

This essay is based on observations in various classrooms. All three studies, with four teachers in the first, six teachers in the second and five teachers in the third, constitute the basis for the results. The studies have been previously reported in part (Lilja 2015; Lilja 2013a; Lilja 2013b; Lilja 2011; Claesson 2008; Claesson 2005; Claesson 2002; Claesson 1999) and the empirical material has now been used again because it is a rich source where a detailed picture of the everyday classroom emerges. The material that is used in this essay does not contradict the material that was not selected. Rather than interpreting all the relevant situations, we have chosen to cite only data from a total of four teachers in this essay. The teachers were selected because each represents one of the teaching strategies found in the material, and because they are working both in compulsory school and in upper-secondary school. All observations were carried out in a similar fashion, where the main focus was on the teacher and notes were taken for 250 days in total, with the notes transcribed and interpreted. This means that what we present here represents a long-term pattern of observations and in this essay we are able to give only a few examples. We switch between general and specific events. In terms of selection, in Claesson's studies the teachers, after answering a survey, applied to participate in the studies; in Lilja's study, schools in various socio-economic areas were contacted and the participating teachers were recommended by a headmaster or colleague.

According to Ricoeur (1988), the emancipation of the action from the acting person gives an independence that he compares to the semantic autonomy of the text. The action leaves a trace. The analysis started with the selection of situations that were interpreted as having to do with order and discipline. When it comes to capturing an action, Ricoeur (2009) suggests that the action can become an object of scientific study without losing importance, through a special kind of objectification. This implies that the action is a pattern that is described and interpreted according to its internal connections. Hermeneutics implies a constant contextualisation, in that there is a constant oscillation between the whole and the part. The selected situations were read several times and organised in different ways before the presented results appeared. The context has been crucial to our interpretations, but the parts have also been necessary for us to get a sense of the whole picture when it comes to order and discipline in various classrooms. After the analysis was complete, four situations were chosen for this essay.

Results

The teacher's authority is not self-evident just because he or she is a member of a profession with a fairly high status (Levinsson 2013; Lilja 2013a; Frelin 2010; Wedin 2007; Claesson 1999). However, our empirical material shows that teachers do not plan their lessons primarily with the thought of maintaining discipline. Rather, they plan to give their pupils opportunities to learn the intended content of the lesson. In the classroom studies presented here, we have nevertheless identified three different strategies for teaching that affect the teacher's ability to maintain discipline: individualisation, group instruction, and an oscillation between individual and group instruction.

Individualising the teaching

Adam is a science teacher at an upper-secondary school in an area with a large number of immigrants. Adam regards every pupil as unique, and should be met with unique questions from the teacher, which is his way to encourage pupils to search for knowledge independently. Adam has come to a conclusion that education in an environment such as his must be designed according to these ideas, and his teaching follows the same structure during every lesson and in all classes. For him, teaching boils down to the idea that every pupil should have the opportunity to ask the teacher questions that result from their own curiosity within the domain of science. This implies that the pupils cannot always study the same content at the same time. Adam tells the pupils to formulate a question of their own, and then asks them to describe in writing how they are going to get the answers to their own questions. Adam's idea about individualisation implies that every pupil should get to work with their personal issues in the school laboratory where they are expected to carry out various experiments.

In the classroom, Adam moves around assisting pupils one at a time, and the conversations he has with his pupils can be described as being of a Socratic nature or using open questions, which he himself hardly ever answers. His idea is that pupils should also take notes about what they are studying.

> – I do not know what to write, one girl says.
> – Can't you write what you learnt about plants and water? Adam asks.
> – Why do we have to write so much? another pupil asks.

> – In order to know what you think about the topic, a third pupil answers.
> – So you can see that we have developed, says a boy with a glance at Adam.
> – Do *I* have to know that? Adam responds.

In this situation, it appears that while one pupil does not know what to write, another wonders why they have to write so much. They try to get Adam to tell them what the point of writing is, but they don't really get a clear answer. Adam responds, as often is the case in the classroom context, with a new question.

From the observations in the classroom, it is clear that some pupils are passive.

> – Honestly, I have not learnt anything at all, says a girl who seems restless.

She wants Adam to tell her how things are linked, but it is clear that Adam wants her to figure it out on her own.

The implications of this way of teaching are that many pupils have a unique opportunity to have Adam's support, but that many pupils are also left to their own devices, and far from everyone can find their own interesting question, or develop the question independently in the classroom environment. So instead, many pupils deal with other things that do not have any bearing on the aim of the lesson. Several pupils are chatting with each other while Adam has long conversations with one or sometimes two pupils at a time.

From a discipline perspective, although some pupils have a lot of support, many pupils seem to be left without guidance and with unanswered questions that seem to make them anxious and frustrated. Therefore, the pupils who are left behind may not have the opportunity to expand their horizons in such a way that they have opportunities to learn the intended content of the lesson. Instead of working with their assignments, they do other things. Some of them seem to think it is nice to decide for themselves what to do, and they chat about various things that interest them. Other pupils take advantage of the opportunity to get 'private tuition' from their teacher, and they seek Adam's attention and develop well in the subject. Adam continues with his way of teaching even though he does not reach all his pupils. To sum up, individualising teaching causes some problems. The largest problem from an order and discipline point of view is that too many pupils are left alone in the classroom, and this means that Adam loses many pupils' interest and attention. Most of all, he loses the pupils who do not understand what the teaching is about from the start. The working environment in the classroom, where many different activities are going on, is confused, and a good many activities have nothing to do with science.

Working with the whole class

If individualisation does not work, would it be better to teach the whole class at the same time? John is a history and civics teacher at an upper-secondary school. He is directed towards the whole class and gives lectures. John is also deeply engaged with his subjects and prepares each lesson carefully.

On one occasion, John gives the class a description of the historical background to the conflict between Jews and Muslims in Israel.

> – It's 1914. What happened then?
> – The First World War, a pupil answers.
> – Yes.

John moves while he speaks. He walks back and forwards, looking at the pupils and talking with enthusiasm.

> – And now they do a thing that is really momentous.

He describes how countries were formed and their borders set after the First World War.

> – It was decided over all of their heads.

John is completely engaged in the content and this is reflected in his body language. However, John is unsure how to deal with these classes because they are vocational training classes and they do not relate to the teaching in the same way as the classes he has been accustomed to teaching. Most of John's experience has been in a school where pupils brought paper, pens, and folders, wrote down what he said, and attended exams. Now things have changed and John has no alternative teaching strategies. Like Adam, John does not change his teaching when he notices that some of the pupils are not focused on the goal for the lesson. He works in the way that he worked before, and that is as far as his horizon reaches. So what he does is to prepare even more, but he prepares more of the same, and not all the pupils appreciate that. Some skip lessons; some do not listen at all. The pupils' and Johns' horizons do not meet in a joint goal for the lesson.

It seems this method of teaching, addressing all the pupils in the class at the same time, is not always successful either. This despite the fact that the method corresponds to the convention used in schools for over a century: pupils sit facing forward, silent, and listen to the teacher. In this case, by using just one teaching method, John loses his pupils; many of them are neither motivated nor interested—not in the subject and not in working. This means that the pupils do not expand their horizons when it comes to the subjects John teaches. Their horizons might even shrink when the pupils experience their education to be useless.

From a discipline perspective, neither the method of addressing the pupils as a group and only having sparse communication between teacher and pupil nor individualisation seem to work. When the pupils lose interest in what John says, they move their focus to other things that interest them more. Some of the pupils even go so far as to not attend lessons, as they consider something else to be more meaningful. Other pupils who are actually in the classroom deal with other concerns than the teacher intends.

Oscillating between the individual and the class

Some of the teachers in our studies show an ability to have a relationship with the class, with small groups, and with individual pupils almost simultaneously. These teachers consider the relationship with the pupils to be a determining factor in successful teaching. An example of such a situation is when Susanna, who teaches pupils aged 7 and 8, is going to read a story for her pupils.

The pupils are gathered in a circle on the floor and Susanna sits on a small chair. She is going to read a detective story and the pupils are supposed to figure out who is the thief in the story. Susanna begins to read with empathy: she uses her voice and she seeks eye contact with her pupils when she takes short pauses. Despite this, it does not take long before two of the pupils begin to talk to each other. They lose interest in the story and talk about something they regard as more important. This interferes with Susanna's reading and disturbs the other pupils who want to listen. Susanna interrupts her reading and asks them to be quiet. They oblige for a little while, but soon they start talking again. This time Susanna looks at them with stern eyes as she leans towards them and says to them with a firm voice. 'Now I want you to be silent.' When Susanna has reprimanded the two pupils, she reverts to her former posture and tone of voice, and continues to read with enthusiasm. However, two other pupils start to quarrel with each other. Max has a wooden bead on the floor in front of him and Carl grabs it, which Max does not like. Max, irritated, tries to take the bead back, but Carl refuses. Susanna interrupts her reading for the third time, gets up from her chair, takes three steps forward and takes the bead from Carl without saying anything. Susanna keeps the bead in her hand as she sits down again. She looks Max and Carl in the eye before she continues reading again with a friendly voice. A peaceful and quiet mood settles over the group. Now there is calm in the circle and Susanna finishes the story.

In this situation, the teacher has a plan for the lesson and has set an object for what she wants her pupils to learn. In order for the teacher and the pupils to be directed towards the same object, Susanna needs to have an individual relationship both with her pupils and with the whole class. However, it turns out that some of the pupils do not have the same goal for the lesson as the teacher and they start to talk and argue with each other. In this way, they disrupt both Susanna's reading and the group's opportunities to learn the intended content. To resolve the situation so that the lesson can continue undisturbed, Susanna needs to deal with what is happening in such a way that all the pupils are directed towards the same goal. The consequence of Susanna's teaching, where she oscillates between those who need extra attention and the whole class, is that it finally makes the pupils do what she has planned. From a disciplinary perspective, Susanna handles the situation by rebuking the pupils who disrupt the lesson. The other pupils who want to listen to the detective story are met with empathy and commitment. In this way, she resolves the difficulties together with the children, who for a moment are caught up in issues other than the detective story. Susanna's pupils have the opportunity to expand their horizons in terms of the lesson content.

Another example of oscillation between the individual and the group is a lesson in biology with Peter, who is a teacher of Year 9 pupils who are going to do a test. Jeanette is often absent from the lessons, but today she is in the classroom. However, she does not have enough knowledge to answer the questions in the test, and so Peter lets her do it with support from her biology book. Jeanette finishes her test quite quickly and gives it back. Then she leans back against the wall and puts her feet on the chair next to her, puts in her earphones, and starts to paint her fingernails. While the other pupils are still deeply absorbed in their tests, a sharp smell of nail polish spreads through the classroom. No one seems to react—neither the teacher nor the rest of the pupils.

In a conversation after the lesson, Peter is asked if pupils are allowed to do a test with support from the book, and to paint their nails during the lesson. Yes, he says, but only Jeanette, who is a special pupil and needs special conditions. School is not particularly important for her and if she is put under pressure, she leaves the classroom. Peter's task as a teacher is to give all pupils the opportunity to succeed based on their individual abilities, which means that Jeanette has her own rules.

The consequence of Peter's teaching ideas is that he strives to make it possible for his pupils to find their own horizons of opportunity, and then choose to act and thereby extend their knowledge in the subjects Peter teaches. Because Jeanette feels trusted and is given rules that she can accept, she chooses to attend Peter's lessons to a greater extent than she does others. Peter can, to some extent, push her to work, and because of that she does not disturb the others by talking and disrupting the lessons. Peter meets her needs, and Jeanette respects the limits Peter sets up for her. The other pupils accept Jeanette's special conditions, as Peter treats all his pupils as though they have equal value. Many of them want to perform well in order to get high grades and advance in the education system, and he gives them what they need: interesting teaching and an expectation that they are capable of doing well. The pupils appear in different ways to the teacher, and Peter also responds to them in different ways depending on who they are. From a disciplinary perspective, this implies that the mutual trust that Peter and his pupils have for each other means that the pupils want to make an effort to do a good job.

Susanna and Peter thus change their ways of teaching when they notice that they have lost some of their pupils' attention during the lesson. Their oscillation between individual pupils and the entire group contributes to the pupils and the teacher being directed towards the same object, and in that way the pupils' horizons expand. The oscillation also contributes to the pupils seeing their opportunities to learn, and the mutual trust between teacher and pupils means that the pupils choose to do the work needed for them to learn. When teachers can talk to the class as a whole and at the same time meet their pupils' different needs, this benefits individual pupils, different groups in the class, and the class as a whole.

Discussion

Dealing with pupils who disturb order in the classroom and pupils' lack of motivation is a part of the teacher's practice, and it is an aspect of a teacher's work that is often discussed among politicians and in the press. These discussions tend to highlight problems with discipline as a reason for pupils' declining results in national and international tests, and both politicians and the public have suggestions about how discipline could be improved. Often you will hear that things were better in the past. But what do we mean by 'the past' and what was better? Does this mean the Lancaster era when the teacher was supposed to be quiet? Or is it the reactions to this method, when the pupils were supposed to put up their hands if they wanted to say something and could be punished physically if they did not behave? Or is it perhaps the humanist values, such as those advocated by John Dewey and Ellen Key? A look back in history shows that the view on what order in a classroom means has changed. That pupils need to be disciplined in some way is a fact that was valid a hundred years ago as well as today, but with regard to the question of how it can be achieved, there are several answers. This essay focuses on a present-day perspective, the relational perspective. Of the fifteen teachers who participated in our studies, four of whom we have discussed in this essay, we see that the teachers who have the ability to oscillate between seeing the individual pupil and meeting the needs of the whole class are the teachers who are most successful both in terms of order and discipline in the classroom, and also when it comes to giving the pupils opportunities to learn the content of the lesson.

By using the phenomenological and hermeneutical concept of the horizon (Husserl 1970; Merleau-Ponty 2008; Berndtsson 2001), we have been able to show how differences between teachers' strategies—the teachers' horizons, for example—affect the pupils' opportunities to expand their horizons when it comes to the intended content of different lessons. Adam was a teacher whose mind was clear when it came to teaching, and his teaching can be compared to the pedagogical humanist values described above. His horizon was stuck at one, and only one, basic idea of learning and teaching. Adam's method gave only a few pupils the opportunity to expand their horizons. The result was that many pupils did not realise what their opportunities to learn really were.

John's teaching horizon was also fixed. He had only one way to teach and that was to give lectures. His ideas might be influenced by behaviourism in the sense that he did not regard the pupils as individuals, but perhaps more as a bowl to be filled with knowledge. His teaching methods can in some ways also be compared with the Swedish Normal Plan, introduced by Rudenschöld in the nineteenth century, in that not all pupils had the opportunity to broaden their horizons or to choose the activity needed in order to learn more history. Most of John's pupils chose an activity that neither encouraged learning nor order in the classroom.

These two ways of teaching differ from Susanna's and Peter's methods, and they also differ from the three historical ways of teaching described in this essay, since for Susanna and Peter, learning happens in the gap between the teacher and the pupils (Biesta 2009). Through the interaction with the pupils, and through an oscillation between the individual and the group, Susanna and Peter manage to engage their pupils in such a way that the pupils give themselves the opportunities to expand their horizons.

Bollnow (1989) considers a teacher's belief in the pupils to be crucial when it comes to how they succeed in school. The pupils need a teacher who sees their capabilities and expands their horizons, and who dares to act without being afraid to fail, according to both Bollnow (1989) and Buber (1990). By comparison, the 'classroom management' approach, where detailed strategies are common features (Lewis et al. 2014), risks viewing pupils as objects: as all pupils are treated in the same way regardless of the reason for pupils' disruptive behaviour and regardless of pupil needs. This method can be perceived as both overly theoretical and bureaucratic. The mission of the school is to educate children and young people, and when pupils do not want to be educated as planned, it is still the teacher's assignment to persevere. The didactical knowledge of our study is that to achieve this, at least in a Swedish school context, an ability is required of the teacher to build relationships with pupils and to teach with the individual pupils' needs and the group's best interests simultaneously in view. The didactical consequence of this essay is that order and discipline is embedded in teaching activities. Where teachers in the past had to be flexible in both content and methods, teachers today need to be all that, i.e. flexible in content and methods and flexible towards their pupils too.

References

Ambjörnsson, R. (2013), *Ellen Key: En europeisk intellektuell* (Stockholm: Bonnier).

Aspelin, J. & S. Persson (2011), *Om relationell pedagogik* (Malmö: Gleerups).

—— (2015), *Inga prestationer utan relationer* (Malmö: Gleerups).

Bengtsson, J. (2013), 'With the lifeworld as ground: A research approach for empirical research in education: The Gothenburg tradition', *Indopacific Journal of Phenomenology*, special issue, 13, 1–18.

Berndtsson, I. (2001), *Förskjutna horisonter: Livsförändring och lärande i samband med synnedsättning.* (diss., Studies in Educational Sciences, 159 (Gothenburg: Acta Universitatis Gothoburgensis).

—— S. Claesson, F. Friberg & J. Öhlén (2007), 'Issues about thinking phenomenologically while doing phenomenology', *Journal of Phenomenological Psychology*, 38, 256–77.

Biesta, G. (2009), 'Good education in an age of measurement: On the need to reconnect with the question of purpose in education', *Educational Assessment, Evaluation & Accountability*, 21/1, 33–46.

Biesta, G. (2004), 'Mind the Gap! Communication and the Educational Relation', in C. Bingham & A. M. Sidorkin (eds.), *No Education without Relation* (New York: Peter Lang).

Bingham, C. (2004), 'Let's treat authority relationally', in C. Bingham & A.M. Sidorkin (eds.), *No Education without Relation* (s. 23–38) (New York: Peter Lang).

—— & A. M. Sidorkin (2004), No *Education without Relation* (New York: Peter Lang).

Bollnow, O. F. (1989), 'The Pedagogical Atmosphere', *Phenomenology + Pedagogy*, 7, 5–63.

Buber. M. (1990), *Det mellanmänskliga* (Ludvika: Dualis).

Claesson, S. (1999), *'Hur tänker du då?' Empiriska studier om relationen mellan forskning om elevuppfattningar och lärares undervisning*, Göteborg Studies in Educational Sciences 130 (Gothenburg: Acta Universitatis Gothoburgensis).

—— (2002), *Spår av teorier i praktiken* (Lund: Studentlitteratur).

—— (2004), *Lärares Levda kunskap*, Göteborg Studies in Educational Sciences, 217 (Gothenburg: Acta Universitatis Gothoburgensis).

—— (2008), 'Life-world phenomenology and empirical studies', *Nordisk Pedagogik*, 2–4, 123–34.

—— (2011), *Lärares hållning* (Lund: Studentlitteratur).

Dewey, J. (1959). Democracy and education an introduction to the philosophy of education (Text-book series). New York.

Frelin, A. (2012), *Lyhörda lärare: Professionellt relationsbyggande i förskola och skola* (Stockholm: Liber).

Frelin, A. (2010), *Teachers' Relational Practices and Professionality* (diss., Uppsala: Institutionen för didaktik, Uppsala universitet).

Gadamer, H. G. (2005), *Truth and Method* (London: Continuum).

Hartman, S. (2005), *Det pedagogiska kulturarvet: Traditioner och idéer i svensk undervisningshistoria* (Stockholm: Natur och Kultur).

Husserl, E. (1970), *The Crisis of European Sciences and Transcendental Phenomenology* (Evanston: Northwestern University Press).

Landahl, J. (2011), 'Ljudet av auktoritet: Den tysta skolans uppgång och fall', *Scandia*, 77/1.

Larsson, E. & J. Westberg (2011) (eds.), *Utbildningshistoria* (Lund: Studentlitteratur).

Levinsson, M. (2013), *Evidens och Existens: Evidensbaserad undervisning i ljuset av lärares erfarenheter* (diss., Gothenburg Studies in Educational Science, 339; Gothenburg: Acta Universitatis Gothoburgensis).

Lewis, T. L. Mitchell, B. S. Trussell, R. & Newcomer, L. (2014), 'School-Wide Positive Behavior', in E. T. Emmer & E. J. Sabornie (eds.), *Handbook of Classroom Management* (Abingdon: Routledge).

Lilja, A. (2011), 'Arbetsallianser i klassrummet', in S. Claesson (ed.), *Undervisning och existens* (Gothenburg: Daidalos).

—— (2013a), *Förtroendefulla relationer mellan lärare och elev* (diss., Gothenburg Studies in Educational Science, 338 (Gothenburg: Acta Universitatis Gothoburgensis).

—— (2013b), 'Body, Space and Time—And their influences on trustful relations in the classroom', *Indo-pacific Journal of Phenomenology*, special issue 13, 1–10.

—— (2015), 'Hur lärande kan möjliggöras och hindras i skolan', in J. Bengtsson & I. C. Berndtsson (eds.), *Lärande ur ett livsvärldsperspektiv* (Malmö: Gleerups).

Merleau-Ponty, M. (2008), *Phenomenology of Perception* (London: Routledge) (first pub. 1962).

Montessori, M. (1976), *Barndomens gåta* (Jönköping: Seminarium).

Montuoro, P. & Lewis, R. (2014), 'Student Perceptions of Misbehavior and Classroom Management', in E. T. Emmer & E. J. Sabornie (eds.), *Handbook of Classroom Management* (Abingdon: Routledge).

Nobel, A. (1991), *Filosofens knapp* (Stockholm: Carlsson).

Pedersen, J. (2004), *Vägar till värderingar och värden: Skolans sociala fostran i läroplanstexter och pedagogisk praktik* (Linköping: Institutionen för beteendevetenskap, Linköpings universitet).

Ricoeur, P. (2009), *Hermeneutics and the Human Sciences* (Cambridge: CUP) (first pub. 1981).

Ricoeur, P. (1988), *Från text till handling: En antologi om hermeneutik* (Lund: Symposion).

Rinne, I. (2015), *Pedagogisk takt i betygssamtal: En fenomenologisk hermeneutisk studie av gymnasielärares och elevers förståelse av betyg*, diss., Gothenburg

Studies in Educational Science, 364 (Gothenburg: Acta Universitatis Gotho-burgensis).

SAOL (2018), *Svenska Akadamiens ordlista*, http://svenska.se/saol/.

Simonsen, B., Fairbanks, S., Briesch, A., Myers, D. & Sugai, G. (2008), 'Evidence-based Practices in Classroom Management: Considerations for Research to Practice', *Education & Treatment of Children*, 31/3, 351–80.

Utbildningsdepartementet (Ministry of Education and Research) (2010), *Skollagen* 2010:800.

van Manen, M. (1991), *The Tact of Teaching* (Alberta: Faculty of Education, University of Alberta).

—— (1997). Researching lived experience: Human science for an action sensitive pedagogy (2.nd ed.). Ontario: Althouse press.

Wedin, A.-S. (2007), *Lärares arbete och kunskapsbildning. Utmaningar och inviter i den vardagliga praktiken*, diss., Linköping Studies in Pedagogic Practices, 2; Linköping Studies in education and psychology, 113 (Linköping: Institutionen för beteendevetenskap och lärande, Linköpings universitet).

Abstract

The use of video to record classroom activities has revolutionized classroom research by making it possible to revisit a classroom practice many times and view it from various research perspectives. This essay discusses various aspects of video-based classroom research in relation to a large international video project. By describing three types of studies within the same project, we show that a combination of macro– and microanalysis has the potential to reveal hidden dimensions of teaching and learning. A systematic overview and macro-level analysis can serve as a tool to generate research questions for in-depth micro-level analysis. The hidden dimensions of algebra teaching that were identified in these studies concerned, for example, the use of manipulatives and pupil engagement in algebra. We describe how video data can be used for research purposes as well as teachers' professional development, and argue that video recording classroom activities enables us, both as researchers and as teachers, to enter classrooms and increase our understanding of classroom cultures across time and space.

CHAPTER 8

Video studies in classroom research

Hidden dimensions of teaching and learning

Cecilia Kilhamn, Elisabeth Rystedt,
Rimma Nyman & Britt Holmberg

A contribution to classroom research

The increased use of video to record classroom activities has made the classroom available for research across time and space, making it possible to revisit a classroom many times and view it from different perspectives. As a result, comparative studies of a qualitative nature and in-depth analyses of authentic classroom practices highlighting classroom interaction can now be added to the field of didactic research. The aim of this essay is to illustrate and discuss the use of classroom videos to enhance mathematics education research. Drawing on research conducted as part of an international video study about algebra teaching, three different types of studies will be briefly described in this essay to illustrate a range of approaches that can be used to analyse the same video data. Together, these studies address different aspects of the didactic situation involving the three corners of the didactical triangle: the teacher, the pupil, and the mathematical content (Brousseau 1997).

This essay builds on classroom videos from the VIDEOMAT pro-ject,[1] where researchers from four countries recorded and shared video data showing introductory algebra lessons with pupils aged 12–13 (see Kilhamn & Röj-Lindberg 2013 for a more detailed description of the project design). Taking a socio-cultural approach, the first phase of the project seeks to analyse between and within countries concerning algebra teaching and learning, for example identifying and comparing instructional strategies, classroom interaction, and pupil reasoning. Five consecutive introductory algebra lessons were video recorded in four or five classes in each of the countries: Finland, Norway, Sweden, and the US (California). The videos were coded, partly transcribed, translated and shared. Initially the videos were treated as data and analysed in search of hidden aspects of algebra teaching that might be worth pursuing in a more in-depth analysis. In a second phase, the classroom videos were used to prompt teachers to discuss their own and other's practices in focus groups, in order to investigate how teachers could make use of classroom videos to enhance their own practice.

The design of VIDEOMAT builds on a tradition of large-scale comparative video research in mathematics education, starting with TIMSS video studies in 1995 and 1999 (Stigler et al 2000) and followed by the Learner's Perspective Study in 2000 (Clarke et al. 2006). These studies collected video recordings of mathematics classrooms from different countries with the aim of finding country-specific patterns of mathematics teaching that could potentially be related to pupil learning. In contrast, VIDEOMAT treats the comparative aspects as a means of collecting a wider range of examples of teaching the same topic in order to find commonalities and particularities that will reveal hidden dimensions (see Table 8.1). It is an assumption of the project that many aspects of a classroom practice stay hidden because they are taken for granted, and will emerge only if they are contrasted with a practice where they do not occur. In classrooms where the same overarching content goals are addressed, explicit comparisons may help illuminate aspects which otherwise can be hard to detect. The seeking of similarities and differences across culturally distinct settings is an analytical, bottom-up process, which reveals details that would not be noticed without comparison. Taking on board the criticism directed at large-scale international video comparisons for their assumption of the existence of an international

	TIMSS video studies 1995, 1999	LPS Learner's Perspective Study 2000	VIDEOMAT 2011–2014
School year	Year 8	Year 8	Year 6–7
Number of countries	7 countries	12 countries	4 countries
Number of lessons	≈100 lessons, one from each classroom	≈360 lessons, 10 consecutive lessons from each classroom	≈90 lessons, 5 consecutive lessons from each classroom
Content	Wide range of mathematical topics	Wide range of mathematical topics	Introductory algebra: introducing variables
Aim	Finding distinct patterns of mathematics teaching and lesson structure.	Investigating consistency and variation of lesson structure in mathematics teaching.*	Finding tacit and unknown dimensions of algebra teaching.

Table 8.1. Overview of three international video studies in mathematics education.
* More countries joined in later, expanding the initial aim of the LPS project so that it can today be expressed more in terms of "a network of researchers with common interests in classroom studies in an international context" (Niss, Emanuelsson & Nyström, 2013, p. 984)

curriculum, the question of what is the same and what is different is part of every analysis. The analytical aim of the VIDEOMAT project as a whole is to reveal embedded features of an enacted curriculum that might pass undetected without a comparison. By sharing video data across countries, each group of researchers can view their own data against the background of data from classrooms with different socio-cultural settings where similar content is dealt with. This essay illustrates how, in a large body of classroom activities incorporating social and cultural differences between countries and classrooms, patterns and intriguing phenomena can emerge, revealing new dimensions of algebra teaching.

The data corpus consists of video recordings of five consecutive introductory algebra lessons in seventeen classrooms (Table 8.1). A mathematics classroom is here defined as the space where a specific group of pupils (a class) have a mathematics lesson of 40–60 minutes, taught by a specific teacher. Three cameras were used to capture (*i*) the teacher, (*ii*) the whole-class activities, and (*iii*) one pair or group of pupils chosen by the teacher to be representative of the class. The first four lessons in each classroom were teacher-planned according to the local curriculum and the fifth lesson was researcher-designed to include some elements of common activity in all classrooms involved. The topic of introductory algebra was chosen as the common content, because of the accumulated evidence of the problematic transition from arithmetic to algebra and the conclusion that such problems relate more to the failure of educators to offer suitable conditions for mathematics learning than to pupils' cognitive limitations (Cai & Knuth 2011; Kaput et al. 2008). The teachers who participated in this project were recruited from among teachers who were inclined to seek opportunities for professional development as mathematics teachers.

The following sections will present three examples of studies emanating from the same set of classroom video data, but answering different types of research questions. First, we describe how we produced an overview of the data using a coding system developed within the project, as an example of knowledge gained from a macro-level comparative analysis. Second, we give an example of a micro-level study where only one section of one classroom video has been analysed in depth, chosen from the larger set of videos because it emerged as an explicit example of an interesting phenomenon. The third example is an analysis of data from the second phase of the project, where the original video data was used as a starting point for teachers' discussions about instructional practices. At the end of the essay, we return to a more general discussion of the contribution of video studies to comparative analysis and the development of instruction.

Macro-level comparative analyses of video data

When a large amount of video data is collected, it is necessary to create an overview of the data to help single out lessons and phenomena for in-depth analyses. In this project, the overview was also used to compare instructional strategies and classroom interaction across classrooms. To this end, a coding system of mutually exclusive coverage codes was developed, describing features of the classroom that are of relevance in a socio-cultural research tradition (Säljö

2000). Each of the four teacher-planned lessons in every classroom was described in a lesson log and coded with respect to types of activity and interaction in the classroom. Activities were coded as mathematical or non-mathematical, and as either whole-class teaching or pupil work (Jacobs et al. 2003), and from this initial analysis more specific codes emerged. Since the mathematical content of the project is an introduction to algebra, and specifically an introduction to variables, we decided to specify in the codes when new concepts or procedures were introduced (I) in a whole-class setting, as opposed to when the same setting was used to follow up (F) on work already done and concepts previously met. We also saw that it was not always the teacher who conducted the whole-class activity, and so we coded these activities as led by either the teacher (T), a student (S),[2] or collaboratively by teacher and student (TS). Pupil work was coded in accordance with the main type of interaction going on (individual or group work). As a last subcategory, the student group (SG) codes also indicated what kind of notation or documentation was requested from the pupils: individual (I), shared by the group (G), or none (N). Each activity that lasted at least 30 seconds was thus assigned a code describing the main activity in the classroom (Fig. 8.1).

The coding system helped us identify and quantify the use of lesson time for different types of activities and interactions. Comparisons revealed a large variation in lesson structure across classrooms, both within and between the four countries. Although no general conclusions can be drawn at a national level, the variation sheds light on issues that are taken for granted or avoided in some classrooms, and highlights aspects of the lesson structure that varied, which generated questions for further analysis.

When comparing across the whole data set, it was possible to pick out lessons that seemed similar but differed in some aspect. One such comparison is between the two classrooms, Finland S4 (School 4) and California S2T2 (School 2, Teacher 2) (Fig 8.2). In both of these classrooms, approximately one-third of the time in the four teacher-planned lessons was spent on pupil work (SI+SG) and almost two-thirds on whole-class instruction (IT+FT). The percentage of

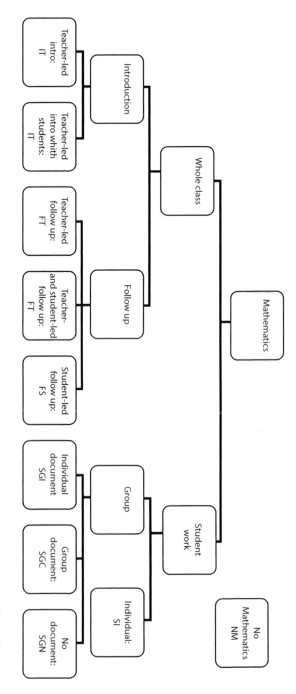

Figure 8.1. Overview of three international video studies in mathematics education.

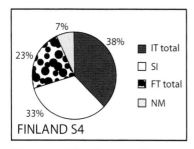
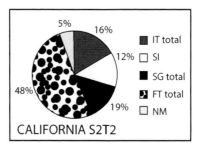

Figure 8.2. Distribution of lesson time in two different classrooms: Finland S4 and California S2T2.

time spent on non-mathematical activities in both classrooms was roughly the same (5–7 per cent). Despite these similarities, the codes reveal two very different teaching approaches. In Finland S4, there was no group work at all, whereas in California S2T2, pupil work was more often in groups than individual. In Finland S4, two-thirds of the whole-class instruction was spent introducing new concepts or giving instructions, and only one-third on follow-up activities, compared to California S2T2, where three-quarters of the whole-class activities—in fact almost half the lesson time—was used on follow-up activities. Despite the similar distribution of lesson time on the level of whole-class instruction versus pupil work, and the similarity of the content matter, it is very likely that the learning opportunities and the enacted learning goals were quite different, building more on pupils' own work and reasoning in the Californian classroom than in the Finnish one. The results of this kind of analysis generate questions concerning, for example, the extent to which each of the approaches offers pupils opportunities to develop reasoning skills, make conjectures and generalisations, revise ideas, listen, and communicate. In short, the quantitative analysis helped us to identify lessons where a more detailed observation and qualitative analysis could reveal new insights. The initial comparison thus supplied contrasting examples for a more fine-grained analysis.

Although algebraic reasoning without the use of written symbols constitutes the core of what is called early algebra (Cai & Knuth 2011), developing fluency in written representations is ultimately an essential part of algebra. Early algebra builds on contexts of

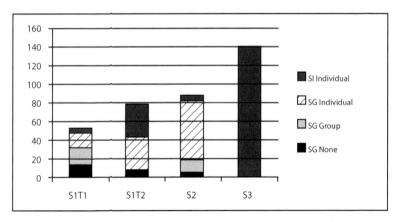

Figure 8.3. Lesson time in minutes spent on student work, differentiating between types of documentation (Kilhamn & Hillman, 2014).

problems, interweaves existing topics from early mathematics, and gradually introduces and extends pupils' own representations into formal representations such as symbolic notation (Carraher et al. 2008). The focus on the introduction of variables was a way for the project to direct its research interest towards the point in the learning trajectory where formal symbolic notation is one of the learning goals. For that reason, a coding of pupil documentation was introduced to indicate when and how pupils were given an opportunity to use algebraic notation. Four Swedish classrooms were compared in terms of how much time out of the total of four lessons (each lesson being 40–60 minutes) was spent on pupil work where some kind of written documentation was produced (Kilhamn & Hillman 2014). It is clear that the practices of writing in the algebra classrooms were all distinctly different (Fig. 8.3). In Classroom S1T1 for example, only twelve minutes out of four lessons involved activities where pupils were asked to write something, whereas in Classroom S3 pupils worked with individual written exercises for 140 minutes. The question is in what way these differences constrain or afford the learning of symbolic algebra. Again, we see how the results highlight an aspect that *may* influence pupil learning, hence generating research questions needing a more detailed, theory-driven analysis. Our second example describes such an in-depth analysis of an episode that was chosen from the larger set of lessons with the help of the overview and the possibility of accessing a sequence of lessons.

Micro-level analyses of video data

Using an inductive approach (Derry et al. 2010), the video corpus was initially subject to a broad search for possible connections between whole-class instruction and pupil problem-solving in algebra. Whenever a didactically interesting phenomenon emerged, it was singled out for a micro-level analysis. In the project design, the first four lessons described in the overview were followed by a fifth lesson in which all the participating pupils worked in small groups to solve three algebra tasks distributed by the researchers. This generated a body of video data on small-group problem-solving where it was possible to look for connections to the specific instructions they had been given. The case study described here is an analysis of a 26-minute-long discussion where three pupils solved a task involving an equation that was also expressed as a word problem. The case stood out as an example of a specific phenomenon: when pupils on their own initiative apply previous experiences of manipulatives as a resource in a new situation. In the video data, we could see that this class had spent three of the preceding four lessons using manipulatives to build an understanding of equation-solving on a concrete level. Fig. 8.4 shows a picture of the manipulatives in the form of boxes and beans used during those lessons. The unique instance of an episode where pupils spontaneously made explicit connections between lessons provided an opportunity to investigate the pros and cons of using manipulatives in mathematics—a didactical issue for mathematics teachers in all countries.

In line with the socio-cultural research tradition, a dialogical approach was used to analyse pupils' communication (Linell 1998). In a small-group discussion, pupils' reasoning is articulated and therefore becomes accessible for analysis (Sfard 2001). During a 26-minute-long interaction, the pupils made a total of 282 interactive turns, here termed utterances. These were transcribed verbatim. In addition, the video data also provided an opportunity to capture, at least partly, the complexity of a small-group discussion with its manifold interactional phenomena, such as gesture, gaze, movement, and facial expression, which deepen the verbal communication and written representations and help make sense of the situation.

The analytical construct of contextualisation was applied with the aim of investigating 'how and why a certain way of reasoning takes form and what it contains in terms of mathematical potential' (Nilsson 2009, 64). The discussion was analysed in terms of how the pupils contextualised the task and how they moved between different contextualisations. The given task provided the pupils with two contexts: a 'Zedland' context and an equation context (Fig. 8.5). The manipulatives used in the preceding lessons provided a third: a boxes-and-beans context. The results of our analysis show that the pupils were quick to recontextualise the given task in terms of boxes and beans, finding a correct value for x. However, although they spent another 20 minutes discussing their solution, they did not arrive at an answer to the original question posed in the context of Zedland. The final solution from this group was 'there are 30 grammes in each

Figure 8.4. Boxes and beans displaying the equation $2x = x + 2$ where x is the unknown number of beans in each box. The string symbolises the equals sign.

In Zedland, the cost of shipping a parcel is calculated using the following equation: $y = 4x + 30$, where x is the weight in grams and y is the cost in zed dollars.

A parcel that costs 150 zed dollars to ship can be written using the following equation: $150 = 4x + 30$.

How many grammes does that parcel weigh?

Figure 8.5. Algebra task discussed in the group, adapted from the TIMSS 2007 survey (Foy & Olson, 2009).

parcel'. Their answer made sense in the boxes-and-beans context where x represents the unknown number of beans in each of the four boxes, but not in the Zedland context, where x represents the number of grammes for one specific parcel.

A general conclusion from this study was that although pupils are able to mobilise resources that are helpful in specific cases, additional problems might arise when they try to comprehend general algebraic principles. This case supports the claim made by Mason (2008) that learning about an abstract principle (in this case an equation) through the introduction of a concrete manifestation (in this case boxes and beans) requires pupils to see the general through the particular. The results highlight the importance of giving pupils opportunities to comprehend the particular position of symbolic mathematical representations when dealing with mathematical concepts. While a symbolic representation describes something general, concrete representations always describe something particular, and no particular example incorporates the rich meaning of a mathematical concept.

The aim of the study was to investigate how pupils made use of an earlier algebra activity with manipulatives as a resource when solving an equation expressed in a word problem (Rystedt et al. 2016). The interest was in understanding, as Dysthe (2003) suggests, a little bit more of what happens or does not happen, and the reasons for this. In this example, we have shown how a broad corpus of video data initiated and formed the background for a small-case in-depth analysis based on an interest in the use of manipulatives in mathematics. The example illuminates a phenomenon on the pupil-content axis of the didactical triangle, exposing a didactical consequence, which is that teachers would do well to connect the use of manipulatives to abstract mathematical concepts if they are to provide pupils with powerful learning opportunities.

Using classroom videos to support professional development

Our final example of how video-recorded classroom activities can enhance research and support practice is an analysis of focus-group discussions (Boddy 2005) from the second phase of the project, where the original video data was used as a starting point for teachers' discussions about instructional practices. In preparation for the focus-group sessions, the eight participating Swedish teachers were handed recordings and overviews of their own lessons, along with instructions to select episodes from the films that they wanted to discuss. After three weeks of preparation, the teachers were invited to focus-group sessions at the university (Fig. 8.6). There were two focus groups (three teachers in one and five in the other), and each group met for seven one-hour sessions to discuss a range of topics. During the first three sessions, the teachers discussed the episodes they had chosen from their own lessons, and in the second round of four sessions they discussed episodes chosen by teachers in the other participating countries.

One of our research questions concerned the topic of interest and engagement (Ainley 2012) during classroom interaction about introductory algebra. The aim of the study was to gain insight into the way interest and engagement are perceived by teachers, and how they attempt to enhance pupil engagement in algebra. To direct the focus-group discussions towards interest and engagement, the teachers had been asked to select episodes where they could see that the pupils were engaged in algebra, and to think about how they as teachers engage pupils in the algebra content they were dealing with. The session commenced with an introduction of the topic by the researcher, then one of the teachers continued by showing his/her chosen episodes, which initiated a discussion about engagement

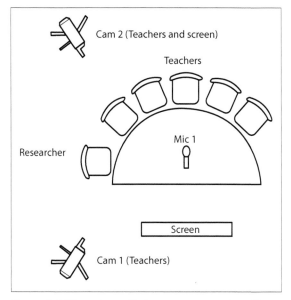

Figure 8.6. The set-up of a focus-group session. Classroom video episodes were shown on the screen (Nyman, 2015).

and how it was, or could be, enhanced. Each teacher showed his or her episode(s) in turn, explaining and discussing why each episode was chosen and in what way it visualised engagement.

The findings consist of a video portfolio of episodes chosen by teachers, along with teachers' utterances (their interactive turns) when commenting on one another's episodes. The two group discussions on the topic of interest and engagement were video-recorded and transcribed, resulting in a total of 588 utterances that were taken to represent the meaning of interest and engagement as interactively constructed by the eight teachers. Two researchers analysed the discussion in an iterative process, revisiting both the transcripts and the videos several times. In the transcripts, the researchers identified indicators of engagement corresponding to an existing model (Helme & Clarke 2001; Nyman 2015) and didactical strategies to enhance pupil engagement brought up by the eight teachers (Nyman & Kilhamn 2015). The main results indicate various ways of describing, initiating and sustaining pupil engagement on the activity level of the didactical contract (Brousseau 1997), relating more to activities and social interaction than content—the recognition of pupils' achievements, for example, or the way individual solutions could be presented in whole-class interaction. The presented video episodes showed whole-class or group interaction about algebraic expressions, representations, the structure of equations, and patterns, but despite the moderator's attempt to direct the discussion towards content-related issues, the participants kept referring to the activities rather than the algebra content as being interesting and engaging. Although the mathematical content was at the fore in the focus-group sessions, the teachers' discussions focussed more on the social aspects of the didactic contract, thus placing the research results closer to the teacher–student axis of the didactical triangle. Based on these results, we would argue that much could be gained if teachers were to focus more on content-related issues in order to engage pupils.

The video recordings from the lessons were central to the teachers' discussion of the interactive aspects of interest and engagement in algebra. Since the teachers were given the videos early in the process, they had time to reflect and carefully choose their episodes. During the focus-group interaction, the classroom videos gave access to detail and provided a sense of authenticity and recognition in relation to the topics discussed. Ideas were shared and validated within the group. It can be concluded that with access to video data, teachers could discuss their own and one another's lessons, and reach a consensus based on and strengthened by empirical evidence of classroom practice.

Another research question for the focus-group discussions concerned what knowledge the teachers acquired when they discussed episodes of their own choosing from their own teaching. As preparation for a second focus-group session, the teachers had been asked to choose episodes showing anything they thought it relevant to discuss in relation to the teaching of introductory algebra. What kind of episodes did they choose, and what kind of knowledge was it possible to develop through the discussion? Two video-recorded sessions of 54 and 60 minutes from one focus group with three teachers were transcribed verbatim. The transcripts were analysed

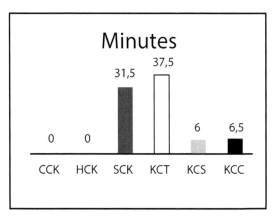

Figure 8.7. Total number of minutes of the discussion related to each MKT category.

using the framework Mathematical Knowledge for Teaching (MKT) (Ball et al. 2008). This framework, which builds on Shulman's notion of pedagogical content knowledge (1986), includes categories that describe different aspects of mathematics teachers' knowledge. It was used to characterise what the teachers discussed, not to assess their knowledge. Although a researcher moderated the session in order to support the discussion, it was the teachers who decided which episodes to watch, what questions to ask, and what to discuss about each episode. Each 30-second section of the discussion was coded in accordance with the topic discussed. If it was related to mathematical content in any way, it was coded as one of the MKT categories. Through this theoretical approach, the analytical focus was directed towards the teacher–content axis of the didactical triangle.

Our analysis and coding show that the teachers spent most of the time discussing specialised content knowledge (SCK) and know-ledge of content and teaching (KCT) (Fig. 8.7). Issues related to knowledge of content and pupils (KCP) and knowledge of content and curriculum (KCC) were mentioned to a lesser extent, and the remaining two categories—common content knowledge (CCK) and horizon content knowledge (HCK)—were not raised at all. The results indicate that the classroom videos served as a useful vehicle for initiating discussions about issues related to a deep and specialised understanding of the content, such as various ways a variable can be used in different tasks, and aspects of importance for teaching, such as various ways of presenting the content in class. We could see that the teachers reflected on their way of teaching when they discussed episodes of their own choosing from their own classrooms. In particular, they discussed things they could have done differently based on what they saw in these episodes. The opportunity to watch an episode several times while choosing and preparing, and again during the discussion, was mentioned by the teachers as being helpful for the development of their teaching. Our results strengthen the idea that teachers involved in research projects about their own teaching as *insiders* contribute to their own development in teaching, but can also contribute to research when a researcher who is an *outsider* takes part in the project (Jaworski 2004). The study shows that discussions about education using classroom videos as a tool can give teachers opportunities to develop mathematical knowledge for teaching, and could therefore be effective in teacher professional development.

Discussion

In this essay, we have described the use of video to record classroom activities for both research purposes and professional development in mathematics education. The greatest advantage with video data is the possibility of returning to a classroom practice, watching a video many times in search of patterns of similarities and differences in order to identify episodes of interest for further analysis. In this way, questions closely related to practice can become the focus of research. Another advantage is the possibility of sharing classroom data among researchers and teachers. Rich classroom video data can be analysed from different perspectives to answer a wide range of research questions. To this end, it is necessary to have a large corpus of video data to start with, and good quality recordings that capture all activities in the classroom. Naturally, there may also be disadvantages with video recordings. The presence of researchers and a camera in the classroom can have an impact on pupils and teachers

(Clarke et al. 2016). However, considering the recent development of technical tools and social media where pupils and teachers frequently take pictures and videos both in and outside class, it is plausible that such impact will be less noticeable in the future. The more a group of pupils are subject to video recording, the less attention will be paid to the camera. In the VIDEOMAT project, all pupils and their parents were asked to give informed consent to participate, with an option to agree for us to use the data either for research purposes only or for research purposes and teacher education. In a few cases when consent was not given, the pupils in question were given the option of participating in class during the video-recorded lessons, but were placed outside the range of the camera. In this way they could participate, and be heard but not identified. This turned out to be a workable compromise. If some pupils had been kept out of the classroom, the recorded lesson would have lost authenticity and ethical value. Since it is difficult to anonymise video data, it is important to be sensitive as to who is given access to the original videos. Transcripts, overviews, and coded summaries are good alternatives to the actual videos when wider groups of researchers or teachers are involved.

We would like to end with some reflections from the Swedish teachers at the end of the second phase of the project. In the first round of focus-group sessions, they had watched and discussed video episodes from their own classrooms. Questions about things that were not visible in the video could be easily answered, which helped give the discussion focus and depth. In contrast, during the subsequent session when episodes were shared between groups with no teacher present who could answer questions, the discussion some-times petered out into uncertainty, with remarks such as 'Well we don't know why the teacher did this', or unanswered questions about what happened in the previous or following lesson. When watching the episodes shared between countries, the teachers acknowledged different cultures and curricula with comments such as, 'Perhaps this is a common way of doing it in [that country]' or 'It may seem strange to us, but we don't know anything about their curriculum'. These comments suggest that we need to be very careful when conjecturing about teaching and learning in the classroom in cultures that are unknown to us. Short video episodes need to be embedded in rich descriptions of the classroom culture and curriculum if they are to be used to argue for or against different didactical strategies. In the use of video as a tool for the development of instruction, discussing your own teaching or that of others in unknown contexts will ultimately be two very different things.

A combination of macro– and microanalysis, like the studies generated by the VIDEOMAT project, shows the wide potential of video studies. The systematic overview and macro-level analysis served mainly as a tool to generate more interesting research questions. Attention to detail as described in the microanalysis and a collaborative reflection as described in the focus-group discussions serve to generate quite different types of knowledge, which is valuable for the research community and practising teachers alike. Although in-depth analyses were made of the data each team had recorded and was best acquainted with, it was through macro-level comparisons that interesting episodes were found. A similar effect was seen in the focus-group discussions, where teachers were given the opportunity to view their own classroom in relation to other classrooms. The teachers had more to say about their own teaching than about one another's, but noticed different things about their own teaching as a result of also watching episodes from other classrooms. Comparisons made it possible to detect and scrutinise previously hidden aspects of the classroom. The examples given here shed light on some factors that have didactical consequences for teaching and learning in algebra classrooms. We have seen that the use of manipulatives requires a thorough abstract knowledge of algebra on the part of the teacher; that teachers need to become aware of the possibility of making use of the content to engage pupils in algebra; and that video analysis can be instrumental in developing teachers' mathematical knowledge.

In this essay, we have shown how video data can be used for research purposes as well as for professional development. New dimensions of teaching and learning mathematics were highlighted through quantitative comparisons as well as in-depth analysis of classroom work and teachers' discussions. Using video to record classroom activities has enabled us, both as researchers and teachers, to enter classrooms and increase our understanding of different classroom cultures, temporally and spatially. In particular, the large-scale comparative point of entry helped us to find potentially interesting and hitherto unknown dimensions of the mathematics classroom, to pursue further using theory-driven in-depth analyses.

Notes

1 The VIDEOMAT project was funded by the Joint Committee for Nordic Research Councils for the Humanities and the Social Sciences (NOS-HS) through a grant to the Linnaeus Centre for Research on Learning, Inter-action and Mediated Communication in Contemporary Society (LinCS).

2 In this coding procedure the letter (S) for student was used when referring to pupils of age 12-14 years participating in the study (Kilhamn & Röj-Lindberg, 2013).

References

Ainley, M. (2012), 'Students' interest and engagement in classroom activities', in S. L. Christenson, A. L. Reschly & C. Wylie (eds.), *Handbook of research on student engagement* (New York: Springer Science).

Ball, D. L., M. H. Thames & G. Phelps (2008), 'Content knowledge for teaching: What makes it special?' *Journal of Teacher Education*, 59/5, 389–407.

Boddy, C. (2005), 'A rose by any other name may smell as sweet but "group discussion" is not another name for a "focus group" nor should it be', *Qualitative Market Research: An International Journal*, 8/3, 248–55.

Brousseau, G. (1997), *Theory of didactical situations in mathematics* (Dortrecht: Kluwer Academic).

Cai, J. & E. Knuth (2011) (eds.), *Early algebraization: A global dialogue from multiple perspectives* (Berlin: Springer).

Carraher, D., A. Schliemann & J. L. Schwartz (2008), 'Early algebra is not the same as algebra early', in J. J. Kaput, D. Carraher & M. L. Blanton (eds.), *Algebra in the early grades* (London: Routledge).

Clarke, D., C. Keitel & Y. Shimizu (2006) (eds.), *Mathematics classrooms in twelve countries: The insider's perspective* (Rotterdam: Sense).

Derry, S., R. Pea, B. Barron, R. Engle, F. Erickson, R. Goldman & B. Sherin (2010), 'Conducting Video Research in the Learning Sciences: Guidance on

Selection, Analysis, Technology, and Ethics', *Journal of the Learning Sciences*, 19/1, 3–53.

Dysthe, O. (2003), 'Om sambandet mellan dialog, samspel och lärande', in O. Dysthe (ed.), *Dialog, samspel och lärande* (Lund: Studentlitteratur).

Foy, P. & J. F. Olson (2009) (eds.), *TIMSS 2007 International Database and user guide. Released items. Mathematics—Eighth Grade* (Boston: TIMSS & PIRLS International Study Center) http://timss.bc.edu/timss2007/items.html.

Helme, S. & D. Clarke (2001), 'Identifying cognitive engagement in the mathematics classroom', *Mathematics Education Research Journal*, 13/2, 133–53.

Jacobs, J., H. Garnier, R. Gallimore, H. Hollingsworth, K. B. Givvin, K. Rust et al. (2003), *TIMSS 1999 Video Study Technical Report: Volume 1: Mathematics Study, NCES (2003-12)* (US Department of Education; Washington, DC: National Center for Education Statistics).

Jaworski, B. (2004), 'Insiders and outsiders in mathematics teaching development: The design and study of classroom activity', *Research in Mathematics Education*, 6/1, 3–22.

Kaput, J. J., D. Carraher & M. L. Blanton (2008) (eds.), *Algebra in the early grades* (New York: Routledge).

Kilhamn, C. & A.-S. Röj-Lindberg (2013), 'Seeking hidden dimensions of algebra teaching through video analysis', in B. Grevholm, P. S. Hundeland, K. Juter, K. Kislenko & P.-E. Persson (eds.), *Nordic research in mathematics education, past, present and future* (Oslo: Cappelen Damm Akademisk).

Kilhamn, C. & T. Hillman (2014), 'Structural and Pedagogical Diversity in Swedish Grade Six Algebra Classrooms', in O. Helenius, A. Engström, T. Meany & P. Nilsson, E. Norén, J. Sayers, M. Österholm (eds.), *Development of Mathematics Teaching: Design, Scale, Effects: Proceedings from Madif 9, The Ninth Swedish Mathematics Education Research Seminar*, Umeå, 4–5 Feb. (Linköping: SMDF).

Linell, P. (1998), *Approaching dialogue: Talk, interaction and contexts in dialogical perspectives* (Philadelphia: John Benjamins).

Mason, J. (2008), Making use of children's powers to produce algebraic thinking', in Kaput, Carraher & Blanton (eds.), *Algebra in the early grades* (New York: Lawrence Erlbaum).

Nilsson, P. (2009), 'Operationalizing the analytical construct of contextualization', *Nordic Studies in Mathematics Education*, 14/1, 61–88.

Niss, M., J. Emanuelsson & P. Nyström (2013), 'Methods for Studying Mathematics Teaching and Learning Internationally', in M. A. Clements (ed.), *Third International Handbook of Mathematics Education* (New York: Springer)

Nyman, R. (2015), 'Indicators of student engagement: What teachers notice during introductory algebra lessons', *International Journal of Mathematics Teaching & Learning*, 15/3, 1–17.

Nyman, R & Kilhamn, C. (2015), 'Enhancing engagement in algebra: Didactical strategies implemented and discussed by teachers', *Scandinavian Journal of Educational Research*, 59/6. 623–37.

Rystedt, E., O. Helenius & C. Kilhamn (2016), 'Moving in and out of contexts in collaborative reasoning about equations', *Journal of Mathematical Behavior*, 44, 50–64.

Shulman, L.S. (1986), 'Those who understand: Knowledge growth in teaching' *Educational Researcher*, 15/2, 4–14.

Stigler, J. W., R. Gallimore & J. Hiebert (2000), 'Using video surveys to compare classrooms and teaching across cultures: Examples and lessons from the TIMSS video studies', *Educational Psychologist*, 35/2, 87–100.

Sfard, A. (2001), 'There is more to discourse than meets the ears: Looking at thinking as communication to learn more about mathematical learning', *Educational Studies in Mathematics*, 46, 13–57.

Säljö, R. (2000), *Lärande i praktiken: Ett sociokulturellt perspektiv* (Stockholm: Prisma).

Abstract

This essay addresses some of the methodological challenges of conducting research on teaching and learning in the classroom. In particular, it looks at how talk in the classroom develops, and how communication patterns are constructed over several lessons. Such investigations require an analysis of individual moments as well as longer sequences of teaching and learning, and there are few examples in the literature. The aim here is to describe one research approach, and then use it to investigate how subject-matter progression is achieved in that particular classroom. The data is from a sequence of lessons in biology, in a classroom characterised by pupils' active role in teaching and learning. The research approach is described and illustrated empirically with three short episodes from the classroom. The episodes together marked something of a turning point in the pupils' learning, and show some communicative processes involved when a genetic explanation is introduced when teaching biological evolution. These conversations, involving pupil objections, pupils taking not-knowing positions, and traditional patterns of teacher questioning, capture significant moments for the pupils' continued learning. The essay considers research timescales, and suggests adding a fourth dimension—the potential for change—to the classical didactical triad.

CHAPTER 9

Teaching and learning in the science classroom

The methodological challenges of research

Miranda Rocksén

Studies of classrooms confirm them to be arenas of great complexity. By investigating the relationship between teaching and pupils' opportunities for learning, the studies in this volume contribute to the empirical base of didactics as a science of teaching; this essay's contribution is a methodological discussion of possible approaches to research timescales. Research results from the tradition of science education, and more specifically teaching and learning about biological evolution, are used here to develop a research approach to empirical materials that considers the many timescales of classroom interaction.[1] The essay takes two questions that are critical to professional teachers as its starting points, namely how to reach moments of joint understanding, and how to achieve subject-matter progression in the classroom.

The science education research tradition has had much to say about the difficulties associated with teaching and learning specific science topics. The topic of biological evolution includes teaching and learning about concepts that involve several biological organisational levels and long-term perspectives, such as the development of life, biological adaptation, and biodiversity (for example, Skolverket 2011). The description of the development of life on Earth involves long time spans, in which rates of survival and reproduction explain evolutionary changes over many generations. Biological adaptation refers to how survival in a specific environment is promoted by an increase in certain heritable trait frequencies of a population (Rector et al. 2013). Biodiversity refers to biological variation on various organisational levels, including genetics and species populations. Research has shown these concepts are demanding to understand, teach, and learn (for an overview see Smith 2010b). Additionally, for some teachers and pupils and in some religious contexts, evolution is perceived as a controversial topic (Smith 2010a). All these aspects present teachers and learners with certain challenges, as the empirical examples presented here will show.

Some of the documented difficulties in the area of biological evolution are connected to the many biological organisational levels that concepts in this area involve. Biology teachers have to develop strategies for how to move between referring to an individual organism and explanations on the level of the population of species in their communications with pupils. The introduction of the genetic level is critical, for it allows the teacher to differentiate between the different levels of biological organisation. The analysis in this essay identifies the precise moment when the genetic level is introduced for the first time in a teaching sequence about evolution. This moment occurs when one pupil asks a question during a whole-class discussion, and it is possible to study the details of the teacher's response both on the spot and in the following lesson. This essay therefore describes a significant turning point in the investigated lesson sequence.

The essay explores communication in a classroom where pupils take an active role in the teaching and learning. This context is perhaps not the most common for discussions about classrooms as arenas for communication. In past research, teachers' ways of asking questions have traditionally been an object of study (Mehan 1979; Sinclair & Coulthard 1975). However, these ways of asking questions are also distinct patterns, which from a methodological perspective it is feasible for research to focus on—these patterns may be easily observed in recordings of short episodes of classroom communication. The results from that research tradition illuminate the dominant position of teachers in the classroom, as well as pupils' restricted opportunities to contribute and talk, which has implications both for teaching practice and for teacher education and professional development.

An issue that is less investigated is how talk in the classroom develops and how communicative patterns are constructed over several lessons. This is true for the didactic tradition in science education (see Duschl et al. 2011) but also for research about classroom communication. How do science teachers and pupils attain those moments of mutual understanding? How is topic progression achieved? How do teachers ensure continuity in the classroom communication with only one or two lessons per week for a given group of pupils? To answer such questions, research approaches need to be developed that capture and analyse what happens both in short episodes and over longer periods of time in the classroom.

The reported case study demonstrates an approach based on open, incomplete, and unfinalised units of analysis (Matusov 2007). This means studying moments and patterns of communication in one classroom is an analysis of a combination of short episodes, classroom activities, individual lessons, and the full sequence of lessons in a curricular unit. The aim here is to describe one research approach and to use it to investigate how subject-matter progression is achieved in one particular classroom. Although the approach is developed in the context of teaching biological evolution, it can be applied to the study of other curricular topics too.

Knowledge of classroom interaction and its consequences for research methodology

Starting from a broad perspective, teaching and learning activities can be understood on several timescales (Lemke 2000 & 2001). This recognises that whatever the research focuses—parts of lessons, lessons, school days, curricular units, semesters, academic years—the teaching and learning activities take place in various spaces inside the walls of the classroom, with each space contributing to the communicated meaning (Hipkiss, in this volume). Inside the classroom, teacher and pupils participate on different terms, and by using different strategies the teacher acts as a coordinator of the communication (Cazden 2001).

Among the strategies used by teachers is IRE dialogue—teacher Initiation, pupil Response, teacher Evaluation—or follow-up (Mehan 1979; Sinclair & Coulthard 1975; Wells & Arauz 2006). In the teaching of the science subjects, IRE dialogue is prevalent (Lemke 1990; Mortimer & Scott 2003), and science teachers seem to have particular difficulties in establishing alternative patterns of communication (Scott et al. 2006). From a research perspective, the frequent use of IRE dialogue in the classroom raises questions about alternative interpretations (see, for example, Lee 2007), as well as the possibility of communicative patterns over other timescales—patterns over several lessons may still exist even if they are difficult to detect, after all. This suggests that focusing too much on IRE patterns might be misleading, and that the functions of IRE dialogue in the classroom might not yet be fully understood.

For the researcher, a range of possibilities exists for investigating how the communication in the classroom proceeds. This includes examining the structure and chronology of the teaching (for example, lessons), and delimitations and sequentialities constructed by the participants (certain activities or projects). Take the example of Ball and Wells (2009), who focus on one teacher's annual project with pupils in Year 4, building vehicles. They conclude that the absence of follow-up moves by the teacher increased over the years, as well as the proportion of 'unsolicited "offers" of information' by the pupils (2009, 378). A second example is Engle (2006) who investigates the framing of time in a four-month-long unit in Year 5, with 34 sessions (1.5 hours each) about endangered species, a study which illuminates how one teacher's frequent use of references to previous and future sessions frames the unit as part of various open, on-going activities and the pupils' participation in these activities. A third possibility is exemplified by Aguiar et al. (2010), who investigate pupils' 'wonderment questions' during lesson sequences about thermal physics and energy transformation in Year 7. That study shows how the character of pupils' questions requires the teacher to adopt different strategies, which has an impact on how the teaching develops. These three studies share an interest in various timescales for classroom teaching and learning, although they identify separate units of analysis as being relevant to their particular object of study, to wit changing patterns of communication in an annual project, interactional framing of classroom activities lasting four months, and developing patterns of classroom communication over a sequence of lessons.

Mercer (2008) writes of a lack of methodological guidance for studying the development of talk in the classroom. He claims that the temporal context of classroom talk includes historical and dynamic aspects, mostly related to the institutional and cultural context, but also to the individual speakers' historical and future relations, leaving it contingent on the emerging conversation (Mercer 2008, 44). For research, the methodological challenge is capturing how knowledge resources become jointly constructed in the communication—the idea of a dialogic trajectory. One conclusion of Mercer's is that there is a need to conceptualise how different levels of human activity are linked.

Ludvigsen et al. (2010) discuss the concept of time and its analytical potential in understanding learning by looking at intersecting trajectories of participation. In order to better understand the use of, for example, books and computers, Ludvigsen et al. find it useful to establish how the timescales of longer processes have an influence on much shorter timescales. The suggestion is a combination of perspectives: a vertical in-depth analysis of moment-to-moment interactions and longitudinal timescales using a horizontal perspective.

In addition to the dimension of time that describes the continuous flow of events, Molenaar (2014) suggests the relative arrangement of multiple events as another dimension of time. She stresses that the interval varies according to the phenomena under study, and therefore that artificial divisions into units of time have large implications for research results. As an alternative to defining units of analysis, a methodology based on open, incomplete, and unfinalised units of analysis has been suggested (Matusov 2007). This could potentially be used to capture, identify, and distinguish details of phenomena such as those Molenaar (2014) refers to as reoccurring patterns of interaction (for example, cyclic working processes), non-reoccurring patterns (learning how to read), or irregular interaction changes (building collaborations from chaotic interaction). Topical progression can be understood as an established pattern of classroom communication, and therefore in this essay a more open and undefined unit of analysis is thought better suited to the study.

Moments and patterns in eleven lessons about evolution

By looking at one research approach to a unit about evolution in biology in Year 9, it is possible to gauge how subject-matter progression is achieved in this particular classroom. An early decision in the project was to focus on the teaching of a curricular unit about evolution. This made it possible to start with unfinalised units of analysis (Matusov 2007) and to study various phenomena that appeared within the delimitation of the sequence of lessons.

The teacher who volunteered for the project, who was well known to the group of 23 pupils, planned the eleven lessons independently from the research team. The pupils were 15 years old and in their final term of Swedish compulsory school. It was decided that the teacher's and pupils' informed consent to participate should be combined with information for the pupils' legal guardians, and that those pupils who chose not to participate would be placed out of shot when filming the classroom. When reporting results, the names of individual pupils and teachers were anonymised and pictures from the data were processed to protect the privacy of the informants.

The eleven lessons were 50 minutes long and distributed over a period of four weeks. Four video cameras were used to capture the detail of what happened during the lessons: one was focused on the teacher, two on two pupil groups, and one provided an overview of the classroom. The video cameras gave multiple perspectives on what was going on in the classroom and were a highly valuable resource. Everything the teacher said was recorded using a wireless microphone, and the recording transcribed. The talk in two pupil groups was transcribed in part, primarily when the pupils were working on particular tasks. In total, 38 hours of video recordings were collected.

The theoretical framing in dialogical theories of communication (Linell 2009) provided analytical tools and perspectives on classroom communication. Dialogical theories include a number of theoretical and epistemological assumptions about the human mind and human action, in which relations and dynamics are fundamental: 'But dynamics in situations and traditions—contextedness on different timescales—is assumed to be an essential property of human activities, rather than just products of irrelevant variations' (Linell 2009, 432). This implies a perspective that views human activity as constantly changing and constituted by reflexivity. One consequence of using this framework in research is the nature of the presented results. Research, for example, may establish and represent how participants construct relations between space and time, such as between previous activities and on-going activities in the classroom. When applied to the study of classrooms, this means viewing teaching as being primarily a communicative activity, which allows the multiple timescales of teaching and learning to be taken into consideration. The respective positions and contributions of teachers and pupils are studied as equally legitimate communicative projects (189–90). Three theoretical principles guided the current analysis: the principles of joint construction, sequentiality, and act–activity interdependence (187). The principle of joint construction states that meaning is jointly constructed in the interaction between participants; the principle of sequentiality implies that every utterance is understood by establishing the position of this utterance in the sequence of actions. In the analysis, this is taken into account by identifying responsive and projective properties of the particular utterance, for example how it is in part a response to a previous contribution and at the same time points towards a particular response. The principle of act-activity interdependence implies that a particular conversation is understood as the realisation of a communicative activity distributed over larger timescales.

The video recordings were watched several times, and evolving topics, on-going activities, and specific discussions were document-ed. By combining different units of analysis, three separate studies were developed. The first involved mapping the activities and ways of participation offered to pupils in the classroom. The second study involved identifying instances where the meaning of frequently used specific words and themes were jointly constructed, and assembling them into collections to be analysed for possible patterns in specific situations. The third study involved investigating how the teacher and pupils in their communication linked the eleven lessons together into a curricular unit about evolution.

Three episodes are used here to illustrate the approach as a whole. Taken from lessons 5 and 6, they shed light on some of the processes involved when a genetic explanation is introduced in the sequence of lessons about biological evolution. The episodes represent reoccur-ring and non-reoccurring patterns or irregular interaction changes (Molenaar 2014), in relation to the progression of topics in the classroom communication as a whole. The three episodes took place in the same classroom, which was equipped with a fume cupboard and sinks, tables arranged for groups of pupils, a teacher's desk, and a whiteboard on one of the walls. Episode 1 is whole-class teaching, and episodes 2 and 3 are from interaction in small-group activities. The three episodes are presented chronologically.

Episode 1 (Lesson 5)

The teacher stands in front of the class, making notes on the whi-teboard about adaptation in relation to three explanatory models of the evolution of life on Earth: creationism, Lamarckism, and Darwinism. A central topic is the survival and extinction of species.

> Lesson 5 [18.00–18.51]
> Teacher: But Darwinism says that there isn't so much that can be done [about it]—some are adapted from the start, and they made it.
> Pupil: But that's what I find so tricky, when you say it like that, be-cause then it ends up as if it is the same thing as crea…creationism.
> Teacher: As creationism.

Pupil: But if we say it like this, yes, some are—some are like this from the start—then it's a mixture.

Teacher: Yes, yes, and I get it, I get it [pupil]. We will talk about that pretty soon—about mutations and the variation of traits, because it is clear that from the start maybe we don't have such large variations of traits... But then we have to start talking about the first life on earth, and the first life on earth is not one little single-celled organism, but it is in many places at the same time. But I understand that it [that way of expressing things] fools you into thinking that everything was decided from the start.

One pupil objects to the teacher's statement in response to what the teacher has just said: 'some are adapted from the start, and they made it'. The pupil says 'that's what I find so tricky, when you say it like that', indicating that similar expressions have been heard on other occasions. Although the pupil's utterance does not take the form of a question, it requires the teacher to explain further. The pupil then repeats 'some are like this from the start' and points to how this makes it hard to differentiate between the three models written on the board. The teacher agrees that the message is unclear saying: 'yes, yes, and I get it, I get it'. The repeated phrase is a strong confirmation that the objection is reasonable at this point. The teacher actually suggests that the current lesson will clarify the perceived difficulty by introducing a genetic explanation.

The topic for discussion—survival and extinction of species—is addressed in four of the eleven lessons. In the final lesson, it is the teacher who brings it up, asking why certain bacteria survive—a question that requires pupils to combine several concepts to provide an explanation (reproduction rate, survival rate, population of species, mutations, and hereditary traits). Following this topical trajectory, Episode 1 marks a point where the discussion about causes for species' survival and extinction for the first time is transposed across biological organisational levels, from the population of a species to the genetic level of hereditary traits. The conversation indicates that the teacher and the pupil have a common goal: to talk about how the three models explain the survival and extinction of species and identify the key differences between them. Analytically, a shared communicative project is established among several of the pupils, if not all (see Episode 2), and distributed over the lessons in this unit. Even though the teacher had already planned to introduce the genetic level, it is the objection made by the pupil that provides the teacher with an opportunity to explicitly introduce the genetic level to the class. The conversation represents a moment of mutual understanding and becomes a resource or common point of reference in the subsequent classroom communication. The analysis shows that the contribution made by the pupil in Episode 1 has a significant role for how the topic of survival and extinction of species develops over the lessons in this classroom.

Episode 2 (Lesson 6)

A small-group activity is initiated. The teacher writes a question on the whiteboard: Will a mutation in a muscle cell be transferred to any children? There is a short pause and then one of three pupils sitting in a row by one table addresses the question. One after another, the pupils claim not to know the answer. After a few exchanges, one of the pupils turns to look at the screen of a laptop placed on the table; the other two pupils remain quiet. For ten seconds all three pupils are silent and the teacher approaches them.

> Lesson 6 [20.16–20.36]
> Teacher: What do you think?
> Pupil 1: I have no idea
> Pupil 2: Something has to be transferred
> Teacher: Then you have to return to sex education: why? What is needed? Use your knowledge: what is necessary for a new individual?

The teacher, in approaching the silent group and asking what they think, is in response to the question written on the board, and to the apparent silence of the members of the group. It encourages the pupils to respond and elaborate on their thinking, while not necessarily requiring a correct answer. The first pupil repeats the claim not to know the answer and the second pupil contributes a conclusion that something ought to be transferred to the children. The word 'transferred', which is part of the question on the board, is repeated, and by using the word 'something' this pupil indirectly requests a clarification from the teacher. Then the teacher suggests that knowledge about sex education may be useful and asks several quick questions about how traits are transferred between generations. In the initial conversation between the pupils in the group, they demonstrate not-knowing positions: one by one, they claim not to know the answer. What the teacher does when approaching the group is to show that knowledge resources are available. The teacher thereby indicates that their not-knowing position may be an orientation, and possibly a consequence of a reluctance to work with the task.

Analysing pupil participation over the eleven lessons gives an insight into how activity roles are distributed on a larger timescale. This shows that the not-knowing position is a pattern of interaction that recurs in the classroom, together with a contrasting pattern where pupils take a knowing position. The ten seconds of silence in Episode 2 is part of the wider pattern. The two positions—knowing and not-knowing—have an impact on the communication and the different opportunities for learning that pupils are provided with by participating in the communication. Analytically, Episode 2 indicates that at this stage this group of pupils does not share the communicative project initiated by the teacher: to give an answer to the key question about genetic inheritance written on the whiteboard. The not-knowing position is problematic for the progression of the teaching, and requires the teacher to develop communicative strategies. In this particular classroom, the teacher organises small-group activities, which enables her to leave her position at the front of the classroom, approaching and giving support to groups of pupils.

In the attempt to understand how topical progression is achieved in the classroom, the teachers' query constructions before the small-group activities are analysed with regard to what kind of answers they are looking for. This shows that in lessons 1, 5 and 8, the teacher asks 'What is your view on why—' or either/or questions. In lessons

6, 7 and 11, the increasing complexity is represented by questions such as 'How will it be affected by—?' and 'What happens if—?' In Lesson 11, questions such as 'Why do we get—?' and 'Why do some—?' are used by the teacher. These last questions are found to be requests for causal explanations of sequences of events. This illuminates how the small-group activities manifest an increasing complexity over the course of the sequence of lessons with a more specialised vocabulary expected from pupils in the later part of the sequence. Analytically, the teacher's query constructions provide a distributed perspective on the principle of sequentiality. The questions and small-group activities indicate the teacher's strategy for achieving topical progression in the unit. She co-ordinates her teaching by listening and talking to the pupils. When talking with groups of pupils, the teacher identifies and responds to pupils' difficulties either during the small-group activity or in one of the upcoming lessons. Compared to Episode 1, Episode 2 does not easily transform into a moment of mutual understanding, although the pupils' responses provide the teacher with important information.

Episode 3 (Lesson 6)

The teacher leans with both arms on a table where three pupils are sitting. The pupils are working with questions from a textbook. The page is open at a couple of pictures, and one question asks whether the particular traits shown will be inherited by any offspring.

> Lesson 6 [42.31–42.51]
> Pupil: The white moose.
> Teacher: Will it have white offspring, okay, why?
> Pupil: Greatest chance.
> Teacher: Why?
> Pupil: Cause.
> Teacher: Can you explain why?
> Pupil: Cause it's not become white during its life, it has not been painted or anything.
> Teacher: If you in fact had that trait.

Pupil: [nods]
Teacher: In one's cells, is that what you are saying [pupil]?
Pupil: [nods]

Episode 3 illustrates a well-known question–answer, teacher–pupil type of dialogue, in which the teacher asks the pupil to explain something. The teacher is not satisfied with the short answer first given by the pupil, and asks three why questions in short order. Then the pupil makes a contribution that the teacher accepts: in this case the pupil suggests some causes for white fur colour and rejects the possibility of them being heritable traits. Analytically, the well-known feedback pattern (IRE) facilitates a common content orientation in the communication, a prerequisite for establishing shared communicative projects. The pupil's response shows an understanding of what might count as an acceptable response to the teacher's question and provides the teacher with important information. This can be seen in the way the teacher immediately uses the response and develops an explanation for the contrasting case: white fur colour as a heritable trait. Explanations for natural phenomena have a central position in the sciences, and in this classroom pupils develop their skills in providing explanations for various phenomena. The question–answer dialogue creates a moment of mutual understanding about how to explain physical attributes by distinguishing between acquired and genetic traits.

Lesson 6 marks the half-way point in the unit. In the next lesson (Lesson 7), the teacher leads a whole-class review of the main study question. Seen from this sequential perspective, the pupil in Episode 3 contributes information that is useful to the teacher in the planning of the next lesson.

Summary

The three episodes illustrate aspects identified as significant in relation to the achieved topical progression. They provide an insight into some of the processes involved when the genetic level is introduced when teaching biological evolution in this particular classroom.

Episode 1 is from whole-class teaching and is an example of one pupil's objection about details in the teacher's way of expressing herself. This is not a criticism, but a contribution to the construction of mutual understanding about the survival and extinction of species in the evolution of life. Episode 3 is from a small-group activity, and exemplifies a question–answer dialogue in which the teacher is provided with information about how the pupil distinguishes acquired from genetic traits. The two episodes capture communicative strategies used by the teacher for handling some of the demanding aspects of this topic discussed in the literature (Smith 2010b): the multiple biological organisational levels involved and the long-term perspectives. Episode 2 is also from a small-group activity, and is an example of how activity roles are distributed in the classroom and how the teacher handles the challenge of teaching pupils who take a not-knowing position. There are many possible reasons as to why they take this position, for example talking about sexual reproduction in this context possibly evokes reluctance among some pupils. By including several timescales in the analysis, the understanding of what goes on in the three episodes is expanded to include the relation between individual conversations and the topical progression achieved over the sequence of lessons.

Multiple timescales in a science of teaching

The previous section describes one research approach for investigating how pupils' contributions to the classroom communication influence the topical progression achieved in a curricular unit. The investigation shows some patterns of communication over the sequence of lessons, and some communicative strategies in short episodes of a conversation. In this classroom, the combination of the progression in query constructions and providing many chances for pupils to participate and have discussions in small groups, creates a classroom organisation with rich opportunities for the teacher to interact and catch up with individuals and groups of pupils. The small-group situations have at least two things in common. Firstly, the contexts in which pupils are asked to explain and reason about a problem strategically chosen in relation to the topic of biological evolution. Secondly, these discussions are characterised by their informality. This is shown in the teacher's and pupils' posture, tone of voice, and interactions, as for example in Episode 3 when the teacher is leaning on the pupils' table in a relaxed position.

For the whole class, Episode 1 shows how the contribution of one pupil drives communication forward and enables the teacher to move the topic of conversation from addressing adaptation at the level of individual organisms to include the genetic level and explanations at the level of the population of species. This occasion marks the end of a longer discussion in Lesson 5, where pupils' difficulties in previous lessons are openly addressed. Looking at the sequence as a whole, it seems this particular discussion represents an irregular interaction change (Molenaar 2014)—a kind of turning point—in the sequence of lessons. In this way, the combination of several units of analysis provides insight into communicative strategies used in the achieved topical progression, with lessons 5 and 6 representing a phase of transposing the topic from the level of individual organisms to the genetic level. The essay shows how the achieved topical progression includes regular changes in terms of reoccurring and non-reoccurring patterns, as well as irregular changes in the classroom. These findings contribute to our understanding, not only about the teaching and learning of evolution, but also of how patterns of classroom communication are constructed over several lessons.

The didactical consequences from this study concern how, as a teacher, to take notice of the short conversations with pupils and their possible contribution to the whole of the teaching. The many scientific concepts included in the science subjects demands a continuous evaluation and exploration by science teachers of the ways these are addressed in classroom communication. For the professional teacher, this is part of their everyday work. Paying close attention to the pupils and their difficulties, and using their contributions to develop the future teaching, are skills a teacher develops. This does not mean that there are simple strategies for how to do this. What this essay attempts to show is teaching as a complex communicative activity. In the preparation for this activity, the teacher mobilizes knowledge about the content, knowledge about pupils' learning about the content in general, and knowledge about the particular group of pupils. By paying close attention to the communication in the classroom during teaching, the teacher may recognise potentials for change and consider how to develop the teaching on different timescales. The research presented here does not attempt to prescribe particular teaching practices, but illuminates details and gives an overview of some communicative strategies that are found in this example of the teaching of biological evolution. The essay provides an opportunity for individual and collegial reflections by teachers, in the firm conviction that the development and evaluation of best teaching practices is primarily a task for the teaching profession.

This essay includes a methodological discussion of the approaches to timescales in research, and illustrates a possible research approach to empirical material that touches on the many timescales of classroom interaction. It has previously been indicated that multiple-scale video analysis has the potential to significantly contribute to the understanding of how content is taught and learnt (Klette 2007), and this essay constitutes one such example. In order to better understand the continuous flow of events characterising classroom teaching and learning activities (Lemke 2000; Ludvigsen et al. 2010; Mercer 2008; Molenaar 2014) new research approaches are called for.

This volume offers a spectrum of research approaches, and the present essay embraces an empirical and analytical perspective on didactics. It indicates the need for a coherent science of teaching based on empirical and analytical studies, a science of teaching that does not necessarily impose answers to the questions of how (as well as why, to whom, when, and where) teaching ought to be conducted. In relation to the didactical triangle, this essay does not explore the relations between teacher, content, and pupil. For the lesson sequence studied, the interaction in the classroom can be described in terms of movement in all directions within an area inside the didactical triangle. The focus in this essay is, however, not primarily on the teacher, nor the pupil, nor the content itself, neither is it on one of the relations represented by the sides of the triangle. What the three episodes are supposed to illustrate to the reader are situations in which all three relations are significant for the continuation of the sequence of lessons. One way of illustrating this could perhaps be to add a dimension to the triangle, turning the triangle into a prism with an apex representing time. This would add a fourth dimension to the classic didactical triad: the potential for change.

Note

1 For further details of the project, see Rocksén 2015. The data used for illustration has previously been published elsewhere, where details about methods and analytical procedures can be found (Rocksén 2016 & 2017; Rocksén & Olander 2017). The writing of this essay was financially supported by the Swedish Research Council (dnr 349–2006–146) through the Linnaeus Centre for Research on Learning, Interaction and Mediated Communication in Contemporary Society.

References

Aguiar, O. G., Mortimer, E. F., & Scott, P.H. (2010), 'Learning from and responding to students' questions: The authoritative and dialogic tension'. *Journal of Research in Science Teaching,* 47/2, 174–93. doi:10.1002/tea.20315

Ball, T., & Wells, G. (2009), 'Running cars down ramps: learning about learning over time'. *Language and Education,* 23/4, 371–90. doi:10.1080/09500780902954281

Cazden, C. B. (2001), *Classroom discourse: the language of teaching and learning.* (Portsmouth: Heinemann).

Duschl, R., Maeng, S., & Sezen, A. (2011), 'Learning progressions and teaching sequences: a review and analysis'. *Studies in Science Education,* 47/2, 123–82. doi:10.1080/03057267.2011.604476

Engle, R. A. (2006), 'Framing interactions to foster generative learning: a situative explanation of transfer in a community of learners classroom'. *Journal of the Learning Sciences,* 15/4, 451–98. doi:10.1207/s15327809jls1504_2

Klette, K. (2007), 'Trends in research on teaching and learning in schools: didactics meets classroom studies'. *European Educational Research Journal,* 6/2, 147–60. doi:10.2304/eerj.2007.6.2.147

Lemke, J. L. (1990), *Talking science: language, learning and values.* (Norwood, NJ: Alex Publishing Corporation).

—— (2000), 'Across the scales of time: artifacts, activities, and meanings in ecosocial systems'. *Mind, culture, and activity,* 7/4, 273–90. doi:10.1207/S15327884MCA0704_03

—— (2001), 'The long and the short of it: Comments on multiple timescale studies of human activity'. *The Journal of the Learning Sciences*, 10/1–2, 17–26.

Linell, P. (2009), *Rethinking language, mind, and world dialogically: interactional and contextual theories of human sense-making.* (Charlotte, NC: Information Age Publishing).

Ludvigsen, S., Rasmussen, I., Krange, I., Moen, A., & Middleton, D. (2010), 'Intersecting trajectories of participation: Temporality and learning'. In Ludvigsen, S., Lund, A., Rasmussen, I., & Säljö, R. (Eds.), *Learning across sites: new tools, infrastructures and practices.* (London: Routledge).

Matusov, E. (2007), 'In Search of the Appropriate Unit of Analysis for Sociocultural Research'. *Culture & Psychology*, 13/3, 307–33.

Mehan, H. (1979), '"What time is it, Denise?": Asking known information questions in classroom discourse'. *Theory into practice*, 18/4, 285–94. doi:10.1080/00405847909542846

Mercer, N. (2008), 'The seeds of time: why classroom dialogue needs a temporal analysis'. *The Journal of the Learning Sciences*, 17/1, 33–59. doi:10.1080/10508400701793182

Molenaar, I. (2014), 'Advances in temporal analysis in learning and instruction'. *Frontline Learning Research*, 6, 15–24. doi:10.14786/flr.v2i4.118

Mortimer, E.F., & Scott, P.H. (2003), *Meaning making in secondary science classrooms.* (Maidenhead: Open University Press).

Rector, M. A., Nehm, R. H., & Pearl, D. (2013), 'Learning the language of evolution: lexical ambiguity and word meaning in student explanations'. *Research in Science Education*, 43/3, 1107–33. doi:10.1007/s11165-012-9296-z

Rocksén, M. (2015), *Reasoning in a Science Classroom* (Gothenburg Studies in Educational Sciences, 365; Gothenburg: Faculty of Education, University of Gothenburg), http://hdl.handle.net/2077/38324

—— (2016), 'The many roles of "explanation" in science education: A case study', *Cultural Studies of Science Education*, 11/4, 837–68. doi:10.1007/s11422-014-9629-5

—— (2017), 'The temporality of Participation in School Science: Coordination of Teacher Control and the Pace of Students' Participation', *Scandinavian Journal of Educational Research*, 61/4, 377–93. doi:10.1080/00313831.2016.1147070

—— & Olander, C. (2017), 'A Topical Trajectory on Survival: An Analysis of Link-Making in a Sequence of Lessons on Evolution', *Research in Science Education*, 47/2, 451–72. doi:10.1007/s11165-015-9509-3

Scott, P.H., Mortimer, E.F., & Aguiar, O.G. (2006), 'The tension between authoritative and dialogic discourse: a fundamental characteristic of meaning making interactions in high school science lessons'. *Science Education*, 90/4, 605–31. doi:10.1002/sce.20131

Sinclair, J. M., & Coulthard, M. (1975), *Towards an analysis of discourse: the English used by teachers and pupils.* (London: Oxford University Press).

Skolverket (Swedish National Agency for Education). (2011), *Curriculum for the compulsory school, preschool class and the school-age educare 2011* (SKOLFS 2010:37; 2011:19) (Stockholm: Skolverket), http://www.skolverket.se/publikationer?id=3984

Smith, M. U. (2010a), 'Current Status of Research in Teaching and Learning Evolution: I. Philosophical/Epistemological Issues'. *Science & Education,* 19/6–8, 523–38. doi:10.1007/s11191-009-9215-5

Smith, M. U. (2010b), 'Current status of research in teaching and learning evolution: II. Pedagogical issues'. *Science & Education,* 19/6–8, 539–71. doi:10.1007/s11191-009-9216-4

Wells, G., & Arauz, R. M. (2006), 'Dialogue in the Classroom'. *Journal of the Learning Sciences,* 15/3, 379–428. doi:10.1207/s15327809jls1503_3

Abstract

This volume grew out of a series of conversations between researchers with different specialisations in the Swedish field of didactics. Thinking about the similarities, differences, and possibilities of our work, we compared research interests and outcomes from our respective fields, finding similar questions in different research contexts, compatible methodological starting points and challenges, and a shared ambition to contribute to classroom practice. The classroom—an arena for organised and intentional teaching and learning—offers both focus and a natural delimitation to our shared interests. Further, the empirical studies we worked on were rooted in scientific didactics (Hudson 2007), all featuring a focus that could be framed by the traditional didactical triangle of pupils, teacher, and content, but with different emphases. This is a distinct feature compared to the larger field of classroom studies (cf. Sahlström 2008), and also compared to the field of didactics (cf. Öhman 2014; Hopmann 2007). Further, the complexities of understanding, predicting and shaping instances of teaching and learning in the classroom in combination with the fundamental character of such research point to its potential value. An interest in these questions is in no way limited to the present volume (see, for example, Klette 2007), but looking at this collection of work as a whole, we discern a potential research direction that we refer to here as didactic classroom studies. The individual studies in this volume have some distinctive common features, while still having clear interfaces with the wider research community.

CHAPTER 10

A potential research direction for didactic classroom studies

Christina Osbeck & Åke Ingerman

This essay, then, interrogates the idea of didactic classroom studies as a research direction as it is found in the essays in this volume. With an analysis of the similarities and differences between the essays in certain specific respects—research questions, theoretical and analytical framing, and the character of and connection to didactical traditions—we chart the variations and commonalities across the contributions, and from that go on to formulate suggestions for the further development of this research direction. The underlying claim in this approach is thus that the studies in this volume—with its limitations in terms of fully reflecting didactic classroom studies and the authors being based at the same university, albeit with different specialisations—together comprise an interesting case of variation, which on reflection will provide the means with which to address the challenges of didactic classroom research and to find a way forward as a potential research direction.

Didactic classroom studies

In articulating didactic classroom studies as a research direction, we first characterise the situations our research focuses on, and from that formulate a broad research question that functions generatively and distinctively for the research direction.

The first characteristic of didactic classroom studies is its focus on the classroom as an arena for organised teaching and learning. The classroom is in most cases one or a limited set of specific physical locations in school designated for teaching and learning. At the same time, it is not the physical layout that primarily makes a classroom a classroom. It is the organised activity of teaching and learning that makes a classroom into an intentional practice that teachers and pupils meaningfully engage in. Classrooms are an important social arena for these actors, with societal impact; however, from a didactical perspective, the interest in the classroom can be understood as focused on the core activity of teaching and learning. This is a multilayered interest, where 'The term "teaching" focuses on the activity of teachers. At the same time, it presupposes a relation to a person taught (or often a group of persons), and in this sense refers to a social phenomenon. [...] The fundamental character of teaching concerns the relation between what the teacher does and the learning environment on one hand, and the result as expressed by the learner(s) on the other hand' (Svensson 2016, 276). The present studies share a clear empirical concern with the classroom and its activities, but also a systematic, scientific character. They represent a spectrum of theoretical and analytical stances, empirical contexts and scales, but they nevertheless share a common connection to the heartlands of didactics.

The second characteristic of didactic classroom studies concerns didactics. Didactics as a field has a common core (Hopmann 2007; Hudson 2007) of considering teaching and learning as intentional, and simultaneously having autonomy, both as autonomy for teachers and pupils, but also as autonomous activities per se—having a non-determinate character, because they are unfolding events. This equates to a firm conviction that the professional, committed teacher is at the heart of successful schooling (in line with many studies outside didactics as summarised by Hattie 2009 and others), and that teaching that facilitates pupils' intellectual engagement, both immediate and continuous, is associated with positive learning outcomes (see, for example, Freeman et al. 2014). The teachers' professional facilitation of pupils' engagement is part of the common core of didactics: a commitment to *Bildung*. It also points to what is acquired in the classroom: the educative constitution of meaning from the subject matter (of teaching). In this way, the teacher, the pupil, the content, and their relationships as manifested in teaching and learning together constitute the core focus of didactics, which is also expressed in the didactic triangle.

Contextual didactic classroom studies

A specific advantage with didactic classroom studies is that they are able to focus on teacher and pupil interactions around specific content taught and learnt in a specific context. In the classroom, these complex, contextual interrelationships are dynamically shifting, interacting, and folding in on themselves in both the short and long term. Even if the contextual character of teaching and learning is implied in didactic classroom studies, it is important to stress that drawing conclusions without clear links to contextual factors can easily go awry. We point to two main groups of such contextual factors. One group is situational, temporally shifting, and individual factors. The other group is underlying structural factors in the physical, temporal, and social organisation of the classroom, which are not explicitly attended to in the classroom. Even though both these groups of factors are ingrained in events and constituted meaning, they are in themselves not the primary knowledge interest in didactic classroom studies. However, the complexity that classroom studies makes visible also means that a strongly reductionist research approach can be avoided. Didactic classroom studies focus on wholes of teaching and learning, as argued by Svensson (2016), recognising that relevant phenomena of teaching and learning are inextricably intertwined. This means that these contextual and complex reflections, from a systematic and scientific stance, can ensure the results being both directly useful in practice and firmly based in (educational) science, thus remaining true to the potential for didactics to be a teachers' professional science (Ingerman & Wickman 2015).

Didactical consequences for classroom teaching

Didactic classroom studies examines classrooms for aspects that can be theorised, using components already established in the field of didactics. The studies concentrate on teaching and learning activities and educational events in the classroom. Such events have a direction, which necessitates a recognition that later events are shaped by teachers' and pupils' intentional actions. As Klette argues, the relational dynamics are not well understood and 'There is a need for more integrated frameworks that link instructional activities and procedures (the how) with thematic patterns (the what) and modes of interaction (the who) patterns' (2007, 148). Contributing to the development of such an integrated framework seems a worthwhile ambition for didactic classroom studies.

Following Klette's proposed interlinking, we identify didactical consequences as a concept of core interest. The focus on consequences highlights any attempts to relate outcomes or later events to earlier events along this chain of events and outcomes that are didactical in nature. This may be done in terms of the teacher's intentions, or in terms of possibilities or consequences for pupils' intellectual engagement with their educational progress towards *Bildung* on the individual level. There are two main directions that are relevant to follow here. The first concerns the direct outcomes of classroom events in terms of pupil learning. The second concerns how intentions, conditions, or previous actions constrain or open up for further didactic action. Teachers' didactical actions and choices largely determine the course of events, and the how, the what, and the who. They shape classroom situation structures and overarching conditions (for example, time limits, group size, communicative patterns, available artefacts, and curriculum) that may impose limits on subsequent didactical choices. It is not the structures themselves that are worth describing, although that would be a perfectly valid exercise; instead, it is the structures' didactical consequences for the situation in question.

The focus on didactical consequences also opens up for discussions about potential didactical actions based on the empirical patterns and the results of didactic classroom studies. New teaching situations may arise when we learn from previous outcomes. Didactical consequences are best understood as an analytical trope, pointing to when processes are investigated and how different parts relate and depend on one another. Contextual dependency and the small scale of the studies often mean that conclusions about consequences are tentative, but it remains important to identify the relationships and consider their meanings.

The studies in the present volume tackle didactical consequences in a variety of ways. For example, Kullberg and Skodras look at pupil outcomes in terms of examples used (a core aspect of didactics in the mathematics classroom) and Osbeck looks at the didactical consequences of a discourse established in different classrooms in terms of both pupil outcomes and possible lessons. Ingerman and Booth consider the pathways that student discussions may take as a consequence of a variety of tutor interventions; Rocksén, the different ways in which the teacher 'listens' to the pupils, and the consequences for subsequent didactical choices. Lilja and Claesson look at how relationships may constrain or enable teacher didactic action, particularly in terms of discipline. Didactical consequences are similarly the focus of Hipkiss's investigation of classroom designs.

These are the grounds for suggesting that didactic classroom studies—a scholarly enquiry into didactical intentions, choices, and conditions in the classroom, and their interactions and consequences—form a distinct research direction. The key components can be phrased as an overarching research question: What are the didactical consequences for classroom teaching and learning of the specific conditions, structures, events, contents, and teacher and pupil priorities and their various interrelationships?

This question has the great advantage of acknowledging the contextual nature of teaching and learning, and therefore the importance of keeping relationships between teacher, learner, and content intact within the study, even though the emphasis necessarily varies from study to study. Thus, the set of results arising from the studies reported here attempts to provide a scientific basis for our understanding of why and how certain learning outcomes come about, and why positive conditions for the intentional relationship between teaching and

	Aims and research questions
Osbeck	'concerns the kinds of communication patterns in the two classes that may contribute to an understanding of the identified differences in achievement and development'
Kullberg & Skodras	'illustrate how teachers used systematic variation in and between examples'
Ingerman & Booth	'develop an analytical understanding of learning in small groups within the research paradigm of phenomenography and the variation theory [...] what constitutes the quality of a group discussion in terms of what is discussed, the character of the discussion, and the appropriate, effective didactical framing of group discussions [...] what different approaches employed by tutors can support or hinder different groups in their discussions'
Sofkova Hashemi	'exploring the significance of digital mediation and multimodal text design for pupils' understanding of specific content, and with it the role that teacher's scaffolding may have in such a modified learning environment with access to digital technologies [...] observes how 8-year-old pupils make meaning from an instructional text composed by peers on computers'
Hipkiss	'discuss classroom design: how a school subject is understood from its design, what teaching and learning activities take place there, and how participants interact [...] focus on when, where, and how subject-specific language is used'
Lilja & Claesson	' to find the patterns in the way teachers handle discipline in their everyday teaching. [...] what teaching strategies are available, and which appear to be successful'
Kilhamn et al.	'to illustrate and discuss the use of classroom videos to enhance mathematics education research'
Rocksén	'methodological discussion of the approaches to timescales in research, and illustrates a possible research approach to empirical material that touches on the many timescales of classroom interaction' 'how talk in the classroom develops and how communicative patterns are constructed over several lessons' 'How do science teachers and pupils attain those moments of mutual understanding? How is topic progression achieved?' 'How do teachers ensure continuity in the classroom communication with only one or two lessons per week for a given group of pupils?'

Table 10.1. The aims and research questions of the essays in this volume.

learning may emerge. Some studies dwell on the elements in teaching practice that have been developed for the purposes of the research (or changed to enhance the focus of research), others look at the contours of well-established practices, and yet others discuss what may constitute quality in such studies or appropriate methods to adopt.

The essays in this volume present a range of studies of immediate relevance to this research direction. In what follows, we therefore consider the full range of research questions set out in the essays, paying particular attention to their theoretical and analytical framing, empirical design, didactical tradition, knowledge claims, and ethics. By highlighting the challenges of didactic classroom studies, we hope to contribute by pointing the way forward—a potential research direction for the field.

The classroom studies

In order to describe and compare the essays' research questions, it is necessary to chart the *aims and potential knowledge contribution* of each of the eight. There are thus three key issues addressed in this section. First, how to interpret the essays' knowledge contributors in their didactical focus on teachers, pupils, and content? Second, to what degree is the spotlight on the relationships between these factors? And third, to what extent does the focus fall on other conditions and structures in the classroom? Based on the research questions and knowledge contributors (as we interpret them) of the essays, we have judged the degree to which each essay concentrates on these aspects (Table 10.1).

Communication patterns are the centre of Osbeck's essay and are here understood as a combination of pupils' and teachers' discussions about the teaching content. As teachers' perspectives, pupils' perspectives, and content are intertwined in this communication, it means that the interrelationship between these three aspects is very much in focus. At the same time, the complexity of the content in itself and how it is structured cannot be said to be at the centre to the same degree as in, for instance, Kullberg and Skodras's study, described below. Osbeck presents some information about the conditions and structures in the two classes studied, and also stresses their potential importance to the communication patterns (how long they have worked together and the number of pupils in class) but the structures are not the focus of the study as in, for instance, Hipkiss's study.

Kullberg and Skodras's essay concerns the teachers' work with mathematics education, together with the complexity of the content. The focus is on how the content is presented and the order in which examples are presented so as to demonstrate a systematic variation. In one of the studies referred to, the order of the examples originates from specific teaching material; in the second study, the pupils' perspectives have a more prominent position and in that way, the study also demonstrates that the examples given, as such, may not be sufficient for a specific pattern to be obvious to the pupils and for certain insights to be gained. The teachers' explicit demonstration of the patterns and what these patterns show, through the use of questions, communication, and notes, may be central. The interrelationship between the teachers' acts and the structure of the content is shown to be central to the pupils' understanding, although in this specific study it is the structure of the content and the teachers' use of these structures that are in the foreground. Other structures or conditions in the classroom are only touched on in passing.

The students' perspectives and their group interactions are the focus of Ingerman and Booth's essay, with a research emphasis on learning. It is the varying quality of group discussions, and the tutor's way of responding to that varying quality, that are the specific interest questions. This also means that the learning object itself—how it is addressed, interpreted, and understood—is of special interest too. The interrelationship of these factors is central, while other classroom or group conditions/structures which might influence the work are not part of the research, even if small groups can be held to be conditions for learning.

Socio-technological changes—how the requirements for multimodal reading skills among pupils have increased—are addressed in Sofkova Hashemi's essay, and in this sense classroom conditions and structures too. But the research interest in this essay is the semiotic choice of the pupils: their preferences and meaning-making of audio, video, and text which in itself is the subject matter of the lesson. The pupils' work and preferences are also described in relation to their communication with their teacher. This means that the research interest is high when it comes to pupils' meaning-making in relation to certain content, and a bit lower when it comes to teachers' actions, as well as conditions and structures.

In Hipkiss's essay, the classroom conditions and structure are the centre of the research. The design of the classroom is in focus, and how this design creates meanings, provides specific venues in the classroom (controlled by specific actors), and how this in turn creates a certain power and distance in the relations between teachers and pupils—with consequences for whether and how subject-specific language is used. The affordances of the classroom, as well as the influences on and interrelationship between actors and communicated meaning, is the focus of the analyses, while the pupils and the teachers are not in focus in the same sense, and conceptual tools for these descriptions are not provided.

In Lilja and Claesson's study, the teachers' relationships with the pupils in the classroom are focused on as conditions for teaching and learning. Although it takes two people to form a relationship, a particular interest is taken here in the teachers and how they constitute these relationships. Moreover, the consequences that these relationships have for discipline and order are central in this study, since they are defined as when 'the teacher and the pupils are directed towards the same object and that the pupils have the opportunity to expand their horizons', the study could be understood as also taking aspects of the content into account. Complexity of content is not part of the research focus; for instance, attention is not paid to how difficulties in being directed towards the same object may differ depending on the character of the object—for example, a detective story or water and plants, which are examples given in this essay. It can be said that a medium degree of research focus is on the interrelationship between the didactical aspects.

The research aims of the two remaining essays are concerned with research methodology. In this summary we have chosen to concentrate

	Not in focus	In focus to a low degree	In focus to a medium degree	In focus to a high degree
Teachers (T)			AMH, SSH	CO; AK & CS; Ål & SB; AL & SC; MR; CK et al.
Pupils (P)			AK & CS; AL & SC; AMH	CO; SSH; Ål & SB; MR; CK et al.
Content (C)		AL & SC	CO; AMH	SSH, AK & CS; Ål & SB; MR; CK et al.
Interrelationships (T-P-C)			AK & CS; SSH; AL & SC	CO; Ål & SB; AMH; MR; CK et al.
Conditions & structures		Ål & SB; AK & CS; SSH	CO; CK et al.	AL & SC; MR; AMH

Table 10.2. The extent to which the essay's focus is the teachers, pupils, content, interrelationships, or conditions and structures. The essays are labelled with the initials of the author(s).

on the studies the authors refer to in their second-order methodological research. Both Rocksén's and Kilhamn et al.'s essays are based on comparisons of video data. For the former, there are many recordings from the same classroom; for the latter, the recordings are from several classrooms. Both consider the structure of the classrooms; however, Rocksén's contribution does so to a greater degree, since the timescale is one of the most central factors that the study uses when examining the development of communication patterns. Kilhamn et al.'s overarching focus is the organisation of classroom work as a central structuring factor, but they also have other central research objects, such as teacher perspectives and the pupils' ability to make use of experiences from one problem-solving context in another context. By focusing on educational communication patterns in the classroom, as both essays do, both teachers' and pupils' utterances about content are found to be of importance, as is the interrelationship between these aspects. In both studies, the communication patterns concern content, and the research interest in this respect is in-depth in character.

The research focuses of this volume can be set out in tabular form (Table 10.2). It demonstrates one of the hypotheses that has driven this present project, namely that classroom studies to a large extent develop knowledge about teachers, pupils, and content in interrelational senses—they realise the ambition of designing didactic studies with distinct consequences for teaching and learning, understood as necessarily involving certain meanings and content. Furthermore, it may also be noted that the kind of content focused on in these studies is confined to the specific classroom episodes studied. Certain content themes and how these are dealt with, rather than school subjects as such, or different conceptions of school subjects (for example, Englund & Svingby 1986; Lindmark 2013) are the focus.

Evidently, there are not large differences in the extent to which the factors of interest are addressed in the essays. Despite this, it seems as though the teacher is the factor that is emphasized most frequently. Given that didactic studies often have an interest in the learning intended by teaching, and teachers' actions can be understood as strategies to ensure particular learning outcomes, this could be thought as a reasonable finding.

The factor paid least attention is classroom conditions and structures. If teaching and learning can be understood as contextual, and structures such as the design of the classroom have the kind of impact that Hipkiss's essay indicates, this is a noteworthy finding. This means that the classroom to a large extent is the place and space where teaching and learning are in progress, and that research is being conducted without paying sufficient attention to what this context means, and how it differs from or resembles the contexts of other similar studies. A substantial interest in classroom conditions and structures would seem to be a priority for the further development of didactic classroom studies as a research direction.

Theoretical and analytical framing

The kinds of theoretical and analytical frameworks that the essays draw on differ (Table 10.3), and in addition the ways in which the frameworks are used varies. Nevertheless, it is common to all frameworks that they broadly address how learning (or meaning-making) is understood, how it can be enhanced (which is an important perspective in relation to teaching), and how knowledge may be

	Theoretical and analytical framing
Osbeck	Sociocultural perspective
Kullberg & Skodras	Variation theory
Ingerman & Booth	Variation theory
Sofkova Hashemi	Social semiotic
Hipkiss	Social semiotic
Lilja & Claesson	Hermeneutic; phenomenology
Kilhamn et al.	Socio-cultural research tradition, a dialogical approach to communication Mathematical Knowledge for Teaching, MKT (Cf. Pedagogical content knowledge, PCK)
Rocksén	Dialogical theories of communication

Table 10.3. Theoretical and analytical framing of the essays.

interpreted. The explicit connection to a theoretical and analytical framework is important if the studies are to be thought characteristic of scientific didactics (Öhman 2014).

In variation theory, the 'learner comes to discern new dimensions of variation, thereby developing the capability of experiencing the phenomenon in qualitatively different, more complex and powerful ways' (Ingerman & Booth). A pupil's opportunities to learn can be enhanced by teaching processes in which critical aspects of the object of learning are clarified (Kullberg & Skodras). In Rocksén's essay, teaching processes are described as 'being primarily a communicative activity'. Such an understanding is also a central perspective in the essays by Osbeck and Hipkiss, who like Rocksén, focus on the communicative patterns and collective meaning-making in the classroom, with an eye to content-specific language and its expression (in Osbeck, for example, in the form of speech genres). Due to these differences, the frameworks allow detailed analyses of various kinds, concerning different aspects of teaching and learning processes in the classroom (which are understood as essential), even if on an overarching level the frameworks can be understood as addressing similar phenomena.

The essays differ concerning the degree to which they are driven by theory or by empirical data. It is obvious in some of the theory-driven essays that it is due to such an approach that it has been possible to produce analyses of a highly systematic and specific nature (for example,

Rocksén), which in turn is a solid basis for conclusions and further research. However, when the empirical observations are as thorough and rich as they are in these essays, it is not surprising that a knowledge contribution may emerge from the studied classroom practice which may go beyond the knowledge contribution of a previously chosen framework (for example, Sofkova Hashemi). How such empirical and theoretical knowledge interests can be combined is a challenge that these kinds of classroom studies must contend with. One apparent risk is that a theoretical framework is presented with specific concepts that are not used in the analysis, while other concepts that are not clearly presented or sufficiently anchored are used.

Besides the traditional division between theoretically and empirically driven research projects, there are also essays that have a basis in current public debate and where the project has been developed in response to such concerns (for example, Lilja & Claesson). In educational research, there is a certain closeness between the practice, public debate, and politics that constitute the conditions for research in the field. This also brings particular challenges when it comes to clarifying the concepts that are currently in use.

Many of the theoretical perspectives researchers use are so well known to them that they are taken for granted. This is an extra challenge in didactic studies, where different types of theories may be necessary, for instance one type of theory to conceptualize learning and teaching and another to discuss central content (see, for example, Kullberg & Skodras). In order to have full transparency, it is of course important to clarify all the theories at work.

Empirical design

The amount, sort, and representation of the data that the essays in this volume draw on vary. However all studies draw on quite extensive material (Table 10.4). Working with wide-ranging material, as is often the case in classroom studies, involves questions about its selection for closer analyses. This means that the selection and representation of data are issues that are present to a high degree during the whole research project and not only at the beginning of a study, during the

	Observational data
Osbeck	80 lessons (3 classes; 1 academic year) 4 lessons analysed and quoted from
Kullberg & Skodras	2 studies: Study I: 5 lessons (2 referred to); Study II: 1 Learning Study – processes over one academic year (2 lessons referred to)
Ingerman & Booth	1 physics course; 7 student groups analysed, 2 groups quoted from
Sofkova Hashemi	1 thematic work; 6 lessons; 2 lessons analysed and quoted from
Hipkiss	5 classrooms; 29 hours; 3 lessons quoted from
Lilja & Claesson	3 studies; 15 teachers, 250 days; 4 lessons quoted from
Kilhamn et al.	17 classrooms; 85 lessons, summaries but no single lesson quoted from
Rocksén	1 thematic work; 1 class, 11 lessons, 2 lessons quoted from

Table 10.4. Observational data.

selection of schools, classrooms, teachers, and pupils from whose activities the empirical material is generated. It seems to be important to distinguish between choices concerning (a) all observations that are made in a project, (b) the observations that are analysed for a certain study and (c) the observations quoted in the presentation of the studies (here, the essays). Besides the observational data, other kinds of data are often used, such as educational materials, interviews, and questionnaires. A large amount of observational data gives certain opportunities, for instance when it comes to specific comparisons where many factors need to be almost the same to allow a certain factor of interest to be pin-pointed (for example, Kilhamn et al.; Osbeck). Thanks to rich data produced over time, it can also be possible to follow the development of communication patterns and the establishment of joint constructions of meaning (for example, Rocksén). The fact that the selection of data in several steps, as described above in (a)–(c), can be understood as crucial in these studies, and imposes high demands on descriptions, arguments, and discussions of these selections. This can be a challenge.

The fact that the empirical material for classroom studies is often much larger than both the material analysed and directly referred to in a specific study, provides classroom studies with both background information and contextual descriptions, which are seldom available in, say, questionnaires and interview studies. How this kind of information is used varies. From the essays in this volume, it is possible to say that many authors have had access to much more information about the studies' contexts than is noted in these essays. To what extent this non-explicit information affected the researchers' selections and interpretations of data, is difficult to know. The fact that broader descriptions of the conditions and structures in the classroom are seldom referred to constitutes a weakness, for instance in relation to chances for the reader to generalise findings by drawing on contextual similarities (Larsson 2009). Perhaps better standards for how to conduct such contextual descriptions could be developed in didactic classroom studies. The issue can also be raised from other angles. If there is a great deal of information that is not being used in classroom studies, might it be possible to conduct better prepared, more directed empirical studies, so that less surplus information is produced? Or is a more extensive secondary analysis of existing material called for?

The kind of observation material that the studies draw on also varies. In the essays, the most frequent way of working with classroom observations is to use video recordings with several cameras in each classroom, complemented by audio recordings (for example, Sofkova Hashemi, Ingerman & Booth, Hipkiss, Rocksén, Kilhamn et al.). The ways of analysing data are related to the available empirical information, which is not only a question of what observations are available, but also about how they are transcribed. Due to the detailed information that video studies have the potential to deliver, it is logical that many of the video-based studies choose to work with detailed communication analyses, where gestures and non-verbal communication are also taken into account. However, this is not always the case, and if so, the added value that detailed video recordings gives (for example in Kilhamn et al.) must be set against the risk to the authenticity of the classroom that is then created by the equipment. This is why field notes can be a preferred method for generating classroom data (for example, Lilja & Claesson). None of the essays in this volume explicitly declare the methods used for transcription of the recordings—in the same way as the selection of material cited is important for the trustworthiness of the study, the ways of observing classroom events and of producing material for analysis from these notes or recordings impact the study's credibility (see also Sahlström 2008).

Just as the ways of generating data for analyses from observations vary between the essays, so do the methods for representing observations and analytical material. Despite the dominance of qualitative analyses of classroom events, the amount of data makes structuring and quantitative representations in the form of tables and figures useful (for example, Hipkiss, Kilhamn et al., Osbeck). Broader patterns become easier to identify. Analyses of classroom design allow plans of the classroom interiors to become central representations (Hipkiss) and the pupils' multimodal educational materials and their interpretations of these materials can be presented simultaneously using innovative tables (Sofkova Hashemi). Also, the transcriptions of the video recordings in the essays vary. In some essays, interpretative summaries of the exclusively visually communicated messages in the films are combined with the verbal quotes in the excerpts; in others, the authors have chosen to focus on the verbal communication and to put interpretative comments in separate text sections. Some data, both transcripts and field notes, are referred to as summarised narratives, both with and without quotations. Thus quotations from classroom observations are used differently depending on the essay, and are given different meanings by different authors. This means that the function of quoted empirical data in a given text—the claim made by quoting it—cannot be taken for granted, and is a key issue that needs to be communicated clearly.

Didactical research specialisations

This volume brings together a wide variety of didactical specialisations that the essays relate to: mathematics (Kullberg; Kilhamn et al.), first languages (Sofkova Hashemi), the sciences (Ingerman & Booth, Rocksén), the social sciences (Osbeck), and general didactics (Hipkiss, Lilja & Claesson). To what degree it is possible or meaningful to link a certain essay to a didactic specialisation varies. In mathematics education, for instance, it is not sufficient to relate the studies to mathematics education generally, but to the knowledge areas that the studies represent, for instance algebra (Kilhamn et al.) or multiplicative structures, the distributive law and the commutative law (Kullberg). This can also be said to be the case for the studies on science (Ingerman & Booth, Rocksén) and first-language education (multimodal texts), while the social studies contribution in this volume has a broader focus ('Introduction to religious studies' and 'Current news'). The two essays that were understood here as contributions to general didactics do not relate to one single subject, but rather to a content interest and specific focuses (discipline and order—Lilja & Claesson; classroom design—Hipkiss). The volume and specificity of previous research vary between different didactic specialisations. Also, the degree of agreement concerning what constitutes important knowledge to teach seems to differ between the research specialisations. The research fields have different conditions, and therefore different strategies for working in a qualified way in these fields must be applied. Didactics is not a single field, but a composite and rather diverse one.

In order to show how much didactical research fields can differ, two examples—religious education and science education—are given. In a Swedish context, religious education (RE) can be understood as a part of the social science education field together with geography, history and civics education. However, putting these four subjects together is a specifically Swedish curriculum construction, which means that the four fields are not necessarily closely related in international educational research. Unlike science education, the various fields must be dealt with separately.

Research in or related to RE is conducted in many different academic disciplines that primarily belong to religious studies, theology, or education. What unites RE research is an interest in institutions where teaching and learning about religion take place, in a Swedish context mainly school and church. This means that RE as an academic discipline in the Nordic countries has to a large extent developed in the faculties of theology (for example, Osbeck & Lied 2012).

RE research, in connection to both schools and religious communities, works today with rather strong international networks both in the Nordic countries and worldwide. However, it can be problematic to compare and to learn from RE school studies conducted in other countries, since the differences in what one defines as RE content are so great (see for example, Schweitzer 2004). In many countries RE is confessional, and even in the Nordic countries there is no common understanding of RE as a school subject.

Swedish RE research has been described as lacking a body of research concerning teaching and learning processes in progress, for example classroom studies (for example, Kittelmann Flensner 2015), which also seems to be the case internationally (Osbeck 2012; Osbeck & Lied 2012). Researchers have been more interested in prerequisites for teaching and learning, for instance concerning the aim of the subject, a disputed question since the 1960s when the school subject was given its neutral, plural position. Pupils' existential perspectives, particularly the 'life questions' (*livsfrågor*) have been comparatively high on the agenda, as have textbook studies. Some evaluative studies do exist, of which several are related to the national evaluations commissioned by the Swedish National Agency for Education (for example, Jönsson & Liljefors Persson 2006). Moreover, it should be mentioned that there is a large body of RE literature that focuses on research on religious studies per se, and which is considered important for RE teaching and teachers (Osbeck & Lied 2012).

Unlike RE, science education is a highly internationalized field, constituted by a huge volume of work during the last 50 years, following the post-sputnik push for development of science education at all levels in the US, which spread across the world. This may be traced, for example, in the discussion of the notion of science literacy (Roberts 2007; Feinstein 2011), and articulations of the goals of science education. The dual focus on science for future scientists and science for all has been a major concern in this discussion. Traditionally, science education has been dominated by pupils' construals of conceptual and procedural knowledge, using individualised perspectives on learning. Later, the field has expanded to include, for example, issues of epistemology and affective factors (such as pupils' perceptions of science and scientists) (Roth 2010), as well as issues of culture, gender, and society, and these now constitute major parts of the field (Lederman & Abell 2014).

That the didactical fields vary when it comes to available research can also be shown through a couple of examples from the Swedish database Swepub. While in September 2017 the keywords 'science education' brought up 690 peer-reviewed contributions, a similar search for 'religious education' results in 107 contributions.

However how well developed, rich, and specific a research field might be, it has consequences for the research quality that can be achieved in certain areas. If the state of the art is vague, unclear, or non-existent, the focus of new research studies is of necessity less directed and specific; a new study has less to draw on, competing research patterns or scientific debate is absent, while the dependence on the subject discipline, on general educational research, and other didactical specialisations increases.

That the didactical research field varies in breadth and specificity is also shown in the essays in this volume, for instance in their references. In addition, the reference lists show a variety in degree of internationalization. Some subjects are more international and not very culturally dependent, whereas other areas such as language, literature, history, or political science are more bound to a specific country. At the same time, the possibility for international comparisons is an issue that could be considered more generally. To what extent are the patterns of findings referred to as 'previous research' comparable to one another and to findings from a Swedish classroom study? To what degree is it possible to compare findings from the studies that are cited? Is there a risk that the use of English as a common language hides the fact that we are researching different phenomena?

Unlike some claims concerning didactical research, the studies in this volume are constituted independently from curricular regulations (for example, Dahlin 1989; Scherp & Scherp 2002). Three of the essays do not refer to the curriculum at all, and the others only touch on it briefly. The relationship with curricula is briefly discussed by Kilhamn et al., who call for caution when comparing classroom processes, since the contexts and curriculum regulations vary greatly. The normative function of curricula can also be assumed to be harder to apply in international comparative classroom studies, where instead the teaching and learning processes can be understood as enacted curricula.

Knowledge claims

Naturally enough, the knowledge claims in the essays are closely related to the aims and research questions (See Table 10.2 above). This means that there is an interest in developing knowledge concerning several of the factors in didactic classroom teaching, since they can be understood as interrelated. In our overview, we have raised the question of whether there might be a potential for development in didactic classroom studies, when it comes to paying attention to the classroom conditions and structures, avoiding treating the classroom as simply a location where teaching takes place, and instead studying how it conditions interaction and in that sense impacts teaching and learning, as Hipkiss, for example, shows. A broader interest in conditions and structures may have the potential for important findings concerning teaching and learning processes in the classroom.

The aims and research questions of the essays result in knowledge claims that can be understood on a variety of levels. Several of the essays make on the one hand claims concerning the specific phenomena and classrooms studied, and also on the other hand broader knowledge claims concerning the phenomenon of which the case study is an example. In Kullberg and Skodras's essay, for example, there is a knowledge claim concerning what was possible for the pupils in the specific classrooms to see when using Muffles' set of examples in multiplication. However, there is also a knowledge claim concerning the systematic variations of examples in teaching as a powerful way to help pupils identify certain phenomena—a knowledge claim that has the contours of a law of a more generic character.

The double knowledge claims, directed at different levels, reflect the fact that classroom studies make validity claims outside the specific empirical context, despite their qualitative case-study format. This broader claim is not always spelled out explicitly, since the grounds for claiming a specific range of validity is not well established for these kinds of studies. In the example used here, we do not see it as problematic to generalise due to the solid theoretical grounding, with research patterns from other previous studies backing up the findings.

The possibility of making broader claims on the basis of didactic classroom studies is key in order to make progress in the field, and to contribute to it systematically and accumulatively. It is reasonable that research should give information that is relevant beyond the specific case studied. Therefore, important directions for didactic classroom studies can be as follows. First, identify when it is possible and reasonable to make broader knowledge claims and generalise from the studies and when not. Second, didactic classroom studies would benefit from systematic, explicit attention being paid to the range of validity for the claims made. And third, summarise general patterns in condensed conceptual terms, and so contribute to further theoretical development in the didactical arena by providing concepts for further analyses (see, for example, Ingerman & Booth).

Didactic classroom studies typically examine contextual 'wholes' of classroom events (Svensson 2016). This implies that controlled, statistical generalisation is not available for claims to a range of validity. As Svensson (2016, 283) notes, 'The openness and uncertainty of descriptions, due to the context-dependent nature and complexity of human and social phenomena, cannot be solved by denial of this character. The traditional escape from the problem to abstract predefined concepts, categories, and variables, and to statistical generalisations, is no solution, and only gives weaker and more uncertain evidence than case-based descriptions have the potential to give.' Thus, it is of limited value to attempt to define a definite range of validity for the knowledge claims in didactic classroom studies. Important aspects of the generalisation will depend on close contextual analysis of the original empirical situation, and comparisons with other situations.

It may be helpful to systematically discuss the potentials that are relevant for knowledge claims rather than the extent to which they are generalisable. Collier-Reed et al. (2009) identified three kinds of potential: collective, critical, and performative. Collective learning potential is the traditional value for contributing to the systematic and collective building of a body of research emanating from, in this case, the research direction. In critical potential the relevance comes from the identification and making visible of an aspect or phenomenon which in a potential range of situations is of importance or in some way problematic—here a single case can give a great deal of leverage. Performative potential, meanwhile, points to innovative relevance, generating new possibilities of didactical action in other classrooms. Several of the essays have strong characteristics of this kind of potential, in that they point to alternative sets of action in the classroom, facilitating change built on research. Here it is important to reflect on the conditions and consequences of realising such performative potential, as change also may take us in unexpected, and even unwanted, directions, especially concerning the contextually very sensitive classroom arena.

A prerequisite for all three kinds of potential regarding the relevance of knowledge claims is a close connection between the empirical case being studied and relevant previous research. Having such a body of previous research to draw on means the researcher must take responsibility for its further development. It is important to point out how certain findings and knowledge claims relate to the extant body of research, and to warn of the limits of the findings and what further research is indicated by the present findings and their limitations.

Research also leads to the discovery of unexpected things, of course. Therefore, it is of great importance to make room for these kinds of findings. To count on unforeseen findings is also a perspective close to the nature of classroom processes and teaching itself. Several of the essays in this volume show that it is the unpredictable utterances of pupils that make it possible for teachers to clarify patterns and statements that theoretically should have been possible for the pupils to understand, but nevertheless were not fully grasped. It is one task of didactic classroom studies to show the unpredictable nature of classroom interaction, and in that sense also the greatness in human interaction and teaching. It is therefore important to develop research designs that have the potential to capture and show this, and allow the possibility of unforeseen findings becoming central knowledge claims.

Didactical consequences

The essays' findings can be considered as important for practice—as having didactical consequences for teaching and learning, both specifically and regarding more general insights. However, to what extent and in what way the essays set out to directly contribute to practice and development varies. Indeed, at least four ways can be identified.

First, classroom studies can be designed to try out methods and approaches that one has reason to believe can be effective. Kullberg and Skodras's essay can be seen as an example of such a study, where the effects of a systematic variation in examples are tried out. Second, classroom studies can contribute to practice and teachers' awareness using approaches where teachers' interpretation of practice and development of practice are part of the research. The teachers increase their knowledge through observations, reflections, and discussions with other teachers and researchers, and the research insights generated in such a way may also be of value, thanks to the teachers' knowledge of these practices. The study presented by Kilhamn et al. is an example of such a design. Third, classroom studies may be designed with the purpose of studying what one has reason to believe to be good practice. It is not clear if there are such studies in these essays; it is not explicitly declared to be the case, but on the other hand, we know that it is quite usual that teachers that are known to be particularly skilled are asked to participate in classroom studies. Fourth, and this applies to the majority of the essays in this volume, classroom studies have an ambition to reveal mechanisms that can be understood as especially favourable—but also particularly unfavourable—when it comes to pupils' opportunities to attain their educational goals.

It is common in educational research to avoid being explicit about what consequences the research may have for practice. A variation of such a standpoint can be seen in Rocksén's essay, where she stresses that the essay should not be understood as an attempt to prescribe teaching practices, since 'the development and evaluation of best teaching practices is primarily a task for the teaching profession.' This is an important statement that reflects respect for teaching as a profession on its own terms, in line with the general tenor of didactics. However, one could also say that the researcher is likely to be the person best placed to interpret the findings and their meanings. From such a perspective, one could consider it to be the researcher's responsibility to interpret the findings in terms of didactical consequences. It is not unlikely that differences in opinions on research implications for practice concern how one interprets the task. To interpret and discuss possible consequences of reported findings is not necessarily to prescribe what constitutes best teaching practice.

It is not possible to summarise the didactical consequences that have been emphasized in the different essays in a specific way. On a more general level, the implications mainly concern the centrality of teachers' and pupils' collective directedness towards learning objects, as well as stressing the importance of clarifying learning objects, and of teachers' awareness and knowledge concerning phenomena that are known to be of importance in order to enhance pupils' learning. The implications also concern teachers' communicative skills, such as their ability to grasp pupils' perspectives and to respond in ways that support the development of pupils' understanding over time. Classroom activities are shown to be complicated activities where different actors and factors can thwart one another's effects, but also compensate for each other's shortcomings, as long as one is aware of aims, available resources, and how to use them. Classroom studies may enhance our collective awareness about these factors and thus have didactical consequences.

Research ethics

The importance of conducting research in an ethically responsible way cannot be stressed enough. Classroom research faces several distinct challenges, among others things due to the close relations that can develop between the researcher and the participants. That means that ethical concerns unavoidably permeate the whole research process. All acts have consequences for others and ethics is about being aware of the power that is linked to that fact, being sensitive to what happens, and responding in wise ways (Kang & Glassman 2010; Løgstrup 1997). A difficulty in classroom research concerns unequal relations of various kinds and levels, which is an argument for caution. At the same time can this ethically caring approach be hard to combine with the critical gaze that educational research demands. However, the close relationship between research and teaching practice means possibilities for development and learning from each other, if difficulties can be addressed and shared in a mutually open and trusting manner. For instance, principles for research ethics—informed consent; 'voice' and ownership; transparency and negotiation; confidentiality, anonymity and trust—have been suggested as tools for both parties to meet around, and in response to which to develop both research and teaching practices (Mockler 2013). The closeness in relationships that characterizes classroom research also increases the opportunities for trust to develop; this in itself can hinder the unfruitful 'teacher bashing' that educational research has sometimes entailed (Dudley-Marling 2005).

Another kind of ethical difficulty that classroom studies struggle with is the protection of individual integrity when working with video recordings. Similarly, the non-controlled, thematic focus of classroom studies constitutes an ethical challenge since there is the risk that it will unintentionally generate sensitive personal data if the pupils happen to make statements about racial or ethnic origins, political opinions, religious or philosophical beliefs, health or sex life. It is of great importance to be well aware of laws and regulations concerning research ethics, even if this can never replace being ethically reflective concerning events that are not regulated but nevertheless demand responsible treatment.

Dealing more fully with the issues of research ethics and classroom studies lies outside the scope of this essay. Here, a few brief comments will be made in relation to the essays in this volume. First, it must be considered a challenge that it has not yet become a routine in each and every study to explicitly pay attention to research ethics—to demonstrate how ethical responsibility has guided the project and has been safeguarded. Second, the issue of confidentiality goes far beyond what is usually reflected in these kinds of studies. It seems to be relevant to distinguish between the confidentiality that it is possible to uphold outside a current practice and inside this practice. Confidentiality inside the practice is almost impossible to achieve. It is likely that the whole school will know that a teacher who is being filmed with mounted cameras is participating in a research study. It is important to be frank about this, and to discuss the possible implications. Third, the possibility of placing non-participating pupils in non-filmed areas of the classroom is not as uncomplicated as it may seem at first glance, and as is sometimes suggested. If the research is informed by a learning perspective where meaning is collectively constructed, it is very hard to remove voices or let certain collective events go unnoticed. It is neither an authentic nor a responsible way to work. Fourth, a specific challenge concerns the sort of studies that work with interventions in practice. As Burner (2016), for example, has discussed, it raises questions about who owns the process and who owns the responsibility for its effects.

Research ethics issues have been more on the agenda lately, especially since the Swedish Act concerning the Ethical Review of Research Involving Humans (SFS 2003:460) was passed. It is reasonable to assume that this can be considered a first step for an intensified discussion to come. We consider such a development an important direction for didactic classroom studies.

Didactic classroom studies— constitution, conditions, continuation

The purpose of this essay has been to investigate the variations and commonalities across the contributions, the emerging potential research direction *didactic classroom studies*, and with such an investigation as a basis, to formulate suggestions for further developments for this research direction. The descriptions and discussions have showed some of the ways these studies are constituted and conditioned. It has also pointed to a potential continuation, in which the research direction becomes more established. This has been done through identifying challenges and discussing possible ways to address them. These further steps are summarised here.

As suggested in the introduction, the analyses have showed how didactic classroom studies largely combine focuses on teachers, pupils, and content. However, this can also bring a dilemma. Observing and showing that a multitude of aspects and factors are at stake, influencing teaching and learning processes, might mean a challenge in limiting the analyses and keeping to the *aim* of the study. At the same time, the analyses of the essays show how broader contextual research perspectives that focus on conditions and structures are not that usual. These observations raise an awareness of the potential importance of working with frameworks that can combine broad structural and contextual perspectives with a sharp focus on specific aspects of the teaching and learning processes of interest.

The importance of an acute awareness of available and possible *theoretical frameworks*, and their strengths and weaknesses for developing didactical knowledge further, is also shown. The framework is of great importance for a consistent and cumulative knowledge production, and a central question is to what field a study contributes by applying a certain framework. For the type of classroom studies exemplified here, another key issue is how the combination of theoretical and empirical perspectives is constituted in the analytical frameworks that are actually put to work. As argued throughout this essay, a focus on didactical consequences needs to be at the core of didactic studies. A theoretical framework must help in this work if it is to be fruitful.

The essays of the volume show a great variety in *empirical designs*. However, the issue of empirical design is not something to consider in isolation, but instead must be related to other aspects of the classroom study. The composition of different parts of a classroom study and the way these are represented in the final text constitutes a whole. The way of representing data, composing the report and writing it, creates in itself trustworthiness. Such trustworthiness presupposes an explicitness about the selection of data to be analysed as well as about the chosen excerpts referred to. The selection of data is made in several steps, which can be seen as crucial for and characteristic of classroom studies, which often work with plenty of data. How the selections are linked to the claims is of course central. Classroom studies give unique opportunities through their production of background information about pupils, teachers and the wider context. An important question concerns how one makes use of this information in a transparent, aware and critical sense so that the advantages of these studies and the information they deliver can be used optimally.

The exemplifications of *didactical research specialisations* and their traditions in this volume and this essay makes clear that didactics is not a single field but rather a multifaceted one. The specialisations have different histories, traditions and current conditions, which have consequences for what it is possible to do and achieve through classroom studies. For instance, the degree of internationalization of these fields and the volume of previous research vary. How research is conducted in powerful ways in fields where available relevant research is largely lacking is an important issue to consider further. At any rate, independently of how large the body of available research is, the issue of what is comparable and to what extent previous studies can be drawn upon—for example, those conducted in other countries where education may have rather different regulations—is a central one.

That the *knowledge claims* of the studies were not specifically concerned with the conditions and structures for teaching and learning processes in the classroom may be of interest in follow-up analyses of other classroom studies. Moreover, the essays show that the knowledge claims vary concerning how specific or general they are. It seems to be important for the development of the field and the knowledge production that the studies are constructed in such ways that it is possible to also draw wider conclusions from a study than those that only concern the single classroom. Clarity concerning what constitutes a case is central, as for the conditions for when broader claims can be made on solid foundations, which needs further attention. The relation between an empirical study, its theoretical framework, and available relevant previous studies should be evident, as well as the importance of encouraging and directing the further research that can be expected on the basis of the presented findings.

That *didactical consequences* of classrooms studies for practice can take different forms and be interpreted in different ways, is shown by the contributions in this volume. Arguing for the importance of didactical implications of classroom studies, stressing that a researcher's interpretations and discussions of the possible implications of reported findings for practice is a central knowledge contribution, is not the same as saying that he or she also should prescribe what constitutes best teaching practice. In this volume, didactical consequences of the presented classroom studies can on an overarching level be understood as enhancing collective awareness about factors that are known to be of importance in facilitating pupils' content learning but also about those known to constrain it. The different essays give different concrete examples of this. In this sense, this volume is not only a contribution to research, but also an offering to practice, to the everyday life of teachers and pupils— something which also can be said to characterize didactic classroom studies. To have the opportunity to contribute in such a process is a joy and a privilege for us as didactic classroom researchers.

The privilege of conducting classroom research must be managed with care. How to protect the integrity and interest of the participants while at the same time providing qualified and authentic knowledge about teaching and learning in the classroom is one of the most fundamental questions of *research ethics*. It is a crucial issue for further possibilities for conducting these sorts of studies. Therefore, it is of the utmost importance for the development of the field, for the direction of further research, that the researchers, in addition to their knowledge of the frameworks, develop ethical sensitivity in terms of identifying ethically critical aspects and finding ways to deal with them. The increasing demands to explicitly address and demonstrate how an ethical responsibility has guided the project and been safeguarded is therefore to be welcomed. To be skilled in research ethics is not only a necessity for members of ethical review boards. It is a part of what it means to be a qualified empirical researcher, a researcher in didactic classroom studies.

The ambition of this volume has been to bring didactic classroom studies together and in that sense to present research of a high standard, and to make the collective challenges visible. This essay, with its condensed presentations of the essays' variations and commonalities, and thus its presentation of challenges, has aimed at contributing to the way forward—a potential research direction—for the field. In this way, we hope that this is not the end, but rather a starting point for further developments of this project. The importance of further discussions and improvements to didactic classroom studies is an urgent issue—for research as well as practice.

References

Burner, T. (2016), 'Ethical dimensions when intervening in classroom research', *Problems of Education in the 21St Century*, 73, 18–26.

Collier-Reed, B. I., Å. Ingerman & A. Berglund (2009), 'Reflections on trustworthiness in phenomenographic research: Recognising purpose, context and change in the process of research', *Education as Change*, 13/2, 339–55.

Dahlin, B. (1989), *Religionen, själen och livets mening* (Gothenburg: Acta universitatis Gothoburgensis).

Dudley-Marling, C. (2005), 'Disrespecting Teachers: Troubling Developments in Reading Instruction', *English Education*, 37/4, 272–9.

Englund, T. & G. Svingby (1986), Didaktik och läroplansteori', in F. Marton (ed.), *Fackdidaktik* (Lund: Studentlitteratur).

Feinstein, N. (2011), 'Salvaging science literacy', *Science Education*, 95/1, 168–85.

Freeman, S., S. L. Eddy, M. McDonough, M. K. Smith, N. Okoroafor, H. Jord & M. P. Wenderoth (2014), 'Active learning increases student performance in science, engineering, and mathematics', *Proceedings of the National Academy of Sciences*, 111/23, 8410–15.

Hattie, J. (2009), *Visible learning: A synthesis of over 800 meta-analyses relating to achievement* (London: Routledge).

Hopmann, S. (2007), 'Restrained Teaching: The common core of Didaktik', *European Educational Research Journal*, 6/2, 109–24.

Hudson, B. (2007), 'Comparing Different Traditions of Teaching and Learning: What Can We Learn about Teaching and Learning?' *European Educational Research Journal*, 6/2, 135–46.

Ingerman, Å. & P. O. Wickman (2015), 'Towards a teachers' professional discipline: Shared responsibility for didactic models in research and practice', in P. Burnard, B.-M. Apelgren & N. Cabaroglu (eds.), *Transformative Teacher Research: Theory and Practice for the C21st* (Rotterdam: Sense).

Jönsson, R. & B. Liljefors Persson (2006), *Religionskunskap i årskurs 9-Rapport från den nationella utvärderingen av grundskolan 2003 (NU03)-Samhällsorienterande ämnen* (Malmö: Malmö Högskola).

Kang, M. J. & M. Glassman (2010), 'Moral Action as Social Capital, Moral Thought as Cultural Capital', *Journal of Moral Education*, 39/1, 21–36.

Kittelmann Flensner, K. (2015), *Religious education in contemporary pluralistic Sweden* (Gothenburg: Göteborgs universitet).

Klette, K. (2007), 'Trends in Research on Teaching and Learning in Schools: Didactics Meets Classroom Studies', *European Educational Research Journal*, 6/2, 147–60.

Larsson, S. (2009) 'A pluralist view of generalization in qualitative research', *International Journal of Research & Method in Education*, 32/1, 25–38.

Lederman, N. G. & S. K. Abell (2014) (eds.), *Handbook of research on science education*, ii (New York: Routledge).

Lindmark, T. (2013), *Samhällskunskapslärares ämneskonceptioner* (Umeå: Umeå Universitet).

Løgstrup, K. E. (1997), *The Ethical Demand* (Notre Dame: University of Notre Dame Press).

Mockler, N. (2014), 'When "research ethics" become "everyday ethics": The intersection of inquiry and practice in practitioner research', *Educational Action Research*, 22/2, 146–58.

Öhman, J. (2014), 'Om didaktikens möjligheter: Ett pragmatiskt perspektiv', *Utbildning & Demokrati*, 23/3, 33–52.

Osbeck, C. (2011), 'Religionsdidaktik som kunskaps- och forskningsfält', in M. Löfstedt (ed.), *Religionsdidaktik: Mångfald, livsfrågor och etik* (Lund: Studentlitteratur).

Osbeck, C. & S. Lied (2012), *Religionsdidaktisk arbeid pågår! Religionsdidaktikk i Hamar og Karlstad* (Vallset: Oplandske Bokforlag).

Roberts, D. A. (2007), 'Scientific literacy/science literacy', in S.K. Abell & N.G. Lederman (eds.), *Handbook of research on science education*, i (Mahwah, NJ: Lawrence Erlbaum Associates).

Roth, W.-M. (2010) (ed.), *Re/structuring science education: Reuniting sociological and psychological perspectives* (New York: Springer).

Sahlström, F. (2008), *Från lärare till elever, från undervisning till lärande: Utvecklingslinjer i svensk, nordisk och internationell klassrumsforskning* (Stockholm: Vetenskapsrådet).

Scherp, H.-Å. & G.-B. Scherp (2002), *Elevers lärmiljö: Lärares undervisning och elevers lärande* (Karlstad: Karlstads universitet).

Svensson, L. (2016), 'Towards an integration of research on teaching and learning', *Scandinavian Journal of Educational Research*, 60/3, 272–85.

Abstract

Recent developments in video technology and supporting method-ological designs have boosted the way for a new generation of class-room studies and today both large scale classroom studies together with targeted and more subject specific studies have contributed to a renewed interest in classrooms designs as a way to gain insights into teaching and learning processes. Today classroom studies serve as the meeting ground for understanding teaching and learning processes capturing different aspects of teaching and learning such as interaction patterns, teachers use of scaffolding techniques and student support, subject specificity such as how the teachers represent content, quality of explanations and tasks, and supporting climate. In this commentary essay I summarize recent developments in classroom studies in terms of technologies, research design and analytical frameworks and relate these developments to the essays in present in this volume. A key argument is how video recordings nurture a new generation of didactical classroom studies which enables us to systematically investigate key features of classroom teaching and learning across grades, content areas, environments and groups of students.

CHAPTER 11

A new generation of classroom studies

Kirsti Klette

Classroom observation studies used as a lens to understand the features of teaching and learning processes are part of a long tradition, whether internationally or in the Nordic countries. Starting in the late 1960s (see, for example, Jackson 1968; Flanders 1970; Brophy & Good 1974; Callewaert & Nilsson 1974; Borgnakke 1979), they have been seen as a more authentic (Nielsen 1985) and reliable way of understanding school and classroom learning. Since the early phase in the late 1960s, classroom research has been established to be a methodological approach that covers the full range of aspects that are central to classroom learning, such as communication processes and interaction patterns (Bellack et al. 1966; Sinclair & Coulthard 1992; Sahlström 1999; Cazden 2001; Andersson-Bakken & Klette 2015), functional classroom activities and instructional repertoires (Brophy & Good 1974; Doyle 1975; Lindblad & Sahlström 1999; Klette 2004 & 2015), and students' role and identities (Nielsen 1988; Lyng 2004; Bakken & Borg 2008; Öhrn 2012)—and, since the late 1990s, subject-specific repertoires and practices (Nystrand 1997; Boaler 1997; Mortimore & Scott 2003; Ødegaard & Klette 2012; Berge & Ingerman 2016). All the approaches listed, and especially the latter (e.g. subject specific approaches), correspond to the *didactic classroom studies* of the present volume. Today, classroom research designs serves as the methodological grounds for at least three distinct research traditions, which, as Erickson (2006) argues, are (*i*) discourse or interaction analyses, which centre on micro-analyses of language and communication; (*ii*) process or product approaches, which concentrate on functional classroom interaction and activities; and (*iii*) teachers' professional knowledge or pedagogical content knowledge, in which the main interests are interaction, the activities linked to the subject matter, and meaning-making linked to content. This concluding essay is especially concerned with the latter position, the use of subject-specific investigations of Swedish primary and secondary school classrooms and beyond.

While video recordings were used in some of early classroom studies (see Sherin 2004), videos were never part of a common toolbox, and for a long time (with the exception of the TIMSS Video Study), audio, together with field notes, classroom diaries, and/or predefined observation schemes, was the basic methodological instrument when gathering *in situ* classroom data. Recent developments in video technology, with small, miniaturised, discrete cameras that support software tools for analysis, together with improvements in methodologies and an integrated methodological design, however, have enabled the combination of in-depth data from classrooms with large-scale data sets, such as student questionnaires and achievement scores (Fischer & Neumann 2012; Klette 2015). Nested, integrated designs and new technologies have paved the way for a new wave of classroom studies along the lines of large-scale classroom studies— hence the Measuring Effectiveness in Teaching (MET) study (MET project 2012), the OECD TALIS Video Study (Decristan et al. 2015; OECD 2016), and the Linking Instruction and Achievement study (Klette et al. 2017). Targeted, subject-specific studies (see for example, Grossman et al. 2013; Lipowsky et al. 2009) have further fuelled interest in classroom research as a way of understanding teaching and learning processes. The contributions to the present volume feed into this with their spectrum of classroom data (videos, field notes, interviews, textual and visual resources, tasks, and, in some cases, achievement scores) used to gauge the multiple meanings of institutional classroom teaching and learning.

Alongside this move in research design, there is plainly considerable consensus on the analytical approaches and frameworks for analysing teaching and learning processes, with an emphasis on teaching and learning as normative and institutional activities that occur at the intersection between the content involved and accompanying students' or teachers' interactions. Thus, frameworks for analysing the dimensions of teaching and learning need to be sensitive to a range of dimensions such as cognitive demands and challenges, pupils' or students' and teachers' communication patterns, and clarity of instruction. These also include teachers' use of instructional activities and scaffolding techniques, and a classroom climate that creates an environment of trust and is open to students' perspectives and needs. If we examine the various frameworks (see, for example, Seidel & Shavelson 2007; Lipowsky et al. 2009; Kane & Staiger 2012; Klette 2015; Nilsen & Gustafsson 2016), five dimensions stand out as especially critical in understanding the key features of classroom teaching and learning: instructional clarity, cognitive demand and activation, discourse features, a supportive climate, and activity structure.

These five dimensions of classroom processes, as distinct analytical approaches —for features of classroom discourse and meaning-making, see, for example, Mortimore and Scott (2003)—or as a coherent framework operationalised at the level of an observation manual—the CLASS observation manual (Pianta et al. 2008), say, or the Framework For Teaching manual (Danielsson 2011)—are often understood as the common analytical ground in today's studies of classroom teaching and learning. Despite their shared basis, however, analytical frameworks vary in how targeted and subject-specific they are, their units of analysis, how fine-grained they are, and whether their primary focus is the teachers' or the students' actions. They further differ in their theoretical and conceptual grounding of teaching and learning and their procedures for analysis. The current volume feeds into this discussion, representing both generic and subject-specific classroom studies and using analytical framings that relate to the entire spectrum listed.

In this essay, I thus comment on the research ambition of the present volume by summarising developments in classroom research designs, especially how recent developments in video design have contributed to renewing and thus vitalising this area of research, including the contributions represented in this volume. I then discuss how the present essays relate to the spectrum of analytical dimensions listed above, or, in other words, how empirical enquiries into subject specificity and unit of analysis turn on conceptions of learning and theoretical approaches.

A new generation of video studies

Scholars agree that video analysis has multiple and significant advantages in developing our understanding of teaching and learning processes (Hiebert 2003; Janík & Seidel 2009; Fischer & Neumann 2012). Clarke and colleagues argue that video recordings '…provide a much richer portrayal of classroom practices than would be possible from any single analysis' (2006, 6). Drawing on video documentations from science classrooms, Fischer and Neumann (2012) claim that video studies are especially interesting for probing quality in teaching, because such studies can capture pupils' and teachers' behaviours in one package.

Video can reveal classroom practices more clearly, facilitate the discovery of new alternatives, and stimulate discussions about the pedagogical choices in each classroom, so deepening educators' understandings of teaching. Video also facilitates the study of complex processes and the integration of qualitative and quantitative analyses. It enables coding from multiple perspectives, and new ways of communicating findings and results. Furthermore, video data can be stored in a form that allows subsequent and novel analyses, fruitful data combinations, and collaborative analyses. Video studies have proved to be valuable tools for investigating instruction both at the level of individual teachers and in larger studies involving samples of teachers from a country or region, as well as between countries or regions. Video analysis allows the identification of subject-specific patterns of instruction and cultural scripts (Stigler & Hiebert 1999).

The growing interest in video can be traced to the rapid development of technology that allows easy storage and online streaming. Video equipment is now miniaturised, portable, remote controlled, and operated by researchers or teachers themselves, thus making such studies feasible and less intrusive on everyday life in the classroom. New technologies have been matched by major developments in coding and processing, software for video data analysis (for example, Studio Code, Interact, Observer XT), and systems and infrastructure that facilitate the sharing of data and targeted and integrative analyses.

One of the benefits of video capture or video data from classrooms is that it enables analyses that combine the subject-specific and generic features of teaching and learning. Video data also provide opportunities to combine different analytical and theoretical approaches to the same data set. Berge and Ingerman (2016), for example, combine variation theory and conversation analysis to understand the features of science teaching and learning among undergraduates. Likewise, Ødegaard & Klette (2012) combine process–product approaches in teaching and learning (instructional format and activity structures) with subject-specific dimensions (conceptual language used, quality of explanations, etc.) when analysing science teaching in Norwegian secondary school classrooms. In the present volume, Rocksén uses different timescales and units of analysis to discuss how pupils' science-related talk develops over time and across sequences of lessons, arguing that several measuring points and a variety of timescales are relevant to understanding how pupils learn.

Recent reviews of coding protocols and frameworks for analysing classroom data (Klette & Blikstad-Balas 2018; Bell et al. in press) have emphasized how analytical frameworks and coding procedures might differ in analytical focus and granularity, in generic versus subject-specific frameworks, and in views and conceptualizations of teaching and learning. Methodological variation needs to be considered too. This refers to how different 'observation systems' (Bell et al. in press) differ in their time segments for coding, explicitness of rubrics and scales for analyses and scoring, and required training and certification. I use these aspects here to evaluate the research goal of the present volume by comparing empirical outcomes with the theoretical and methodological approaches employed.

Analytical frameworks

Developments in video design, then, have paved the way for a renewed interest in shared analytical frameworks and observation schemes when analysing the features of teaching. Earlier observation schemes and protocols were primarily mapping surface structure of teaching and learning (Siedel & Prenzel 2006) and/or trivial aspects of classroom teaching and learning (Ko & Simmons 2010; Scheerens 2014). More recent protocols and frameworks are more targeted, and capture either generic (Pianta et al. 2008; Danielsson 2011) or more subject-specific (Hill et al. 2008; Grossman et al. 2013) aspects of teaching and learning. They have also been thoroughly validated in large-scale empirical studies (Archer et al. 2012), and their consistency is strengthened by the elaboration of procedures for scoring and coding that meet specific certification and training requirements. The different analytical frameworks or protocols might also vary in terms of the aforementioned factors—views on teaching and learning, units of analysis, and teacher and/or pupil/student focus.

The essays in the present volume illustrate different ways of handling these challenges, but none of them use a standard observation protocol or framework. On the contrary, each of the studies uses its own analytical and conceptual framework, consistent with the existing analytical approaches in its respective theoretical tradition (variation theory, interaction analysis, semiotic analysis, etc.), or it draws on existing practices, consistent with prior research conducted in its respective area (for example, Lilja & Claesson, Kilhamn et al.). Below, I comment on the dimensions of the analyses used in the current volume, and argue how the various frameworks and approaches might produce new and significant, but also different and possibly inconsistent findings, guided in my exercise by the following factors: views on teaching and learning, units of analysis, analysing teachers' actions versus pupils' actions, generic versus subject-specific analyses, and individual analyses versus joint analyses.

Views on teaching and learning

The essays presented in this volume use a broad spectrum of theories of learning when investigating classroom teaching and learning, spanning everything from socio-cultural and dialogic approaches to learning, semiotic analysis, and variation theory, to more subject-specific theories required when learning mathematics, for example, as mathematical knowledge for teaching (MKT) (see Ball et al. 2008).

Variation theories and semiotic analyses feature in four out of the nine essays. Kullberg and Skodras, like Ingerman and Booth, use variation theories in their analytical approach, whereas Sofkova Hashemi and Hipkiss both draw on social semiotic analyses. However, while drawing on the same theoretical grounding and framework, the analyses as practices in the same tradition differ radically in scale and preferred analytical concepts. Ingerman and Booth, for example, analyse meaning-making in shared discussions of a joint problem in physics education, showing how groups of students vary in the way they deal with the problem at hand. The authors argue that a more fruitful discussion might occur if the groups were composed more carefully, or if they had a more careful combination of students and tasks that had the appropriate relevance and levels of difficulty. Thus, the authors use variations in content-related communication and discussion as their analytical tools. Kullberg and Skodras also drawing on variation theory, focus on teachers' selection and use of examples in middle-school mathematics classrooms to discuss how the different ways of using and displaying examples provide substantially different learning experiences for the pupils. The authors state that the teachers' careful selection, use and presentation of examples, supported by a clear conceptual focus, are decisive for the pupils' opportunities to experience the content in question. The authors' analytical focus is the selection of examples and supporting visual models and accompanying discussions as representations for possible pathways of content learning in mathematics. Drawing on the same theoretical framework (for example, variation theory), Ingerman and Booth see difficulty level and group composition as constraints to possible learning, whereas Kullberg and Skodras highlight the ways of representing content, as illustrated by the teachers' use of examples as critical for learning. Thus, the authors do not use joint concepts in their empirical inquiries, but rather use variation design (systematic comparison of similar cases and units) as a key strategy. Contrary to many other theoretical traditions that built their analysis around some key concepts or dimensions and categories to be studied (such as types of questions, use of uptake and responses, and turn-taking in interaction analyses), variation theories allow a systematic comparison between two or more similar cases. However, the unit of analysis and key concepts pursued differ substantially.

Two essays, Sofkova Hashemi and Hipkiss, use semiotic theoretical perspectives to underscore an analogous argument. Although drawing on related theoretical frames and views of learning, they use different key categories and concepts in their analyses. Sofkova Hashemi categorises semiotic resources and tools in terms of type and the relative distribution of time spent on writing, speaking, listening, and so on seen in the different classrooms, and qualifies these activities according to multidimensional criteria. Hipkiss, who also draws on semiotic analyses, uses concepts and categories such as monologues, dialogic exchanges and participatory exchanges, together with spatial features, to analyse interpersonal interaction and differential spatial affordances in the classroom. As such, Hipkiss' categories and lenses for analysing her data share more similarities with the concepts used in the essays in which socio-cultural theories (Osbeck) and theories of communication (Rocksén) are the preferred theoretical perspective. The analyses in Osbeck's and Rocksén's essays use conceptual categories, such as open-ended and closed questions, inferential utterances, interpretative utterances (Osbeck), and dialogues versus monologues and teacher-directed dialogues (Rocksén)—all concepts that are not far from those deployed by Hipkiss, drawing on semiotic analyses.

The point to be made here is twofold. First, similar studies with similar theoretical perspectives do not necessarily share a conceptual framework, operationalisation, or reported levels of analysis. Variation theory and social semiotics representing two distinct theoretical traditions offer a set of approaches (variation theory) or a set of concepts/conceptual categorisations that both provide a large degree of freedom when researchers conduct their analysis. Thus, categories at the empirical level may differ substantially between researchers belonging to the similar traditions and pursuing similar theoretical goals.

Second, because of the discrepancies between the theoretical and empirical definitions of categories in the essays, it is tempting to follow the suggestion by Thomas (2007) and Hammersley (2012) that we should look closer at the 'language games' played when referring to theoretical frameworks or theorising. A conceptual level that is closer to the actual analytical work may provide the template for exploring how different categories delineate similar or different phenomena and how they process outcomes, as well as the extent to which these are consistent with higher-order theoretical concepts. This endeavour is only partly done in the present volume. Such an approach that is close to the data and analyses might contribute to strengthening cross-case analyses and syntheses when conducting didactic classroom studies; therefore, it also contributes to more systematic and programmatic research to understand the different theoretical traditions and conceptualisations that teaching and learning might add to our understanding of the formal processes in classroom learning, as will be seen when considering individual analyses versus joint analyses below.

Units of analysis

The essays differ in granularity and unit of analysis, thus putting conceptual demands on both researchers and readers. While a holistic research design (Day et al. 2010b) might have the goal of grasping the multidimensional and complex character of classroom learning, it often suffers from grasping surface aspects (Seidel & Prenzel 2006) of classroom teaching and learning, thus tending to reproduce what we already know (Hammersley 2008). Being explicit about the unit of analysis is one way to reduce these complexities. The unit of analysis could be a single pupil or student, a group of pupils or the entire class, or the teacher or teachers. However, it could also be a single task or a problem-solving phase, or how different series and time segments might produce different conditions for learning, such as the example used by Rocksén in this volume. Preferences connected to the unit of analysis will, however, have strong implications on the empirical focus, the selection of the data required and the presentation of the data.

In the present volume, the unit of analysis focuses on an adjusted version of the didactic triad—teachers' and students' activities, communication and meaning-making linked to a specific content. Kullberg and Skodras, Osbeck, and to an extent Lilja and Claesson are explicit about using teachers as their basic unit of analysis: they draw on data from mathematics or religious education classrooms, as well as look across different classrooms (Lilja & Claesson). Kullberg and Skodras, as well as Osbeck, are explicit about teachers' use of examples as their basic unit of analysis. They differ in their ambition of scale, however. Kullberg and Skodras link teacher strategies to targeted analyses of variations in teachers' use of examples (and supporting scaffolding strategies), and they show how teaching strategies (use of examples in mathematics) and aspects of the content together shed light on pupils' opportunities to learn. Osbeck, on the other hand, discusses teachers' orchestration of classroom communication by using teachers' and pupils' joint classroom talk as the pitch of her analysis, operating on the level of the community or group and on a more aggregated level. Lilja and Claesson, as a third example, investigate teachers' ability to move between instructional strategies as a focal unit for analysing teachers' capacity to maintain discipline in the classroom. However, the way they have conceptualised order and discipline, together with the level of detail, tends to produce rather generic knowledge. A more systematic, targeted focus and unit of analysis might have produced stronger evidence for the claims they make.

Teachers' actions, students' actions, or both?

Three of the essays in this volume explicitly focus on students' or pupils' actions (Sofkova Hashemi, Ingerman & Booth, Hipkiss), one essay focuses on teachers' actions only (Kullberg & Skodras) and the five other essays focus on both pupils' and teachers' actions. As teachers or pupils seldom engage in stand-alone activities but take part in a chain of interactions and interlinked relationships and activities, scholars conducting classroom research need to situate their analyses in a larger landscape and segments of actions and meaning. To analyse learning from pupils' perspective, one most often needs to include the teacher's activities and utterances, as well as those of the other pupils, so that the processes can be understood. Social semiotic analyses, as performed in this volume (Sofkova Hashemi, Hipkiss), represent a distinct approach for keeping track of pupils' perspectives, I would argue, even when teachers' actions are included in the analyses. Their conceptual framing and categories seem to work well when keeping track of the pupils and keeping them in focus. As content cannot be analysed alone, it moves at the intersection between the three key partners—the pupils, the teachers, and the content involved—several of the essays in this volume include the focal content in their analyses. There is, however, as I have argued elsewhere (Klette 2007), a danger for privileging interaction at the cost of in-depth analyses of the content, thus reducing content learning to interaction and communication patterns.

Generic versus subject-specific

Most of the essays argue for a subject-specific approach using the didactic triad as a baseline for their study. Some essays work at the intersection of content and teacher actions, whereas others are interested in how pupils might engage with content as their primary interest. Only one of the essays uses what might be called a subject-specific framework when analysing the focal content: this is Kilhamn et al.'s essay, which draws on mathematical knowledge for teaching, developed by Ball and colleagues (Ball et al. 2008). Whilst not representing subject-specific approaches, variation theory, and social semiotics, three essays in this volume (Osbeck, Ingerman & Booth, Sofkova Hashemi), however, come close to subject– and content-specific analyses, as they draw on a theoretical grounding and a conceptual toolbox that nurture content-related analyses.

These frameworks (variation theory, theory of semiotics) are not subject specific; they are generic and could be applied to all types of content areas. In these cases, the conceptual specificity, together with the granularity, however, produce targeted and thus subject-relevant analyses.

Internationally, several scholars argue for the need for subject specificity when analysing the qualities of classroom teaching and learning. Hill and Grossman (2013) argue that if classroom analyses were to achieve the goal of supporting teachers in improving their teaching, these frameworks must be subject specific and involve content expertise. This will enable teachers to provide information that is relevant for their situation-specific teaching objectives, regardless of whether these are student participation, algebra learning, or group problem-solving. Blömeke et al. (2015) show how a combination of generic factors and subject-specific factors (in their case, mathematics) is required for producing valid knowledge about how different teaching factors contribute to student learning. Klette et al. (2017) use a specific analytical framework (targeted for English-language arts education) to capture both subject-specific and generic goals when analysing the features of Norwegian-language arts and mathematics instruction. One goal in the Klette et al. (2017) study is to analyse how and to what extent subject-specific frameworks might work across different content areas.

Individual versus programmatic analyses

As already mentioned, none of the essays in the present volume systematically develop or draw on the same analytical framework. A more programmatic approach might be required to produce sustainable and robust findings when trying to understand the critical components in classroom teaching and learning. The relational dynamics between classroom teaching and learning are not well understood, and integrated frameworks 'that link instructional activities and procedures (the how) with thematic patterns (the what) and mode of interactions (the who)' (Klette 2007, 148) are needed. One promising way to go forward in the field of didactic classroom studies is to use a more programmatic approach in which researchers with a shared tradition, view of teaching, and learning or subject expertise area address a set of questions and analytical approaches systematically and over time.

Like Grossman and Macdonald (2008), I would argue that to advance in the area of didactic classroom studies our next step should be to move beyond single case studies towards more programmatic research that addresses a set of critical questions over time and in different settings and subject areas. To this end, we need integrative and synthesising manoeuvres that can summarise how different frameworks and conceptual enquiries might produce patterns and possible findings, as well as the use of these to investigate how the range of such findings might vary across contexts, subjects, groups of students, classrooms, and school environments. Likewise, we need common analytical frameworks and instruments that can discern the possible impacts and implications of these across sites and classroom settings. Using variation design to systematically investigate the role of group discussions and the role of examples for learning across school years, subject areas and groups of students could be one way to pursue such a goal. Applying different analytical frameworks and conceptual framings in examining the features and challenges in a specific subject area, such as algebra learning, could be another way. A third approach could be using the same analytical framework in different topics and subjects to push our understanding of the potential power of a specific feature of classroom learning, such as classroom discussion. Reviews of research on the impact of class-room discourses, for example, point to mixed and rather inconsistent findings (Howe & Abedin 2013) about when classroom discourses are productive or are not of critical interest.

A future for content-focused classroom studies

The present volume presents a solid, empirically grounded attempt to understand the complexities of classroom teaching. A special value is how the different contributions take on the challenge of setting out analysis that moves at the intersection of teachers, students, and the content involved. Unlike similar studies, this volume seriously considers the role of content and how the content in classroom learning might produce rather different contexts for learning. One of its strengths, of course, is the spectrum of theoretical perspectives applied by the authors.

Classrooms and students vary, and subject-specific and targeted analyses are required to make this research useful for teachers. We need information about how the features of classroom teaching and learning might work for different types of students, group compositions, and types of learning goals, regardless of whether they are cognitive, social, motivational, and so on. For this, multiple frameworks and instruments are required. Thus, the next phase for didactic classroom studies might be what I have described as a programmatic approach to classroom studies, systematically investigating the key features of classroom teaching and learning across years, content areas, environments, and groups of students.

References

Andersson-Bakken, E. & K. Klette (2015), 'Teachers' Use of Questions and Responses to Students' Contributions During Whole Class Discussions: Comparing Language Arts and Science Classrooms', in K. Klette, O. K. Bergem & A. Roe (eds.), *Teaching and Learning in Lower Secondary Schools in the Era of PISA and TIMSS* (Cham: Springer).

Archer, J., S. Cantrell, S. L. Holtzman, J. N. Joe, C. M. Tocci & J. Wood (2012), *Better Feedback for Better Teaching: A Practical Guide to Improving Classroom Observations* (San Francisco: Jossey-Bass) http://k12education.gatesfoundation. org/teachersupports/teacher-development/measuring effective-teaching/.

Bakken, A., E. Borg, K. Hegna & E. Backe-Hansen (2008), *Er det skolens skyld? En kunnskapsoversikt om skolens bidrag til kjønnsforskjeller i skoleprestasjoner* (Oslo: Norsk institutt for forskning om oppvekst, velferd og aldring).

Ball, D. L., M. H. Thames & G.C. Phelps (2008), 'Content Knowledge for Teaching: What Makes it Special?' *Journal of Teacher Education*, 59/5, 389–407.

Bell, C., K. Klette, M. Dobbelaer, A. Visscher A. (2018), 'Qualities of classroom observation systems *School Effectiveness and School Improvement*, 1–27. An International Journal of Research, Policy and Practice (London: Routledge)

Bellack, A. A., H. M. Kliebard, R. T. Hyman & F. L. Smith (1966), *The Language of the Classroom* (USOE Cooperative Research Project, 2023; New York: Teachers College Press, Columbia University).

Berge, M. & Å. Ingerman (2016), 'Multiple theoretical lenses as an analytical strategy in researching group discussions', *Research in Science & Technological Education*, 35/1, 42–57.

Bjerrum-Nielsen, H. (1985), 'Pedagogiske hverdagsbeskrivelser: Et forsømt område i pædagogisk forskning', *Tidsskrift for Nordisk Forening for Pedagogisk Forskning*, 2, 27–42.

—— (1988), Jenter på østkanten: Når kvinneligheten blir synlig i klasserommet', in H. B. Nielsen (ed.), *Jenteliv og likestillingslære: Kjønnsroller og likestillingsarbeid blant ungdom* (Oslo: Cappelen).

Blömeke, S., J.-E. Gustafsson & R. J. Shavelson (2015), 'Beyond dichotomies: Competence viewed as a continuum', *Zeitschrift für Psychologie*, 3–13.

Boaler, J. (1997), *Experiencing school mathematics: Traditional and reform approaches to teaching and their impact on student learning* (Buckingham: Open University Press).

Borgnakke, K. (1979) (ed.), Project Skolesprog: Skoledage 1–2 (Copenhagen: GMT & Unge Pædagoger).

Brophy, J. & T. Good (1974), 'Classroom research: Some suggestions for the future', in eid., *Teacher–student relationships: Causes and consequences* (New York: Holt, Rinehart & Winston).

Callewaert, S. & B. A. Nilsson (1974), *Samhället, skolan och skolans inre arbete* (Lund: Lunds bok och tidskrift).

Cazden, C. (2001), *Classroom discourse: The language of teaching and learning* (Portsmouth: Heinemann).

Clarke, D., C. Keitel & Y. Shimizu (2006) (eds.), *Mathematics Classrooms in Twelve Countries: The Insider's Perspective* (Rotterdam: Sense).

Danielson, C. (2011), *The Framework for Teaching: Evaluation Instrument* (Moorabbin, VIC: Hawker Brownlow Education).

Day, C. & Q. Gu (2010) *The New Lives of Teachers* (London: Routledge).

—— —— —— D. Hopkins, Q. Gu, E. Brown & E. Ahtaridou (2010), *School Leadership and Student Outcomes: Building and Sustaining Success* (Maidenhead: Open University Press).

Decristan, J., E. Klieme, M. Kunter, J. Hochweber, G. Buttner, B. Fauth, A. L. Hondrich, S. Rieser, S. Hertel & I. Hardy (2015), 'Embedded Formative Assessment and Classroom Process Quality: How Do They Interact in Promoting Science Understanding?' *American Educational Research Journal*, 52/6, 1133–59.

Doyle, W. (1975), 'Paradigms in Teacher Effectiveness Research', paper presented at the Annual Meeting of the American Educational Research Association, Washington, DC, April.

Erickson, F. (2006), 'Definitions and Analyses from Videotapes: Some research procedures and their rationales', in J. Green, G. Camilli & P. B. Elmore (eds.),

Handbook of Complementary Methods in Education Research (American Educational Research Association (AERA) Lawrence Erlbaum).

Fischer H. & K. Neumann (2012), 'Video analysis as a tool for understanding science instruction', in D. Jorde & J. Dillan (eds.), *The World of Science Education* (Rotterdam: Sense).

Flanders, N. (1970), *Analyzing Teaching Behavior* (Massachusetts: Addison Wesley).

Grossman P. & M. McDonald (2008), 'Back to the Future: Directions for Research in Teaching and Teacher Education', *American Educational Research Journal*, 45/1, 184–205.

Grossman, P., S. Loeb, J. Cohen & J. Wyckoff (2013), 'Measure for Measure: The relationship between measures of instructional practice in middle school English language arts and teachers' value added scores', *American Journal of Education*, 119, 445–70.

Hammersley, M. (2008), *Questioning Qualitative Research: Critical Essays* (London: SAGE).

—— (2012), 'Troubling theory in case study research', *Higher Education Research & Development*, 31/3, 393–405.

Hiebert, J. & D. A. Grouws (2007), 'The effects of classroom mathematics teaching on students' learning', in F. K. Lester (ed.), *Second handbook of research on mathematics teaching and learning* (Charlotte, NC: Information Age Pub).

Hill, H. C., M. Blunk, C. Charalambous, J. Lewis, G. C. Phelps, L. Sleep & D. L. Ball (2008), 'Mathematical Knowledge for Teaching and the Mathematical Quality of Instruction: An exploratory study', *Cognition & Instruction*, 26, 430–511.

—— & P. Grossman (2013), 'Learning from Teacher Observations: Challenges and Opportunities Posed by New Teacher Evaluation Systems', *Harvard Educational Review*, 83/2, 371–84.

Howe, C. & M. Abedin (2013), 'Classroom dialogue: A systematic review across four decades of research', *Cambridge Journal of Education*, 43/3, 325–56.

Jackson, P. W. (1968), *Life in the classroom* (New York: Holt, Rinehart & Wilson).

Janík T. & T. Seidel (2009) (eds.), *The Power of Video Studies in Investigating Teaching and Learning in the Classroom* (Münster: Waxmann).

Kane, T. J. & D. O. Staiger (2012), *Gathering feedback for teaching: Combining high-quality observations with student surveys and achievement gains* (Seattle: Bill & Melinda Gates Foundation).

Klette, K. (2004), 'Lærerstyrt kateterundervisning fremdeles dominerende? Aktivitets- og arbeidsformer i norske klasserom etter Reform 97', in K. Klette (ed.), *Fag og arbeidsmåter i endring?* (Oslo: Universitetsforlaget).

—— (2007), 'Trends in Research on teaching and Learning in Schools: Didactics meets Classroom studies', *European Educational Research Journal*, 6/2, 147–61.

—— (2009), 'Challenges in Strategies for Complexity Reduction in Video

Studies: Experiences from the PISA+ Study: A Video Study of Teaching and Learning in Norway', in T. Janik & T. Seidel (eds.), *The Power of Video Studies in Investigating Teaching and Learning in the Classroom* (Münster: Waxmann).

— — (2015), 'Introduction: Studying Interaction and Instructional Patterns in classrooms', in K. Klette, O. K. Bergem & A. Roe (eds.), *Teaching and Learning in Lower Secondary Schools in the Era of PISA and TIMSS* (Cham: Springer).

— — M. Blikstad-Balas & A. Roe (2017), 'Linking Instruction and Student Achievement', *Acta Didactica*, 11/3.

— — — — (2018), 'Coding Manuals as Lenses To Classroom Teaching: Measuring Teaching Qualities', *European Educational Research Journal*, 7/1, 129–46.

Ko, J. & P. Sammons (2010) *Effective Teaching: A review of research and evidence* (Reading: CfBT Education Trust).

Lindblad, S. & F. Sahlström (1999), 'Gamla mönster och nye gränser: Om ram-faktorer og klassrumsinteraktion', *Pedagogisk Forskning i Sverige*, 4/1, 93–111.

Lipowsky, F., Rakoczy, K., Pauli, C., Drollinger-Vetter, B., Klieme, E., & Reusser, K. (2009). Quality of geometry instruction and its short-term impact on students' understanding of the Pythagorean Theorem. *Learning and instruction*, 19/6, 527–537.

Lyng, S. T. (2004), Være eller lære? Om elevroller, identitet og læring i ungdomsskolen (Oslo: Universitetsforlaget).

Mehan, H. (1979), *Learning Lessons: Social Organization in the Classroom* (Cambridge MA: Harvard University Press).

Mortimore, E. & P. Scott (2003) (eds.), *Meaning Making in Secondary Science Classrooms* (Philadelphia: Open University Press).

Nilsen, T. & J. E. Gustafsson (2016) (eds.), *Teacher Quality, Instructional Quality and Student Outcomes* (Amsterdam: Springer).

Nystrand, M. (1997), *Opening Dialogue: Understanding the Dynamics of Language and Learning in the English Classroom* (New York: Teachers College Press).

Ødegaard, M. & K. Klette (2012), 'Teaching Activities and Language Use in Science Classrooms: Scales and Analytical Categories as Pillars for Possible interpretations', in J. Dillon & D. Jorde (eds.), *Science Education Research and Practice in Europe* (Rotterdam: Sense).

OECD (2016), *TALIS 2018: Video study and global video library on teaching practices* (Paris: OECD).

Öhrn, E. (2012), 'Urban Education and Segregation: The responses from young people', *European Educational Research Journal*, 11/1, 45–57.

Pianta, R. C., K. M. La Paro & B. K. Hamre (2008), *Classroom Assessment Scoring System Manual* (Charlottesville, VA: Teachstone).

Sahlström, F. (1999), *Up the Hill Backwards: On interactional Constraints and Affordances for Equity-Constitution in the Classroom of the Swedish Comprehensive School*, Uppsala Studies in Education 85 (Uppsala: Acta Universitatis Upsaliensis).

Scheerens, J. (2014) 'School, teaching, and system effectiveness: Some comments on three state-of-the-art reviews', *School Effectiveness & School Improvement*, 25/2, 282–90.

Seidel, T. & M. Prenzel (2006), 'Stability of teaching patterns in physics instruction: Findings from a video study', *Learning & Instruction*, 16, 228–40.

—— & Shavelson, R. (2007), 'Teaching Effectiveness Research in the Past Decade: The Role of Theory and Research Design in Disentangling Meta-Analysis Results', *Review of Educational Research*, 77/4, 454–99.

Sherin, M. G. (2004), 'New perspectives on the role of video in teacher education', in J. Brophy (ed.), *Using video in teacher education* (New York: Elsevier Science).

Sinclair, J. & M. Coulthard (1992), 'Towards an analysis of discourse', in M. Coulthard (ed.), *Advances in spoken discourse analysis* (London: Routledge).

Stigler, J. W. & J. Hiebert (1999), *The teaching gap: Best ideas from the world's teachers for improving education in the classroom* (New York: Free Press).

Thomas, G. (2007), *Education and theory: Strangers in paradigms* (Maidenhead: Open University Press).

About the authors

Shirley Booth, Professor Emerita, has followed a research interest in student learning and associated teaching in the mathematical, physical and engineering sciences. Phenomenography and the theoretical insights into learning that have emerged from its empirical studies have provided her main methodological framework.

Silwa Claesson, Professor Emerita in Education, has conducted hermeneutical and phenomenological studies – mainly with a focus on the relationship between pedagogical theories and teachers' everyday work in their classrooms.

Sylvana Sofkova Hashemi, PhD in Computational Linguistics and Associate Professor in Education [Utbildningsvetenskap]. Her recent research concerns studies in technology-enriched instruction and analysis of classroom practices in relation to literacies teaching and pedagogy, students' development of communicative skills, textual and multimodal competencies and reflective learning.

Anna Maria Hipkiss, PhD in Swedish language and teaching, and is particularly interested in the affordances of classroom interaction which includes the teaching and learning that takes place in different 'rooms'.

Britt Holmberg, Master in Education, has a specific interest in how students solve subtraction problems, and taught in elementary school for many years before working with training of in-service teachers in mathematics and in teacher education.

Åke Ingerman, Professor in Science and Technology Education at University of Gothenburg has special research interests in Physics Education Research, meaning-making in groups and phenomenography and variation theory.

Cecilia Kilhamn, Senior Lecturer in Mathematics Education at University of Gothenburg and researcher at Uppsala University with focus on teaching and learning in algebra.

Kirsti Klette, Professor at the Nordic Center of Excellence for Research on Education Quality, (QUINT), Oslo University, Norway.

Angelika Kullberg, Associate Professor and Senior Lecturer in Pedagogical work, focuses her research mainly on teaching and learning of mathematics in compulsory school.

Annika Lilja, Senior Lecturer in Pedagogical work with research interests in two areas, namely teaching and learning related to Ethics and Relational Pedagogy.

Rimma Nyman, PhD in Mathematics Education and Senior Lecturer in Pedagogical work. With a school teacher background, her focus of research is pupil engagement in mathematics and mathematics in teacher education.

Christina Osbeck, Associate Professor and Senior Lecturer in Social Studies Education, focuses her research mainly on teaching and learning related to Religious Education [Religionskunskap], which also includes Philosophy of Life and Ethics which are central areas in her work.

Miranda Rocksén, PhD in Subject Matter Education and Senior Lecturer in Pedagogical Work, with a special interest in Science Education and the study of interaction during processes of teaching and learning.

Elisabeth Rystedt, Ph.Lic., has extensive experience in teaching at compulsory schools. She is engaged in a national program for in-service training of teachers in mathematics and in teacher education at University of Gothenburg and Stockholm University.

Christina Skodras, Lecturer in Mathematics Education at the Department of Pedagogical, Curricular and Professional Studies, University of Gothenburg.